THE FIGHTING IRISH

By the same author

Medieval Warfare
The Barbarians
Celtic Warriors
Medieval Warlords
Women Warlords
The Art of Emile Galle
Brassey's Book of Camouflage
Brassey's Book of Uniforms
War in Britain
Where They Fell
In Heroes' Footsteps
Turning the Tide of War
The Mafia at War/Mafia Allies
Camouflage
Highlander
Lucky Luciano
Empire of Crime

THE
FIGHTING
IRISH

Tim Newark

CONSTABLE • LONDON

Constable & Robinson Ltd
55–56 Russell Square
London WC1B 4HP
www.constablerobinson.com

First published in the UK by Constable,
an imprint of Constable & Robinson Ltd, 2012

A copy of the British Library Cataloguing in Publication Data
is available from the British Library.

ISBN: 978-1-84901-515-8

1 3 5 7 9 10 8 6 4 2

To Max Newark,
a tough little soldier

Contents

Acknowledgements		*ix*
List of Illustrations		*x*
Introduction		*xii*

1	On the Banks of the Boyne	1
2	The Wild Geese	11
3	Wellington's Irish Storm Troopers	25
4	Napoleon's Irish Legion	41
5	Latin American Adventures	55
6	Queen Victoria's Invisible Army	71
7	The Emerald Flag	83
8	Frontier Fighting	95
9	South African Irish	109
10	Great War Irish	123
11	Over the Top	137
12	Fascist Crusade	153
13	Churchill's Irish Brigade	167
14	Secret War	181
15	Cold War Irish	193
16	Slaughter in the Congo	205
17	War on Terror	219
18	Blown up in Afghanistan	231

Appendix 1: Irish-Born Winners of the Victoria Cross	*239*
Appendix 2: Irish-Born Winners of the Medal of Honor	*245*
Notes	*251*
Bibliography	*263*
Index	*269*

'*The Fighting Irish* is a must-read for anyone wanting to know how such a small nation can provide some of the world's finest fighting men.'

Captain Doug Beattie MC, 1st Battalion, Royal Irish Regiment

Acknowledgements

Thanks to the following individuals and institutions who helped me in my research for this book in Britain, Ireland and the USA: David Read of the Soldiers of Gloucestershire Museum, Gloucester; Captain Doug Beattie MC, 1st Royal Irish Regiment; Elizabeth McEvoy, Archivist, National Archives of Ireland, Dublin; Irish Newspapers Archive; Terence Nelson, Royal Ulster Rifles Regimental Museum, Belfast; Sean Longden; Kieran Lynch; Gerry White; Robert Doyle; Peter and Ollie Newark for their picture archive; the staff of the British Library, King's Cross, and The National Archives, Kew; Richard O'Sullivan for the Second World War memoirs of his father, Edmund, London Irish Rifles; John Gorman for his memories of Jadotville, and Austin Berry, former mayor of Athlone; Captain Nigel Wilkinson, London Irish Rifles Regimental Association; Henry O'Kane, Royal Ulster Rifles, for his memories of Korea; Glenn Thompson for showing me around the excellent 'Irish at War at Home and Abroad' exhibition at the National Museum of Ireland, Collins Barracks, Dublin; Captain Brandon Gendron, 1st 69th Infantry Regiment, US Army, for showing me the Irish bar of the Fighting 69th at the Lexington Avenue Armory, New York, and Staff Sergeant Brandon Luchsinger; Company Sergeant Major Dominic Hagans, Royal Irish Regiment, for his memories of Iraq and Afghanistan. Special thanks to Chris Newark for his advice and good company in Ireland. Thanks also to my first-class agent Andrew Lownie and excellent publisher Leo Hollis.

List of Illustrations

King William III leads his Protestant army to victory over the Irish Catholics at the battle of the Boyne, 1690. Illustration by R. Caton Woodville. © *Private Collection, Peter Newark's Military Pictures*

The Wild Geese – Jacobite Irish soldiers leave Limerick for France in 1691. © *Private Collection, Peter Newark's Military Pictures*

Theobald Wolfe Tone, founder member of the Society of United Irishmen, commits suicide, rather than be hanged by the British for his part in a projected French invasion of Ireland in 1798. © *Private Collection, Peter Newark's Military Pictures*

British soldiers – many of them Irishmen – storm the ramparts of Badajoz in 1812. © *Private Collection, Peter Newark's Military Pictures*

American Civil War recruiting poster for the Fighting 69th in 1861. © *Private Collection, Peter Newark's Military Pictures*

Royal Munster Fusiliers form a square for a photograph during the Boer War *c*.1900. © *Private Collection, Peter Newark's Military Pictures*

Irish recruiting poster of the First World War, printed in Dublin in 1914. © *Private Collection, Peter Newark's Military Pictures*

Michael O'Leary, Irish Guardsman and Victoria Cross winner, near his home in County Cork, 1915. © *Private Collection, Peter Newark's Military Pictures*

Statue to Father Francis Patrick Duffy in Times Square, New York, inspirational military chaplain to the Fighting 69th in the Great War. © *Author's own collection*

The band and wolfhound mascot of the Irish Guards wearing the shamrock on St Patrick's Day. Painting by Douglas Macpherson. ©

Private Collection, Peter Newark's Military Pictures

2nd Battalion London Irish Rifles, part of the 38th (Irish) Infantry Brigade in the Second World War, advance towards the River Reno in 'Kangaroo' armoured carriers, Italy 1945. © *London Irish Rifles*

Statue to Sean Russell in Fairview Park, Dublin, defaced by swastika graffiti. Russell was an IRA chief who secretly worked with Nazi Germany during the Second World War. A controversial figure, an earlier stone statue to Russell in the same place had an arm and head knocked off, before being replaced with this bronze version. © *Author's own collection*

Seventeen-year-old Private John Gorman in the Congo, shortly after the battle of Jadotville in 1961, in which Irish United Nations peacekeepers fought off an attack by hundreds of Katangan soldiers. © *John Gorman*

The Lexington Avenue Armory, New York headquarters of the Fighting 69th, used as a help centre following the terrorist attack of 9/11 in 2001. © *Author's own collection*

Royal Irish soldiers in Afghanistan in 2008 as part of an operation training the Afghan National Army. Company Sergeant Major Dominic 'Brummie' Hagans in the centre, Sergeant Boyle, right, Major Armstrong, left. © *Dominic Hagans*

Remains of Royal Irish Land Rover after it was blown up by a Taliban roadside bomb in September 2008. Hagans and his crew all survived the blast. © *Dominic Hagans*

Introduction

One evening in 1815, a cattle farmer was sitting on the verandah of his house in the province of Corrientes in northern Argentina, near the border with Paraguay, when he was approached by a stranger – a 'tall, raw boned, ferocious looking man', dressed as a gaucho with two cavalry pistols stuck in his waistband and a sabre in a rusty steel scabbard hanging from his belt. The farmer feared he was a bandit, but when the stranger opened his mouth, he spoke a mangled Spanish with a strong Irish accent.

'I am Don Pedro Campbell,' he announced.

He was, in fact, Peter Campbell from western Ireland, formerly of the 71st Highland Regiment garrisoned in County Galway. What was this Irishman doing so far from home? His dramatic appearance on a faraway plain epitomizes the extraordinary journey undertaken by so many Irishmen in foreign military service.

For hundreds of years, Irish soldiers have sought their destiny abroad. Stepping aboard ships bound for England, America, or Europe, young Irishmen have been hungry for adventure, a self-made fortune, or the means to carry on a cause back home. The horrendous rift caused by differing religious beliefs or a desire for independent nationhood encouraged many Irishmen to travel abroad, seeking allies to help them in their long battle against Britain.

The battle of the Boyne is my starting point for this saga as Irish Catholics and Protestants fought for who would rule their country. As result of their defeat at the hands of the Protestant Williamite forces, many Catholic soldiers sailed abroad to enrol in the armies of the king of France, setting a pattern for future foreign military service. Leaving their birthplace, they travelled with hope and a romantic dream in their heart, perhaps wanting to return home in due course to bring a liberating revolution to their fellow countrymen; frequently, however, they were disappointed and recruited into the armies of foreign tyrants, among them Napoleon Bonaparte.

Many more Irishmen have set sail with less lofty ideals in mind, escaping poverty, or just wishing to make their own way in the world and impress the girls back home. Many of them took employment with the British Army – at one time making up over 40 per cent of Queen Victoria's army. These red-coated Irishmen travelled to all corners of the British Empire, winning new territories and a reputation as fearless soldiers. Some sailed to America and joined in frontier fighting or demonstrated their loyalty to their new homeland in the bloody combats of the American Civil War. Some took the opportunity to carry on their home-born disputes with campaigns against the British Empire in Canada and South Africa.

In the twentieth century, the bitter conflicts of an Ireland seeking independence have been overshadowed by the far greater sacrifice of Irishmen fighting overseas against Germany in two world wars or serving in Cold War expeditions as part of United Nations' armies. This book is about all those Irishmen fighting abroad, their triumphs and their failures in foreign lands, and their individual motivations for risking their lives so far from home.

Sometimes the price of adventure can be high, as Dominic Hagans, Company Sergeant Major in the Royal Irish Regiment found out when his Land Rover was blown up by a roadside bomb in Afghanistan. Badly injured, he was nevertheless keen to return to the battlefield.

'To be honest, if they said to me tomorrow you're going back, my Bergen would be packed,' says Hagans, 'and I'd be on the first plane out, because that's what we are trained to do and that's what we want to do. You don't join the army to drink loads of beer. You join to go to war.'

It is this irrepressible fighting spirit that has made the Irish soldier abroad such a distinctive character, much respected by other nations, and is the inspiration for my book.

Tim Newark, 2009

Chapter 1
On the Banks of the Boyne

The great hatred between Irish Catholics and Protestants reached a climax on the banks of the River Boyne on 1 July 1690. A hundred years of violent animosity born out of the Reformation that split Europe along frontiers of faith would be settled on this boggy land. The river flowed through the town of Drogheda, just two miles to the west of the battlefield. Forty-one years earlier, Drogheda had been the site of a notorious siege in which the Protestant Oliver Cromwell's English Parliamentarians had stormed the town and slaughtered its Royalist garrison – among them many Irish Catholics. This ruthless religious contest between Protestants and Catholics, in which little mercy was shown, fired up the soldiers as they glowered across the River Boyne at each other on that summer morning in 1690. The result of this conflict would echo across centuries of Irish history and determine the fate of many young Irishmen.

Gerald O'Connor was a Catholic teenager when he stood on the banks of the Boyne and he measured his life from the arrival of Cromwell's troops, or as he put it, 'I was born in 1671, twenty years after Ireland had been crushed by the accursed hands of Cromwell.' He had a lofty heritage, being descended from the Earl of Kildare, and his grandfather had fought the English in the 1590s, but his family had not prospered since then and their money had run out. Following the Tudor conquest of Ireland, land had been taken away from Catholic Irish owners and given to mainly Protestant English and Scots settlers – the plantations – and this process was completed during Cromwell's rule. Despite his illustrious lineage, O'Connor's birthplace was a simple thatched house in Offaly standing next to the ruined remains of a castle his family had once owned. He ached to win back their lost wealth and hoped that the battle on the banks of the Boyne might return his family to their once proud position.

When the Catholic King James II arrived in Ireland, he was determined to use the country as a springboard in his campaign to win back the English throne. It had been taken from him by King William III, the former William of Orange, a Protestant Dutch prince who had been invited to depose James in 1688 by an English Parliament who feared James's tyrannical Catholic regime. Gerald O'Connor was one of many Irish aristocrats who had lost their privileged positions thanks to Cromwell's land confiscations and now flocked to the standard of King James, hoping a Catholic victory would bring benefits to them all. Just nineteen years old, he became a captain in an Irish Catholic cavalry regiment.

Although inspired by a desire to right the wrongs inflicted on his country and family by previous English invaders, O'Connor was also realistic about the prospects of Ireland in a war against the Protestant monarch. 'What were the resources of Ireland compared to those of England and Scotland?' he wondered. 'The Exchequer in Dublin was almost empty,' he admitted, 'base money could not procure what we required for the field; we had not the means to make our army a real instrument of war.' He feared their soldiers were no match for the more professional troops hired by William III. The Irish Catholic foot soldiers were poorly trained and ill equipped. The one quality they possessed was their determination to 'measure their swords with the Saxons'. Not only was it a religious war, according to O'Connor; it was a race war too. Such fervent ardour, born out of fury and religious faith, might well win the day, but that was not the whole picture. Another level of conflict had to be added to the forces opposing each other at the Boyne because many of the soldiers present were not Irish at all.

King James II had a strong ally in the king of France – Louis XIV – at that time the most powerful monarch in Europe. Louis was playing a political game with James, using him to build a powerful alliance against the English Protestants and their friends in Europe. The French king wanted Ireland to be part of his Catholic sphere of influence and welcomed Irish troops into French ranks to fight wars on the Continent. In return, he sent 6,000 French soldiers to join the Jacobite army at the Boyne. O'Connor considered them the best infantry they had.

Many of the troops opposing James's soldiers were not Irish either. Although many Protestant Ulstermen rallied to the cause of the Williamites, fearing that a Catholic victory would imperil their own livelihoods, the Dutch king depended on foreign troops to provide his most professional fighters. Alongside his English regiments, these included Dutch, Danes, Germans and Huguenot French – meaning that Frenchmen would fight on both sides at the Boyne. The Irish were in danger of being sidelined in a battle that would decide the future of their own island. This would not be the last time that Irish soldiers found themselves engaged in a fight they hoped would further their own ends but which was in fact part of a larger political strategy.

William III landed at Carrickfergus in the north of Ireland on 14 June 1690 and advanced rapidly southwards towards Dublin. James could have opposed him earlier, but the French commanders in his ranks urged caution and withdrew before the Protestants, refusing to fight them in open country, looking for a strong line of defence. O'Connor and the Irishmen believed this was a mistake, but the Catholics did have the smaller force. William's multinational army numbered 36,000, whereas the Catholic Irish and French were 25,000 strong.

'We made a halt and encamped along the southern bank of the Boyne', recalled O'Connor. 'The position was not without natural strength; the Boyne covered our front, with its broad and deep current; a breastwork had been thrown up at accessible points; the hedges and farmhouses on the southern bank had been hastily entrenched or fortified.' In an age in which firearms and artillery had become more deadly, it was a distinct disadvantage to advance against entrenched guns, but O'Connor noted there were problems with the position. The Boyne could be forded at several points and their flanks attacked by the greater numbers of Williamites. He was also concerned that their route of escape towards Dublin, thirty miles to the south, was blocked by a narrow pass at Duleek.

Catholic anxieties were not allayed by the presence of their commander-in-chief. 'The tent of James was pitched in our rear,' remembered O'Connor, 'he never stirred from it to give heart to his men, and he was to look idly on in the great trial on which we had staked our fortunes.' In contrast, William led his men from the front and was one of the first to arrive on the battlefield to study the river. O'Connor saw the Protestant king ride to the edge of the water and examine the enemy forces before him. Some Irish Catholic gunners took a shot at him and missed, but his personal courage impressed them. 'Would to God we could exchange kings,' grumbled one of the Irishmen.

The morning of the battle dawned bright but O'Connor was dismayed to see the French already riding off the battlefield to secure the Catholic route of retreat at the pass of Duleek. As the cavalry captain had guessed, King William would seek to outflank the Catholics and this he proceeded to do early in the day, sending his cavalry in a race with the French to capture Duleek. In the meantime, Protestant forces surged across fords on either side of the Catholic position. The soldiers of both sides wore a mixture of red, blue and white uniforms reflecting the wide variety of countries they came from, so the only way to tell enemy from friend was to wear different field signs in their hats. The Jacobites chose a white cockade made of paper or cloth to symbolize their alliance with France, while the Williamites wore a sprig of greenery. The sight made an impact on O'Connor as he saw them advance towards his position. 'From Oldbridge for more than half a mile towards Drogheda, the river looked like a thicket of green boughs,' he recalled. 'Loud cheers, mingling with the drums on the northern bank, burst forth from the armed throngs of many races.'

On the left of the Catholics at Oldbridge ford, blue-coated Dutch soldiers waded through the water and used their superior firepower to force back the Catholic Irish infantry. Two-thirds of the Irish were armed with old-fashioned matchlock muskets that were slow to load, while the remaining third held long pikes to protect them. In contrast, the Dutch carried more modern and efficient flintlocks equipped with bayonets, so each Dutchman could function as a musketeer and pikeman, shooting and then thrusting with his steel-tipped barrel. This meant the Dutch had a third as much firepower to bear on their enemies and far fewer misfires.

Splashing through the water, the Dutch poured disciplined volleys of shot into the Catholic Irish and then charged with their bayonets. O'Connor saw militiamen from his home county of Offaly valiantly resisting the attack but they were no match for the well-drilled foreign troops. It was then that O'Connor and his Catholic Irish cavalry led a counter-attack. The dispossessed Irishmen dashed through the gunpowder smoke towards the Dutch, screaming war cries of retribution for past Protestant crimes.

King William looked on nervously as the Catholic Irish horsemen thundered towards his troops clambering up the riverbank, but the Dutch kept their cool, presented their guns and fired a well-aimed close-range volley that halted the Irish cavalrymen. Some tumbled wounded from their saddles, while others turned and rode back up the slope away from the river. They re-formed then charged again, this time clashing with French Huguenots who had followed the Dutch across the Boyne. Sword rang out against sword. 'I did my best in this furious shock of arms and cut down more than one Frenchman,' said O'Connor.

Eventually, despite the desperate hard fighting of the Irish Catholics, the superior numbers and professionalism of the Williamites proved decisive and the Irish Catholics broke, fleeing back towards Dublin. In total, they took 1,500 casualties, while the victors counted 750 dead and wounded. Towards the end of the combat, O'Connor knocked the sword out of the hand of a French Huguenot officer and took him prisoner as they rode back to Duleek. Thanks to the early departure of the French, the pass to Dublin had remained open, but O'Connor couldn't help but wonder that if the Catholic French had fought alongside them at the Boyne they might have won the battle.

If O'Connor was disappointed by the performance of the French, he saved his scorn for King James, who had rapidly left the battlefield and within days had set sail from Ireland to safety in France, leaving the Irish to fight on by themselves. 'James lost two kingdoms by his craven weakness,' said O'Connor, referring to England and Ireland. 'I thank God I never saw him again – he is known in the tradition of our people as "James the Coward".' In fact, many Irishmen called him *Séamus an Chaca* – 'James the Shit'. In turn, the Catholic king criticized his Irish soldiers, telling the wife of one his commanders, 'Your countrymen run well.' To which she responded: 'Yes it would seem so, but Your Majesty would appear to have won the race.' James's behaviour damned for ever the cause of the Stuart kings in the eyes of the Irish and they did little to help later Jacobite rebellions in Scotland in 1715 and 1745.

Two days after the battle of the Boyne, King William and his army marched into Dublin. Their victory ensured the Anglo-Protestant domination of Ireland for over two centuries and triggered the struggle of Catholic nationalists against it. The success of William of Orange in particular continues to inspire the Orangemen of Ulster, who celebrate the battle every July with marches. Some historians have pointed out the multinational character of his triumph. 'Considering the battle', writes one, 'was won by Danes and Dutchmen, French Huguenots and Prussian Brandenburghers, it is almost ludicrous to any one who has the smallest respect for historical accuracy to see Orangemen celebrating the anniversary of the Boyne as their victory.' That ignores the very real contribution of the Ulstermen to the battle, but it does show how the legend of the Boyne has grown in importance over the years, not only for Irish Protestants but also for Catholics, as it set in motion a chain of events that led to another legendary moment that echoed throughout the centuries – the Flight of the Wild Geese.

*

After the battle of the Boyne, while much of the Jacobite army disintegrated, a small core of regiments retreated to Limerick in southwestern Ireland. With King James gone to France, one of his Irish commanders at the battle of the Boyne took over. He was Patrick Sarsfield. Thirty years old and a giant of a man, Sarsfield commanded the respect of his soldiers both for his personal bravery and his loyalty to their cause. Born into a wealthy family in Lucan, County Dublin, he was a second son, but he succeeded to the family estate in 1675 and took receipt of an annual income of £2,000.

Set on a life of soldiering in England, Sarsfield served both King Charles II and James II, rising from captain to colonel. When William of Orange landed in England, Sarsfield went back to Ireland to recruit soldiers for the Jacobite cause. When James arrived in Ireland, Sarsfield stood by him and was rewarded by being created Earl of Lucan, but the king was not so impressed with his military abilities. Physically tough and keen on fighting duels, Sarsfield had a reputation for hot-headedness and James only reluctantly gave him senior army posts. Following defeat at the Boyne, Sarsfield openly criticized the king. 'That man', he told Gerald O'Connor, 'has cursed the soldiers of our race, who had risen in thousands and fought his cause; like all the Stuarts, he is false and double-dealing at heart.'

At Limerick, Sarsfield proved a popular commander-in-chief, scoring a few minor successes against the Williamites, but towards the end of 1691 his troops were hemmed in by King William and awaited the final bloody assault on the town. Cavalry Captain Gerald O'Connor had followed Sarsfield to Limerick and now witnessed the endgame of the tragic struggle that had begun at the Boyne a year earlier. The west side of the town was already in the hands of the Protestant army and they concentrated their assault on a bridge across the Shannon to finish the resistance of the Catholic Irish. In the late afternoon of 22 September 1691, the Williamite forces surged towards the Thomond Bridge over the Shannon. O'Connor noted with pride the resistance of his Irishmen.

> They suffered grievously from the fire of our skirmishers, half concealed in the adjoining gravel pits and quarries. The struggle raged for perhaps two hours; reinforcements were hurried forward from both sides: the outworks fell at last into the hands of the enemy, who, however, had dearly paid for his first success.

O'Connor's Irish troops held the bridge with fierce hand-to-hand fighting, thrusting with bayonets and pikes at the Dutch and other Protestant soldiers. Edged back slowly by the weight of the Williamite horde, the exhausted Jacobites were determined not to give up the bridge, but at that moment one of the few remaining Catholic French officers in the garrison of the town lost his nerve and ordered the drawbridge linking the bridge to Limerick to be raised, condemning those stranded Irishmen to a horrible death. 'Many flung themselves into the Shannon and sank in its waters; some met their deaths in a wild effort against the foe; some sought mercy from their relentless victors in vain.'

Hundreds of Jacobites were butchered on the bridge. 'This frightful catastrophe incensed our army,' said O'Connor, 'already filled with dislike of the French, and began to make the bravest hearts despair.' It was up to Patrick Sarsfield to decide what to do next and although his heart wanted to fight on, his head knew he had run out of options. Rather than condemning his men to a pointless slaughter, he urged a treaty with the Williamites while his soldiers still held their weapons. Eleven days later, the resulting Treaty of Limerick ended the Jacobite war in Ireland and allowed Sarsfield and his soldiers, including O'Connor, to march out of the town with full military honours.

On the surface, the Treaty of Limerick appeared to be a reasonable conclusion to the conflict, allowing freedom of Catholic worship in Ireland and no retribution against Jacobite supporters, but as the Protestant establishment took back control of the country, they violated the agreement and enacted the harshly anti-Catholic Penal Code. The military part of the treaty gave Sarsfield and his soldiers the option to sail to France and take service with King Louis XIV. Many of them decided to do just that. O'Connor was one of them and, although he was clearly one those Irishmen who had no great love for the French and were disgusted by the flight of James II to France, he believed that life in a Protestant-ruled Ireland held little future for him and preferred to trade his fighting skills abroad. This mass exit of fighting Irish Catholics was what became known as the Flight of the Wild Geese – a poetic term first used in the eighteenth century evoking the migratory flight of the birds in autumn.

In November and December 1691, fleets of ships anchored at Limerick and Cork to take away the Irish to their new lives in France. Sarsfield was proud of the more than 12,000 soldiers who had decided to follow him and O'Connor recorded his comments.

> These men are leaving all that is most dear in life for a
> strange land, in which they will have to endure much,
> to serve in an army that hardly knows our people; but
> they are true to Ireland and have still hopes for her
> cause – we will make another Ireland in the armies of
> the great King of France.

This was to be the rallying cry for many Irish soldiers in exile in France. They wanted their service abroad to be turned into an active blow against the tyrannical English, but many were to be disappointed as they became embroiled in military expeditions to further the ambitions of French autocrats.

As the ships were readied for departure, it was hoped that the families of many of the soldiers could join them in their new venture, but there was not enough space for them all. 'Loud cries and lamentation broke from the wives and children who had been left behind,' recalled O'Connor. 'Some dashed into the stream and perished in the depths; some clung to the boats that were making off from the shore; many of the men, husbands or fathers, plunged into the waters; not a few lost their lives in their efforts to reach the dry ground.' It was a tragic beginning to an epic voyage.

Chapter 2
The Wild Geese

When Patrick Sarsfield's Irish soldiers landed in Brest, they received little welcome from the French and spent a cold winter camped in fields in Brittany. Nevertheless, the exiled James II was delighted to see them and hoped that, once re-equipped, they would provide him with a cheap army to help claim back his throne from William III. 'We assure you, and order you to assure both officers and soldiers that come along with you', wrote James to the Irishmen in France, 'that we shall never forget this act of loyalty, nor fail when in a capacity to give them above others a particular mark of our favour.' But James was a powerless dreamer and a guest of the French King Louis, who made it plainly clear that he would employ the Irishmen in his army and on his terms. That suited Sarsfield and his countrymen very well as they had little wish to serve under a discredited former monarch who had ditched them at the Boyne.

By the spring of 1692, once the survivors of a failed expedition to Scotland and other Irish former prisoners of war were brought together with the Wild Geese, the new Jacobite army on French soil numbered almost 15,000. It was divided into six regiments of foot soldiers, two of dragoons, two of cavalry and two of horse guards. James's illegitimate son, the Duke of Berwick, commanded the first unit of horse guards and Patrick Sarsfield commanded the second. With this force, Louis XIV planned to invade England and put James back on the throne. With the addition of 7,000 French troops and a train of artillery, it made a larger combined invasion force than that deployed by William III when he landed in England to take the crown away from James in 1688.

For a few months, the Catholic Irish exiles were very excited as they marched from Brest to the heights overlooking the English Channel on the Cotentin peninsula. There, they waited for the French transport ships to take them to England and strike a blow at the heart of the Protestant regime that had taken so much away from them in Ireland. Gerald O'Connor, Irish Catholic veteran of the Boyne and the fall of Limerick, gazed with wonder at the ships assembled by the French – 'those mighty hulls, with their towering masts and their grim tiers of cannon'.

In preparation for the invasion of England, Louis decided that the French fleet should strike a pre-emptive blow against the English navy, but when news got through that the English had combined with the Dutch to form a fleet that outnumbered the French two to one, it was too late to stop the French battleships and they sailed out to disaster. The fleets pounded away at each other in full view of the hopeful Jacobite exiles standing on the Cotentin cliffs at La Hougue. O'Connor watched in horror as the English ships set fire to French craft anchored nearby. 'I have never understood why our armies did nothing on this day,' he said of the French artillery perched on the cliff. 'It certainly might have given the ships assistance with its guns.'

Overwhelmed by English and Dutch cannon fire, the French fleet was crippled and, having lost control of the Channel, Louis called off the invasion. It was a bitter disappointment for the Wild Geese, who saw it as their only possible ticket back home, and shattered for ever James's dream of recovering his throne. He died nine years later and was buried in Paris. Louis XIV, however, had many other battles to fight and the Irish were redeployed in his service elsewhere in Europe.

Patrick Sarsfield was transferred away from the Jacobite invasion force into the main French army, where he was given the rank of *maréchal de camp* – the French equivalent of a major general – but he never again commanded a substantial force of Irishmen. Some of the Wild Geese became angry at him after the defeat of La Hougue, feeling that they had been left stranded in France and that he was no longer interested in their welfare, but Sarsfield simply accepted the reality of the situation. The best the Irish exiles could hope for was to make a career in the French army and Sarsfield and his comrades grabbed the opportunity. Those Irishmen not considered good enough to find posts elsewhere in Louis' army were recruited into a unit of fellow countrymen under French leadership, known as the Irish Brigade.

Gerald O'Connor was one of the chosen Irish officers who followed Sarsfield into commanding French regiments. He had little to return to in Ireland. The Protestant establishment in Ireland had reneged on the Treaty of Limerick and Catholic estates had been confiscated. O'Connor's family had been proscribed as rebels. 'The few hundred acres that had remained to us', he noted bitterly, 'were bought by the descendant of a Cromwellian settler.'

Shortly after the failed invasion attempt, Sarsfield and O'Connor were ordered to Flanders, where they fought in the French army led by Marshal François Henri de Montmorency-Bouteville, duc de Luxembourg. Sarsfield distinguished himself in battle at Steenkirk in August 1692 against the Anglo-Dutch army of King William III, continuing his struggle against Louis XIV on the Continent as part of the War of the Grand Alliance. Luxembourg personally recommended Sarsfield to the French king, saying, 'we have particularly noticed the valour and the fearlessness of which he has given proofs in Ireland. I can ensure your Majesty that he is a very good and a very able officer.'

After the year's campaigning had ended, Sarsfield and his Irish colleagues relaxed in Paris. O'Connor was much taken by the elegance of French life and recorded his own impressions of the capital. 'I devoted my hours of leisure to exploring the vast and stirring world of Paris,' he recalled. 'Accustomed as I had been to the sight of the poor towns in Ireland I used to gaze with astonishment at these scenes of wonder.' Sarsfield had brought his young wife with him from Ireland, while O'Connor later married a French woman, who was, coincidentally, the daughter of the Huguenot French soldier he had made his prisoner at the battle of the Boyne. Faced with the stern objections of a French Protestant mother, the Catholic Irishman persisted and the Huguenot officer, now returned to France, consented to his former enemy becoming his son-in-law, telling O'Connor that 'though a poor exile, I was a soldier who had a future before him'.

Fighting for Louis XIV began again in May 1693 with the French taking the offensive, laying siege to Flemish towns still in Anglo-

Dutch hands. King William had the best of the action, outmanoeu-vring the French and, by July, the two armies were ready for a major clash. The French outnumbered the Anglo-Dutch forces by 80,000 to 50,000 troops, but William's men were dug in along a two-mile front that passed through the villages of Laer, Neerwinden and Neerlanden. Early on the morning of 29 July, after a massive exchange of artillery fire, the French commander, Luxembourg, ordered his left wing of cavalry and infantry to attack Neerwinden. Patrick Sarsfield, with his rank of *maréchal de camp*, directed a French division as part of this initial assault.

Serving with the French cavalry, Gerald O'Connor witnessed the attack as the Irish marshal led the French in a desperate bid to break through the Anglo-Dutch earthworks, but the storm of cannon fire was too much for them to make any headway. By midday, Luxem-bourg was still sending in more men, hoping by sheer weight of numbers to break through at Neerwinden. Sarsfield and O'Connor rode with the French cavalry as they spurred their horses into action for another attack.

> I was, with Sarsfield, in the line of these brave horsemen;
> they remained under the fire of the breastwork for two
> hours, unable to strike a single blow, but steadily closing
> up their shattered ranks. William [III], I have since heard,
> broke out into an exclamation of praise.

Luxembourg would not let go of the position and by the afternoon his stubbornness began to pay off, as French soldiers pushed past their dead and dying comrades and finally broke into the village of Neerwinden. King Louis' elite household cavalry joined in and the Anglo-Dutch right flank was turned and broken. The French claimed victory; however, as O'Connor surveyed the battlefield he was shocked by the carnage he saw, with bodies strewn throughout the captured village. It was then he received news that Sarsfield had been wounded in one of these final charges and he rushed to his side. 'The noble form of the hero lay on a pallet in a hut,' remembered O'Connor. 'He feebly lifted up his nerveless hand and gave me a letter, which he had dictated … "I am dying", he said, "the most glorious of deaths; we have seen the backs of the tyrants of our race. May you, Gerald, live to behold other such days; but let Ireland be always uppermost in your thoughts."'

It was the beginning of the mythologizing of Sarsfield as a hero of Irish independence. His greatest pleasure on that day was chasing the fleeing Williamites who had hounded him throughout Ireland. Sarsfield was carried to the nearby village of Huy but died there a few days later from his wounds. An alternative account of his final moments had him struck by an enemy musket ball and, as he lay on the ground, lifting his hand covered in his own blood, he gasped, 'Would to God this were shed for Ireland!' The same exhortation was quoted in a twenty-two-page penny history of Sarsfield published in Liverpool in 1875. 'Though his services were lost to Ireland,' exclaimed the author, 'he sustained her honour, and, under the French flag, added to the brilliancy of her annals ... Ireland cherishes gratefully his memory – on the long list of her heroic departed there is no nobler name than that of PATRICK SARSFIELD.'

O'Connor noted sourly that despite this tremendous victory, purchased with so many lives, including Sarsfield's, Luxembourg failed to make the most of it by advancing on Brussels and, instead, allowed King William to reassert control in Flanders. The fighting would carry on for several more years. O'Connor continued serving under the banner of Louis XIV, biding his time until he could face his English enemy again. He was to wait over a decade until the battle of Ramillies in 1706. In the meantime, he would have five children and two of them would eventually fight for the French king too.

*

The Wild Geese were not the only veterans of the battle of the Boyne to end up fighting abroad in continental Europe. Protestant soldiers from the Williamite war in Ireland also took up arms in the epic struggle between France and England. Robert Parker was one of them. The son of a Protestant settler in Kilkenny in southern Ireland, he was brought up with a fervent hatred of Popery. From an early age, he yearned for a military career and in his mid-teens he ran away from school to join a regiment in Ireland. When this unit was absorbed into the army of James II, as a Protestant, Parker was out of a job. He returned home and when, shortly afterwards, both his parents died, he sold his part of the family inheritance and funded his journey to London. There, he joined Lord Forbes's regiment in 1689, which became part of William III's army in Ireland.

Parker fought at the battle of the Boyne and throughout the Williamite campaign. During an assault at Athlone, he nearly lost his life. 'A stone which had been thrown from the top of the castle as I passed under it, fell on my shoulder,' he recalled, 'the effects of which I feel to this day on every change of the weather. This indeed I deserved for being so foolhardy as to put myself on this command when it was not my turn; but it was a warning to me ever after. It is an old maxim in war, that he who goes so far as he is commanded is a good man, but he that goes farther is a fool.'

Parker survived the campaign to serve abroad with the Anglo-Dutch troops in Flanders during the fighting in which Sarsfield died. At the siege of Namur in 1695, he received a bullet in the shoulder, which caused him to have medical treatment for thirty weeks. But Namur was a significant victory for William III and it was out of gratitude for the brave performance of Parker and his fellow Irish Protestants that he bequeathed them the title of the Royal Regiment of Ireland. Parker was soon after appointed the regimental Colour Ensign, the lowest commissioned officer rank, entrusted with carrying the regiment's colours. A few years of peaceful garrison duty followed in Ireland, where Parker met his wife, but in 1701, war broke out again between England and France, and Parker's regiment was back in the front line in Flanders. Parker was promoted to lieutenant.

The War of the Spanish Succession raged until 1714 and it was during this conflict that the Duke of Marlborough was appointed commander-in-chief of the British army and inflicted a series of devastating defeats on Louis XIV. Irish soldiers fought on both sides. The Catholic Irish Brigade fought for the French king, while the Royal Regiment of Ireland served the Protestant monarch throughout most of the campaigns. Robert Parker was at the battle of Ramillies in 1706 when Marlborough wrong-footed the French commander with a feint against one wing before attacking his weakened right flank.

Parker noted that the fearless Duke placed himself at the heart of the action and was nearly struck by a cannonball that killed his equerry as he helped the Duke mount a horse. Gerald O'Connor was also at Ramillies and described how his French cavalry – the Maison du Roi – seized an opportunity to charge at the enemy commander. The Duke was being acclaimed by his soldiers at the time.

> I can still see him as, undaunted and serene, he rode forward amidst the cheers of his troops, shouting 'Corporal John', the name they had given their hero; he was surrounded by his staff, evidently receiving his commands. I fell on his men with my whole regiment; he narrowly escaped being made prisoner – oh! that Heaven was so unpropitious to France – but he was extricated, and my troopers were compelled to retreat.

O'Connor and his French horsemen suffered badly and in the chaotic retreat the Catholic Irishman was lucky to escape with thirty of his comrades to Brussels. 'Our beaten and fugitive soldiery were hunted through the Low Countries,' he recorded. 'They were scattered into little knots and bands of men, ravaging villages and living on reckless pillage.' In Brussels, O'Connor had to avoid being caught by the English and hung as a Jacobite rebel. He eventually disguised himself as a peasant to flee southwards to France.

The plight of the French was not helped by their country being plunged into the worst winter within living memory in 1708. 'The sights I saw and the tales I heard', observed O'Connor, 'would make the bravest of spirits tremble. In some districts the peasantry were simply starved; their villages and cottages were filled with corpses, devoured and mangled by wolves as they lay unburied.' The ice-induced famine extended into the cities, including Paris. O'Connor contrasted it with the mild winters he had known in Ireland.

The victorious march of Parker and his redcoat Irishmen continued. At the battle of Malplaquet in 1709, another success for Marlborough, Parker recorded a dramatic description of how two Irish units – on opposing sides – clashed. The Royal Regiment of Ireland was ordered to march on the enemy sighted in an opening between woods. To the sound of a slow drumbeat, the Irish advanced at a steady pace. Within a hundred paces of their line, the enemy opened fire. What Parker's comrades didn't know at the time was that these enemy soldiers were in fact Catholic exiles of the Irish Brigade. Confusingly, they were also clad in red coats as a sign of their Stuart allegiance.

The Royal Regiment of Ireland halted and executed a perfect display of platoon firing – firing their muskets as alternating sections of the line, rather than in ranks. The French Irish Brigade returned fire in ranks for a second time. Undeterred, Marlborough's Irish reloaded and musketry rippled along their line. For the third time, the French Irish shouldered their guns, but this time their shooting was scattered and less effective. It was then that they broke, running into the woods behind them, chased by a third volley of fire from Marlborough's Irish. It was only when the Royal Regiment of Ireland reached the ground the enemy had been standing on and talked to their wounded that they discovered they were fighting their Catholic countrymen.

'Here, therefore, was a fair trial of skill between the two Royal Regiments of Ireland, one in the British, the other in the French service,' concluded Parker with some soldierly satisfaction. 'For we met each other upon equal terms, and there was none else to interpose. We had but four men killed and six wounded: and found near forty of them on the spot killed and wounded.' Parker ascribed the secret of their success to the heavier weight of their musket balls – sixteen to the pound rather than the French twenty-four to the pound – that made for a more deadly impact, and their superior shooting skills. 'The French at that time fired all by ranks, which can never do equal execution with our platoon-firing, especially when six platoons are fired together.'

Aside from a period of garrison duty in Ireland, teaching tactics to other soldiers, Parker, now a Captain of Grenadiers, stayed in Flanders for the remainder of the war against France. The Royal Regiment of Ireland had acquitted itself very well, winning four battle honours at Blenheim, Ramillies, Oudenarde and Malplaquet. In 1713, however, when it came to winding down operations and preparing for their return to Britain, the Irish felt they were being treated less then generously.

Stationed in Ghent, they were unhappy at the quality of their food, but behind this was a deeper concern that when they were disbanded they would lose all the pay owed to them. A handful of

Irishmen planned a mutiny in which they would kill any officers that opposed them and ransack the Flemish town. When the time came for action, they were joined by a few hundred other soldiers and barricaded themselves in a building, sending their demands to the generals. The commanders responded by bringing in four artillery pieces and Irish Inniskilling Dragoons.

Surrounded, the mutineers hoped to negotiate themselves out of trouble, but the generals insisted they lay down their arms and surrender unconditionally. The leading mutineers proposed to fight it out, but the other soldiers seized them and handed them over, hoping for mercy. 'A court-martial was immediately held,' recalled Parker, 'and ten of the chiefs were found guilty, and executed on the spot.'

While the other British regiments were sent home, Parker and the Irishmen were kept in Ghent for another year. Their loyalty was further tested when they were sent to suppress Jacobites in Scotland during the rising of 1715. The following year, the Royal Irish were sent to Oxford to quell the riotous activities of students. Ordered to leave their swords and muskets in their barracks, the Irishmen took up cudgels and aggressively patrolled the streets of the university town. 'The scholars were never before known to keep so close to their Colleges,' noted Parker. In 1717, he decided to leave his regiment and sold his commission for a good sum. Parker retired to Ireland to live near Cork.

Gerald O'Connor's fighting career also came to an end with the conclusion of the War of the Spanish Succession in 1714, but he stayed in the French army until 1731, when he was sixty years old. He became a major in Lord Clare's regiment of exiled Irishmen, part of the Irish Brigade. His eldest son also took command in this regiment and, on Gerald's retirement, invited him to a regimental banquet. It was to be a disappointing moment for the veteran soldier as none of the assembled officers remembered his old war chief, Patrick Sarsfield.

Further disappointment came when O'Connor returned to his home county of Offaly in central Ireland. Compared to Paris, the city of Dublin seemed mean and squalid; Catholics were discriminated against and regarded as second-class citizens, while his own family had integrated themselves within the Protestant establishment. O'Connor stayed barely six months. When he returned for one more time, the country was ravaged by famine and he was pleased to get back home – to France – where he died at the age of seventy-nine.

'France is no longer the France of the great king,' wrote O'Connor in the year before he died, referring to Louis XIV, who had passed away in 1715. 'But I have hopes for the future of the noble land which has caught to its heart the Irish exiles and has placed them high on the roll of her renowned armies.' He contemplated his old sword, which he had wielded in so many battles, and trusted that his descendants would draw it, 'should the occasion arise in the service of the nation which has given us the [Irish] Brigade, and, whether in good or evil fortune, will prove themselves worthy of their people and their name'.

To France, O'Connor concluded, he owed everything that made life most prized – his wife, children, friends and home. 'I love her as if she were a second mother. Yet my thoughts often turn to our fallen Offaly, the scenes of my boyhood and first youth, to the castle by the lake, to our broken clansmen …' It was to be the lot of so many Irishmen fighting abroad – a passion for their adopted home but nostalgia for their lost land.

*

Patrick Sarsfield and his Jacobites might be the most famous of the Wild Geese, but they were not the only Catholic Irish soldiers to seek a better future abroad in foreign armies. Earlier flights of Catholic Irishmen had supplied warriors for the Spanish king in the sixteenth century. William Stanley was an officer loyal to Elizabeth I during her conquest of Ireland in the 1580s, but he was also a secret Catholic. When he was commissioned by the Queen to raise a unit of Irishmen for service in the war against Catholic Spain in the Netherlands, he took his troops to the Low Countries but switched sides and the Irish joined the army of the king of Spain. In 1588, if the Spanish Armada had destroyed the English fleet, Stanley and his Irish soldiers would have joined the invasion of England.

Throughout the seventeenth century, rebel Irishmen saw Catholic Spain as a possible patron and saviour against Protestant England. Oliver Cromwell's ruthless suppression of the Catholics in Ireland encouraged further military emigration, but by the end of the century, Louis XIV's France had supplanted Spain as the leading Catholic power in Europe and many Irishmen preferred service in the French army rather than the Spanish, where conditions were reputed to be better. Strong links remained, however, between Ireland and Spain and by the early eighteenth century there were three Irish infantry regiments in the Spanish army, called Hibernia, Ultonia and Irlanda. Service in the Spanish army was now not so much about striking back at Protestant England, but about pursuing a profitable career. Aside from Irishmen motivated by religion and nationalism, this was the other great strand of Irish military history – the adventurer travelling the world in search of a fortune. Alexander O'Reilly was one of these Irish soldiers in Spanish service.

Born in County Meath, O'Reilly was taken by his Catholic father to Spain where he was enrolled in a school for priests in Saragossa. At the age of eleven, he decided he preferred the idea of a military life, and as an officer cadet entered the ranks of the Hibernia infantry regiment with its banner of a gold harp on a blue background. In 1741, aged eighteen, he fought against the Austrians, allies of Britain, in Italy in the War of the Austrian Succession (1741–48). Badly wounded in a battle near Bologna, he lay with the dead and wounded all night on the battlefield before he was taken prisoner by the Austrians. O'Reilly must have been impressed by his captors, because when he had recovered from his wounds and was released, he asked for permission to serve with the Austrians, then fighting against the Prussians. His plan was to study the tactics of the Prussians, amongst the greatest soldiers in Europe, and bring this information back to Spain. The Spanish were impressed by his diligence and promoted him to the rank of brigadier.

With money and status assured, O'Reilly was still hungry for adventure and he found this in the New World. In the eighteenth century, the Americas were a wide-open territory where Spain, Britain and France competed for control over wealthy colonies. In 1769, O'Reilly was selected to lead a 2,000-strong expeditionary force to establish Spanish control over French-occupied New Orleans and the territory of Louisiana. The land had been ceded to Spain by the British as a result of their victory over France in the Seven Years War (1756–63). This was to compensate the Spanish for the British having taken their colony of Florida, but it meant the

Spanish had to deal with the French colonists. Just a year earlier, the French settlers had expelled the Spanish governor of New Orleans. It was up to O'Reilly to reassert Spanish authority and this he did with merciless efficiency. Five of the leading French rebels were executed and five more sent to prison in Spanish-held Cuba. The rest were pardoned if they pledged loyalty to the Spanish crown.

Having broken the French rebels and added a major colony to the Spanish Empire, O'Reilly was richly rewarded. He was now no longer simply a professional soldier, but joined the governing classes. Granted the title of the Count of O'Reilly, he was appointed captain general of the military region of New Castile in central Spain – not bad for a lad from County Meath. But, having risen to the upper levels of Spanish society, he then he made a dreadful error. In 1775, O'Reilly was entrusted with the task of defeating the Moorish pirates who were attacking Spanish shipping in the Mediterranean. The Irish general decided to tackle the pirates in their bases along the North African coast and launched a punitive raid on Algiers, but as his soldiers landed on the beaches, the corsairs, who had been given advance warning of the operation, ambushed them. Moorish marksmen picked off hundreds of Spaniards as they stepped off their boats onto the sand and O'Reilly was forced to order a humiliating retreat. Although it was not his fault directly, O'Reilly took the blame for this disaster and his punishment was exile to an island off the North African coast.

The Spanish king valued O'Reilly too highly to let this exile last long and, after a year, he was brought back to command Spanish troops in Andalusia. It was the time of the American War of Independence and O'Reilly helped plan assaults on British possessions in the Caribbean. Almost twenty years later, O'Reilly was still soldiering, and he ended his days as a seventy-year-old general readying himself to oppose Napoleon during the wars of the French Revolution. He died from a stroke before he could test his military skills against Bonaparte. It was an extraordinary military career that showed how far an Irishman could progress in a foreign army. Other ambitious Irishmen in the eighteenth century, like O'Reilly, served in Austrian, German, Swedish, Italian and Russian armies. One even acquired the extravagant title of General Johann-Sigismund Maguire von Inniskillin, when he served the Emperor of

Austria as governor of Carinthia, while another, known as Count Iosiph Kornilovich O'Rourke, rode with the Tsar's cavalry against Napoleon. For many less high-flying Irishmen, however, the road to foreign adventure lay in joining the British Army, and they enrolled in their thousands to fight for that leading Irish-born general – the Duke of Wellington.

Chapter 3
Wellington's Irish Storm Troopers

Arthur Wesley (later Wellesley), the Duke of Wellington – one of Britain's greatest military commanders – was born in Ireland in 1769. His father was descended from an English family that had lived in Ireland for generations, and had been a member of the Irish House of Commons before being ennobled in the Irish House of Lords. Their country house, Dangan Castle, was in County Meath, and their townhouse in Upper Merrion Street, Dublin. Soon after his birth, however, the Wesley family moved to London, where his father struggled to maintain their lifestyle in rented rooms in Knightsbridge. Arthur was sent to Eton, where he would learn to speak without the Irish accent his father considered might be a disadvantage in polite society.

It is frequently suggested that Wellington took no pride in his Irish birthplace. 'Being born in a stable', he is claimed to have said, 'does not make a man a horse.' In fact, this quote was misattributed to him by the nationalist politician Daniel O'Connell, who wanted to repeal the Act of Union that had brought Ireland and Britain together into a United Kingdom in 1801. In truth, Wellington spent much of his early adult life in Ireland and was elected MP for Trim in 1790 and sat in the Irish Parliament. It was during this election campaign that he spoke out against Henry Grattan, leader of the Irish nationalist movement and a distant relation of William Grattan, a soldier of the Connaught Rangers. Wellington understood the turmoil in his island, later saying, 'Show me an Irishman and I'll show you a man whose anxious wish it is to see his country independent of Great Britain.' But he advocated force to keep Ireland part of the Union.

Wellington began his military career as an ensign in a Highland regiment, the 73rd Foot, but served in at least one thoroughly Irish unit, the 18th Light Dragoons (later, the 18th King's Irish Hussars) – known jokingly as the 'Drogheda Cossacks' – as a captain from 1791–93. It was during this time in Dublin, enlivened by much socializing and gambling, that he met the daughter of Lord Longford, but his offer of marriage was turned down by her brother, who considered Wellington to be in debt and having few prospects. Profoundly upset by this rejection, Wellington vowed to dedicate himself to his military career and over the next decade rose steadily through the British Army. After gaining some of his toughest combat experience in India, Wellington returned to Britain as a much admired military commander. Elected an MP to the British Parliament, he was appointed Chief Secretary for Ireland, but gave up his political career in 1807 to continue his soldiering, and was sent to Portugal in 1808. There, he became commander-in-chief of the British Army and fought a six-year conflict – the Peninsular War – against the French forces of Napoleon that had invaded Spain and Portugal.

Irishmen formed a significant part of the British Army in the Peninsular War. At least five regiments were raised in Ireland. These included the 4th (Royal Irish) Dragoon Guards, the 18th King's Irish Hussars, the 27th (Inniskilling) Foot, the 87th (Prince of Wales's Irish) Foot and the 88th (Connaught Rangers) Foot. It has been estimated that of the rest of the foot and cavalry regiments in the British Army, between 30 and 40 per cent of their ranks were also filled with Irishmen. Such a dependency on Irish military manpower was a complete reversal of the situation for much of the previous century.

Following the battle of the Boyne and the Williamite War of the late seventeenth century against James II, the fear of resurgent Catholicism meant that Irish Catholics had been banned from serving in the British Army since 1701. Even Irish Protestants were not officially welcomed into the army as it was thought any Irishman could be a latent papist. But the final defeat of the Jacobite cause at the battle of Culloden in 1746 and Britain's growing military commitments around the globe slowly relaxed the British attitude to Irish Catholic recruits and, by the 1770s, an oath of allegiance to the crown was deemed to be sufficient to allow Catholics to serve abroad in the British Army. The threat of invasion during the French Revolutionary Wars hastened the recruitment of Irishmen, and the Act of Union in 1801 consolidated their valued presence in the British Army. It was a combined force of Irish, English and Scots soldiers that Wellington led to Portugal.

*

From the deck of the transport ship *Samaritan*, docking in Lisbon harbour on 29 October 1809, Dublin-born subaltern William Grattan was very impressed by what he saw. Exquisite buildings stood like an amphitheatre before him, with lush gardens and sumptuous orange groves adding an exotic richness to the view. Yet when he stepped off the ship, he was less than charmed by the local citizens he had come so far to defend against Napoleon and the invading French. 'I confess I was inexpressibly disgusted,' recalled the seventeen-year-old ensign. 'The squalid appearance of those half-amphibious animals, their complexion, their famished looks, and their voracious entreaties for salt pork … was sufficient to stamp them in my eyes as the most ill-looking set of cut-throats I had ever beheld.'

His first night ashore did not improve matters, with packs of hungry dogs howling in the streets while his bed was infested with bugs and fleas. So much so that Grattan commended the French General Jean-Andoche Junot, during his brief occupation of the capital, for shooting the dogs and fining local proprietors for filthy houses.

Grattan's mood improved markedly when he joined his unit, the first battalion of the 88th Foot, stationed at Monforte near the border with Spain. The 88th Foot or Connaught Rangers had been raised in 1793 by General John de Burgh, Earl of Clanricarde, to counter the threat posed to Britain by the French Revolution. They took part in British expeditions to Flanders in 1794, India in 1799, Egypt in 1801, South America in 1806 and the notorious Walcheren campaign in the Netherlands in the summer of 1809, when thousands of troops died from fever. The unit was almost exclusively Irish.

When Scotsman James McGrigor purchased the position of surgeon with the regiment in 1794, he was told by Major Keppel, its then commander and the only other non-Irishman in it, that every one of their fellow officers was from Galway. 'In fact, the officers were not only all Irish', remembered McGrigor, 'but almost all of one sept [clan] or family; all more or less nearly related to the colonel; all of them having raised men, Connaught Rangers, for their rank.' McGrigor was destined to rise to the position of surgeon-general to the Duke of Wellington but always considered himself an old Connaught Ranger, and when he arrived in Portugal during the Peninsular War he took shelter with the 88th.

While Wellington oversaw the construction of defensive lines north of Lisbon, the 88th were plagued by desertions. Many Irishmen had died of fever in Walcheren and of those that survived several wanted to escape the harsh realities of military service by starting a new life in Portugal. This turned sour when some deserters were killed by local bandits, while others were arrested by the local militias for misdemeanours and taken to the nearest British depot, where they were flogged or hanged.

The 88th was part of the 3rd Division, created by Wellington as one of his main fighting formations against the French in Portugal. The divisional commander, General Thomas Picton, arrived with a reputation for enforcing harsh discipline and a fierce prejudice against Irish Catholics. He had two of William Grattan's comrades flogged for stealing a goat. The punishment was carried out in front of the entire division and Picton addressed the 88th, saying: 'You are not known in the army by the name of "Connaught Rangers", but by the name of Connaught footpads!' The Connaughts' commanding officer, Scotsman Colonel Alexander Wallace, was outraged by this insult and demanded that Picton retract his comments when he next assembled the entire division. Picton ignored the request but invited Wallace to dine with him.

When Wallace arrived for dinner, he found all the senior officers of the 3rd Division present. Picton then announced that Wallace had taken offense at his comments about the 88th, and declared: 'I am happy to find that I have been misinformed as to their conduct for some time past.' Wallace accepted the apology with a bow and later told Grattan: 'From that period General Picton and myself were always on the best of terms, and though from prejudice he

often signified that he suspected the Connaught Boys were as ready
for mischief as any of their neighbours, he always spoke of them to
me as good soldiers while I was with his division.'

. In the summer of 1810, the French under Marshal André Masséna
invaded Portugal for the third time, Masséna leading an army over
twice the size of Wellington's. The British commander therefore
adopted a defensive strategy, preferring to avoid any major combat
and wearing down the resources of the invaders. In September,
however, the two armies met at Bussaco. Wellington took a position
on a rocky ridge to block the French advance on Coimbra, a strategically important Portuguese city overlooking the River Mondego.

When battle began, early on the morning of 27 September, a
heavy mist obscured the rocky landscape and French skirmishers
quickly advanced up the slope towards the British Army and their
Portuguese allies. Losing sight of his commander, Colonel Wallace
was compelled to decide alone how to deal with the French snipers
among the boulders below them. He chose to attack and addressed
the 88th.

> Now, Connaught Rangers, mind what you are going to
> do; pay attention to what I have told you, and when I
> bring you face to face with those French rascals, drive
> them down the hill – don't give the false touch, but push
> home to the muzzle!

None of the Irishmen cheered their Colonel, but nonetheless they
formed ranks and advanced towards the enemy with a steely calm-
ness, 'as if the men had made up their minds to go to their work
unruffled and not too much excited', recorded Grattan. They moved
off in a column and as they came within range of the French skirmishers, musket balls took a toll of some of the advancing Irish
soldiers. Wallace ordered the cluster of rocks to be cleared of French
snipers and, once that was achieved, the 88th carried on their march
against the main body of French troops further down the hill.
Unfortunately, it was at this point that the Connaught Rangers
were caught by the friendly fire of their Portuguese allies. Wallace
sent Lieutenant John Fitzpatrick to alert them of their mistake, but
he was hit by two bullets, one in the back from the Portuguese and
one in the front from the French that broke his leg.

Wallace saw no alternative but to engage quickly with the enemy. He dismounted and led his men from the front, running towards the flames of French musket fire. 'All was now confusion and uproar, smoke, fire and bullets,' recalled Grattan. 'In the midst of all was seen to be Wallace, fighting at the head of his devoted followers, and calling out to his soldiers to "press forward!"'

When the French finally broke and retreated in panic, they left behind 200 dead soldiers, including their colonel. Wallace reformed his men in line and advanced to the bottom of the hill where he awaited further orders. Wellington had watched the attack and turned with satisfaction to Field Marshal Beresford, who had previously commanded the 88th and doubted their ability against a superior number of Frenchmen. Wellington tapped the field marshal on the shoulder and said: 'Well, Beresford, look at them *now*!' After the battle, Wellington rode up to the colonel of the 88th and warmly shook his hand. 'Wallace, I never witnessed a more gallant charge than that made just now by your regiment!'

Wallace removed his hat, but said nothing. 'It was a proud moment for him,' wrote Grattan. 'His fondest hopes had been realized, and the trouble he had taken to bring the 88th to the splendid state of perfection in which that corps then was, had been repaid in the space of a few minutes by his gallant soldiers, many of whom shed tears of joy.'

*

Although now allowed to serve together in the British Army, the tension between Irish Catholics and Protestants remained a potent point of conflict within British regiments. Benjamin Harris was born in Dorset, but happened to be in Dublin when a recruiting party for the 95th Rifles arrived in the city. Much taken by their stylish dark-green uniform, he deserted his current regiment and joined the Riflemen. Sailing back to England and surrounded by Irish recruits of both faiths, he noted their hot-headed ways. It was not long before the Protestants and Catholics started fighting each other.

They all carried immense shillelaghs in their fists, which they would not quit for a moment. Indeed they seemed to

think their very lives depended on possession of these
bludgeons, being ready enough to make use of them on
the slightest occasion.

Camped on Salisbury Plain, the Irish Riflemen started dancing
together. To Harris, it looked as though maybe they were seeking
to overcome their centuries-old mutual hatred, but this was merely
a preliminary show of drunken camaraderie to be followed by
more sectarian violence. One Catholic partnered a Protestant in a
jig, but then leapt in the air and, with a loud whoop, dealt the Protestant a blow to the side of the head with a club that laid him out
flat. A mass brawl broke out, which carried on in fits and starts
until the Irishmen ended up rioting in the streets of nearby Andover
and had to be pacified by musket-armed English militiamen.

The 28th (North Gloucestershire) Foot also recruited from Ireland
and one of these soldiers was Charles O'Neil, born in Dundalk in
County Louth. In fact, O'Neil stepped up three times, joining two
other regiments before the 28th. On each occasion, he took the
eighteen guineas bounty paid to every new recruit, rapidly deserted,
and moved on to the next unit. He claimed a higher purpose for
enlisting in the British Army. 'Fathers and mothers were careful to
instil into the minds of their children the glory and honor of a military life', he wrote, 'and the fair young damsels of our own dear
island – for Ireland has charming and beautiful girls – were scarcely
willing to regard any young man as honorable or brave, who did
not enlist, and aim to deserve well of his country.'

O'Neil was just seventeen years old when he arrived in Spain at
the British base of Gibraltar in January 1811. The Sunday after his
British regiment landed, he was ordered to attend a Protestant
Church of England service, but, being Catholic, he refused. For his
disobedience, he was summoned before a court martial and sentenced to 300 lashes. The next day, he was stripped to the waist and
bound to a triangle of three poles in the middle of a large hollow
square of soldiers. One soldier stepped forward, took the 'cat' – a
whip with nine knotted cords – and lashed O'Neil twenty-five
times on his bare back.

I was asked if I would give up; I answered 'No!' The
blood was already flowing freely from my back, yet I

resolved to die rather than submit to what appeared to me
so unjust a requirement. The next soldier then took the
lash, and struck twenty-five times. Again the officer
asked if I would yield, and received the same reply; and
this was continued until the whole three hundred had
been inflicted.

More dead than alive, the teenage O'Neil was taken to hospital
where it took several weeks for his wounds to heal. He later claimed
to have written to Prince Frederick, Duke of York and commander-
in-chief of the entire British Army, stating his case as an Irish
Catholic. Realizing this could be a major cause of indiscipline
throughout the army ranks, the Duke of York subsequently granted
permission for Irish soldiers to worship as they pleased. With his
back still sore, O'Neil marched out with the 28th to do battle with
the French.

*

By the end of 1811, the British and French were seeking command
of the main passes on the Spanish–Portuguese border at Ciudad
Rodrigo and Badajoz. Major but inconclusive battles had been
fought at Fuentes de Oñoro and Albuera and Wellington felt confident enough to go on the offensive and advance into central Spain.
It was then that the many Irishmen in his ranks would see some of
the fiercest fighting of the whole campaign – and none came more
bloody than the taking of the town of Badajoz. Both Charles O'Neil
and William Grattan would bear full witness to its horrors.

Grattan and the Connaught Rangers arrived outside Badajoz on
16 March 1812. The Spanish town was perched above the Guadiana
River and its high ramparts had resisted British assaults for over a
year. Grattan and his fellow Irishmen had grown to hate the stub-
bornly resistant citadel and 'contemplated with delight the prospect of having it in their power to retaliate upon the inhabitants
their treatment of our men'. This malevolence would lead to one of
the blackest moments of the Peninsular War.

The town was held by 5,000 French troops, whereas Wellington
commanded five times as many soldiers encircling it, but after two
failed sieges, the French felt confident in the strength of their rein-

forced defences and were determined not to give up. Wellington began the month-long assault by digging earthworks around the town from which his artillery could bombard its walls. The weather was appalling and Grattan recalled wading knee-deep through rain-flooded trenches.

Deciding to exploit the misery of the besiegers, the garrison commander, General Armand Philippon, launched a raid on one of their gun batteries on 19 March. Grattan and his men were digging a trench at the time. Two thousand Frenchmen poured out of the bastion with fixed bayonets.

> I, on the instant, ordered the men to throw by their
> spades and shovels, put on their appointments, and
> load their firelocks. This did not occupy more than
> three minutes, and in a few seconds afterwards the
> entire trenches to our right were filled with Frenchmen.

The French soldiers had been promised money for every shovel or pick-axe they captured, but, thanks to Grattan's quick-witted response, his Irishmen stood their ground and repulsed the attack, chasing them back to the walls of the town. After the fight, Divisional Commander General Picton, so disparaging of the 88th earlier in the war, strode up and congratulated Grattan and his men.

The heavy rain continued and three days later the pontoon bridge erected by the British over the Guadiana was washed away by the swollen waters. The walls of the trenches dug by Grattan and his compatriots began to dissolve and liquid mud made it almost impossible to move the artillery closer to the town. In the meantime, the French directed their guns expertly at the British positions and many Connaught Rangers were killed as their fire raked the earthworks. On one occasion, a French shell hit a wooden magazine shelter and ignited several kegs of gunpowder.

> The planks were shivered to pieces, and the brave
> fellows who occupied them either blown into atoms,
> or so dreadfully wounded as to cause their immediate death;
> some had their uniforms burned to a cinder, while others
> were coiled up in a heap, without the vestige of anything
> left to denote that they were human beings.

Compared to this, one soldier of the 88th, their company barber, got away lightly with a slight scratch to his face from a flying splinter. According to Grattan, he was an ugly man but complained bitterly about the wound destroying his 'good looks'. Moments later, a French cannonball struck him on the head and knocked it off. Grattan and his comrades quickly drew lots for the valuable soap and razor found in the barber's coat.

The arrival of powerful British howitzers enabled Wellington to intensify his fire on the walls of Badajoz, while Picton and his men managed to seize one of the French bastions. By early April, three breaches had been made in the walls and as news reached Wellington of an approaching French relief army, he ordered a final assault on the town on the 6th. Picton's Division, including the Connaught Rangers, was given the task of scaling the thirty-foot high walls of Badajoz Castle on the northern tip of the town, but first they would have to cross the Rivellas, a branch of the River Guadiana, in front of it. This was meant to be a diversionary attack, as the main British assault would come from the other side of the town, but it evolved into a decisive combat.

'The day passed over heavily', remembered Grattan, 'and hour after hour was counted.' Scaling ladders were passed around to the first assault units at five o'clock in the evening; three hours later, they were told to assemble for action. The rain had stopped and the night was clear. The gun batteries fell silent and all Grattan could hear was the sound of frogs croaking on the banks of the Rivellas. Then the band of the 88th struck up, playing Irish airs – what should have been a stirring moment was in fact made melancholic with the men thinking more of their homeland. At 9.25 p.m., the men moved off towards the castle. Unencumbered with knapsacks, they unbuttoned their shirt collars and rolled their trousers up to their knees, and then the 4,000 men of the 3rd Division waded across the Rivellas. At that moment, French flares illuminated the scene and the defenders suddenly saw the rush of men crowding towards them. Every gun on the enemy battlements opened fire.

The Connaught Rangers and others soldiers of Picton's Division advanced into the storm of shot and those that made it to the redoubt placed their ladders against the base of the castle walls. As they surged up the ladders, they were met by rocks and handgrenades thrown down at them; and for those who reached the top, they were pushed backwards by pikes so that they fell and were impaled on the bayonets of their dead comrades in the ditch beneath.

> Hundreds of brave soldiers lay in piles upon
> each other, weltering in blood, and trodden down
> by their own companions.

The 88th lost more than half their men that dreadful night. General Picton, who was in the midst of the fighting and urging his men onwards, was wounded as he tried to climb a ladder. Nevertheless, the sheer weight of redcoats overwhelmed the defenders in the end.

Elsewhere, British and Portuguese soldiers were suffering terribly, blown apart by French mines or pierced by trunks studded with blades chained to the walls. Between ten o'clock and two in the morning, almost 3,000 of them were killed or badly wounded. Grattan compared the horrible spectacle to a volcano – 'vomiting forth fire in the midst of the army'.

> The ground shook – meteors shone forth in every
> direction – and when for a moment the roar of battle
> ceased, it was succeeded by cries of agony …

Towards the end of the fighting, Grattan was busy placing a barrel of gunpowder under the dam of the Rivellas when he was hit by a musket ball in his left breast. 'I staggered back, but did not fall.' A comrade bandaged him up with a handkerchief and he hid in a ditch. But feeling weak from loss of blood, he eventually forced himself out and staggered back to camp.

As the victorious attackers swept over the ramparts, the French and the Spanish citizens of Badajoz paid a terrible price for their resistance. The sheer frustration of the siege and anger at the terrible assault boiled over in the actions of the redcoats as they ran screaming through the narrow streets of the town. Houses were broken into and looted. Men, women and children were assaulted, raped and slaughtered where they were found. The 28th Foot were not present at the final assault on Badajoz, but some of its officers and men volunteered for service there and Charles O'Neil claimed to be among them and joined in the pillaging. He and his fellow Irishmen broke into a cellar to find something to drink, but instead of barrels of booze they found small kegs for storing butter. Furious, one of the men slashed at one of the firkins with an axe. 'To our great surprise, out rolled whole handfuls of doubloons,' he recalled. The soldiers hacked away at the rest of the barrels and gold coins gushed out.

> Each one of us then took what we pleased. I placed three
> handfuls in my comrade's knapsack, and he did the same
> by me. I then filled my haversack, and even my stockings …
> I soon found that I had stored more money than I was
> able to carry, so I threw part of it in an old well.

Once O'Neil's superior officer found out about the treasure, he had the cellar cleared, bringing out enough gold for eight mules to carry.

Surgeon-General James McGrigor, formerly of the 88th, walked through the streets of Badajoz to witness the chaos.

> In a little time the whole of the soldiers appeared to
> be in a state of mad drunkenness. In every corner we met
> them forcing their way like furies into houses, firing
> through the keyholes of doors so as to force the locks,
> or at any person they saw at window imploring mercy.

He heard the screams of women being raped and the groans of those being tortured. At one point, at the risk of his own life, he intervened as two soldiers of his old regiment dragged away two young women. 'It was only by reminding them that I was an old Connaught Ranger', he wrote, 'who felt for the glory of the corps, that I disarmed their rage towards me and their raised muskets were lowered.'

For seventy-two hours, soldiers sacked the town and drank it dry, but on the third day, order was restored when Wellington had a gallows set up in the town square and threatened to hang any soldier still in Badajoz. It had the required sobering effect. Gibbets and triangles for flogging were erected. 'Many men were flogged', noted Grattan, 'but, although the contrary has been said, none were hanged – yet hundreds deserved it.'

*

Wellington's victories in 1812 proved to be decisive in the Peninsular War. Grattan and the Connaught Rangers shared in this triumph, fighting at the battle of Salamanca and entering the Spanish capital of Madrid. They received an enthusiastic reception with bottles of wine thrust into their hands and young girls kissing them.

'The officers were nearly forced from their horses in the embraces of the females,' recalled Grattan. Towards the end of the campaign, Grattan, now a lieutenant, was entrusted with a budget of fifty Spanish dollars to organize a St Patrick's Day celebration for the officers' mess. Mounted on a mule and accompanied by two soldiers, he made his way to a nearby market town where he found what he was looking for.

> I purchased a number of fine mullet, some hens and
> fowls, and a variety of other matters which I thought
> requisite to garnish our table the following day.

He dispatched the valuable food with the other two soldiers and promised to follow them some hours later: it was not a wise decision. As he rode back through mountain passes, the sun set and he lost his way. He heard the cry of wolves coming closer and, as he slowed to cross the rough ground, three wolves leapt out of the darkness and attacked his mule, one springing at its throat. He discharged a pistol at the animals and his mule bolted away from them. He was never more pleased to get back to his camp. The St Patrick's Day dinner was a great success, except the Connaughts' doctor had too much to drink and mistook a balcony for a door, plunging fifteen feet to the ground.

After four years of campaigning, Grattan took his first period of home leave. He carried with him 265 Spanish dollars and set sail from Lisbon to Portsmouth. There, he changed a solitary gold guinea for thirty shillings and took a coach to London. After a few days of sightseeing, he took a coach to Liverpool and sailed home to Dublin. 'As a matter of course all my acquaintances got round me, and I had to recount all my four years' adventures in the Peninsula', wrote Grattan, 'and, while I was so employed in the drawing-room, my man Dan [his servant] fulfilled his part in the kitchen, and, I have little doubt, did much more justice to the matter than I did.'

By the time Grattan was ready to return to the 88th in the spring of 1814, Wellington was on French soil and Napoleon had abdicated. The Peninsular army was disbanded and Grattan's military career came to an end in 1817. He had to wait until 1848 before he received his Peninsular Medal, the year after he published his two volumes of military reminiscences.

The Connaught Rangers fought their last battle against the French at Toulouse in April 1814 and shortly afterwards embarked for service in Canada. While the 88th would see no more combat against Napoleon, Dundalk-born Charles O'Neil and the 28th Foot were present at the final showdown when the French emperor, having escaped from exile, confronted the Duke of Wellington at the battle of Waterloo in 1815. Part of a massive Coalition army that included Dutch, Belgian and German troops, the British contingent was 34,000 strong, so on the basis of between 30 and 40 per cent of these regiments being recruited from Ireland, at least 10,000 Irishmen stood on the battlefield at Waterloo.

Charles O'Neil was wounded at the climax of the battle as the British charged at the French ranks.

> I bled very freely; and this weakened me so much, that,
> finding it impossible to continue my retreat over the pile
> of dead and wounded with which the field was covered,
> I fell among them.

As bullets struck the bodies huddled around him, O'Neil's biggest fear was of being trampled by the cavalry of his own side. When the Scots Greys charged into the French just fifty yards away from him, he imagined the 'iron heel of the horse' finishing him off. At that moment, the result of the battle seemed to hang in the balance until O'Neil heard the drums of the Prussians coming to join them. The arrival of tens of thousands of fresh allied troops finally turned the battle against Napoleon. In the meantime, O'Neil managed to staunch the flow of blood from his arm by turning his handkerchief into a tourniquet and was taken to hospital in Brussels, where he was told his wounded arm had to be amputated. He refused to have it removed and, in due course, he recovered, spending several months back in England at the Chelsea Royal Hospital.

In 1816, an account was made of the losses of the 28th Foot during the war against Napoleon and, of the thousand men who began the Peninsular War, only seven were still alive. O'Neil was granted a pension of a shilling a day and returned to Ireland in 1818. After twelve years at home, O'Neil swapped his pension for a lump sum of money and the promise of 280 acres of land in Canada. At the age of thirty-seven, he sailed to Quebec, took possession of his Canadian land, and then moved to Worcester in Massachusetts where he spent the rest of his life, raising a family alongside other Irish immigrants.

Chapter 4
Napoleon's Irish Legion

The French Revolution inspired Irish nationalists to dream that they could liberate their own country from British tyranny, and for a few days in December 1796 it looked as though it might come true. Thirty-three-year-old Theobald Wolfe Tone stood on the deck of a French frigate as it sailed towards Bantry Bay in County Cork, heading a fleet of 43 ships and 14,000 French Revolutionary troops to bring liberty to Ireland. Five years earlier, Tone had founded the Society of United Irishmen, which in the spirit of the French Revolution's ideal of fraternity hoped to bring together Irish Catholics and Protestants who shared the same beliefs in reforming their political relationship with Britain. When peaceful attempts at reform failed, Tone saw little alternative but to lead the majority of United Irishmen towards an armed rebellion against the British that would result in an independent Irish republic. The French Revolutionary government agreed. It gave him the rank of adjutant-general, and on 15 December 1796 a French invasion fleet set sail from Brest with the aim of bringing revolution to Ireland.

As Tone watched the grey clouds gather above the sails of the ships as they entered the Irish Sea, the United Irishman had doubts about the ability of the French to pull off the invasion. On a practical level he wondered at their seamanship, and the chosen time of year for the seaborne attack could not have been worse – gales lashed the Irish coast – but he could also have wondered at their motive. Over the previous century, Irish desires for independence from Britain had found keen support on the Continent from French

kings who exploited the conflict as part of their wider Catholic
crusade against Protestant nations. With these kings toppled by
revolution, however, Tone believed that this time it would be different.

Just as poor weather had saved England from the Spanish
Armada, so storms raged across the Irish Sea in December 1796
forcing Wolfe Tone and his revolutionary invasion fleet to sail back
to France. Tone stayed on the Continent determined to argue the
case for further French intervention and when the United Irishmen
organized an uprising in June 1798, he succeeded in getting French
agreement to send troops to their assistance. But, by the time they
arrived, the majority of the Irish rebels had been crushed by the
British and a small French force of 1,000 soldiers landing in County
Mayo was easily overwhelmed. A larger French army of 3,000
troops arrived later in October of that year. Sailing towards the
coast of County Donegal, they were again accompanied by Wolfe
Tone, but this time they were intercepted by a Royal Navy squadron and after a three-hour battle were forced to surrender. Tone
was put on trial and rather than be hanged, he slit his own throat in
prison. The fate of the United Irishmen and their alliance with
Revolutionary France now lay in the hands of two other Irish rebels:
Arthur O'Connor and Thomas Addis Emmet.

Emmet and O'Connor had been arrested on the eve of the 1798
rebellion. As senior members of the United Irishmen – also know as
the Union – they had been taken to Britain and were interrogated
by a Secret Committee of the House of Commons in London, where
they freely revealed their connection with Revolutionary France.

'Sometime in 1795, or the beginning of 1796', recalled O'Connor,
'a letter was received by the Executive of the Union from France,
from some individuals of the Union who had fled from persecu-
tion, in which they mentioned that they believed the French would
be induced to treat with the Union, to free us from the tyranny
under which we groaned.'

A official alliance between the United Irishmen and France had
been formalized with the first of the subsequent armed interventions
coming shortly afterwards. Having explained the full story of their
political relationship with the French to the British Parliament in
August 1798, O'Connor and Emmet were sent to prison in Scotland
at Fort George. It was there that the common interests of the two

United Irishmen began to break down. O'Connor received better treatment than Emmet and the other political prisoners, and Emmet suspected O'Connor of reaching some kind of deal with the British, perhaps even spying for them. This distrust reached such a point that when they were released three years later and sent into exile in France, the two men were determined to fight a duel to settle the matter. Their fellow émigrés managed to persuade them not to, but once in Paris, neither figure communicated with the other and factions of exiled Irishmen congregated around each of them. Both men believed they spoke for the Society of United Irishmen.

In the meantime, Napoleon Bonaparte was subverting the idealism of the French Revolution and transforming its republican government into a dictatorship run by himself. The French revolutionary promise of national self-determination, which had so appealed to the United Irishmen, was being overtaken by Napoleon's desire to create a French empire in Europe. The failure of the armed interventions in Ireland in 1796 and 1798 did little to dissuade Napoleon from planning his own assault on Ireland in 1803, timed to coincide with a major invasion of Britain, but rather than aiding an Irish revolution, Napoleon saw it mainly as a way of distracting the British and driving them out of Ireland. He pledged 20,000 troops to the expedition and wanted most of them to come from an Irish Legion raised from rebel émigrés living in France.

Napoleon's Irish Legion formed at Morlaix in Brittany on 31 August 1803 and was under the overall command of Marshal Augereau and his Corps de Brest, assembled specifically for the invasion. Almost all the officers and men were Irish, but the officers were divided by the rift between the exiled leading United Irishmen, some supporting Emmet, while others followed O'Connor. O'Conner was the more military orientated of the two and accused Emmet of being a coward, while Emmet accused O'Connor of naked ambition and wanting to become the first consul of Ireland, aping the title taken by Napoleon in France. Emmet also feared the Irish were merely being used as cannon fodder to fulfil French imperial designs and, in December 1803, wrote to Napoleon, asking him to explain his intentions for the Irish Legion. The response came a fortnight later.

'He [Napoleon] desires that the United Irish should be convinced that it is his intention to secure the independence of Ireland', said the official proclamation, 'and to give protection, entire and effica-cious, to all those of their body who will take part in the expedition, and enter the French service.'

Napoleon pledged that any subsequent peace treaty with Britain would have to include the independence of Ireland. This was con-ditional, however, on a considerable body of United Irishmen joining the French army.

'Every person who shall embark with the French army destined for the expedition shall be commissioned as French,' Napoleon insisted, but this also came with a promise of protection for the Irish soldiers. 'In case of being arrested and not treated as a pris-oner of war, reprisals will be made on English prisoners.'

At first, this guarantee seemed to convince Emmet of the First Consul's sincerity and he even enthused to fellow United Irishmen about the Legion's new standard, bearing the declaration '*L'indepéndance de l'Irlande – Liberté de Conscience.*' In fact, the final form of the Irish Legion colours accepted by Napoleon in 1804 fea-tured the legend '*Le Premier Consul – Aux Irelandois – Unis*' in a laurel wreath on one side, and, on the reverse, four golden Irish harps in each corner against a green background. The initial uniform of the Irish Legion appears to have included a dark-green light infantry jacket with yellow facings. Emmet termed this yellow 'the second national colour'.

Emmet's tentative support for the enterprise collapsed following events in Paris in the spring of 1804. Moving to secure his dictator-ship over the French government, Napoleon ceased to be first consul and was allowed the title of emperor of France in May, with a coronation to come in December. This shift in power had a direct impact on soldiers in the French army, who were now expected to swear an oath of allegiance to the emperor. This did not sit well with Emmet. 'I am an Irishman,' he said, 'and until necessity forces me to contract ties of allegiance elsewhere, I will hold no situation that is not Irish or obviously directed to the emancipation of that country.'

O'Connor had no such qualms, and his more obliging character made him the preferred choice of the French to speak for the United Irishmen; early in 1804, he was rewarded with the rank of general and assigned to Marshal Augereau's staff in Brest. Once Emmet heard this, he stepped away from his negotiations with the French government and made plans to emigrate to the United States.

Later that year, the tensions between the factions supporting Emmet and O'Connor boiled over into conflict on the parade ground. At midday, on 3 June 1804, the Irish Legion was assembled in Carhaix, near Brest in Brittany, to swear an oath of loyalty to the new Emperor Napoleon. As Captain John Sweeny, an ardent supporter of Emmet, marched in front of the ranks of Irishmen, he made a comment to Adjutant Commander Bernard MacSheehy along the lines that this was the first time he had been asked to make such an oath and wondered how it affected his position as an Irishman loyal to his country. Dubliner MacSheehy replied by saying that France had taken him in as an émigré and that Napoleon had given him a job in his army and that he owed both of them his sworn allegiance – especially as Napoleon was the only chance of independence for Ireland. Sweeny accepted the rebuke and took his place in line. MacSheehy then administered the oath to the entire Irish Legion.

The next day, MacSheehy assembled his officers to sign a document that testified that the oath had been taken by everyone in the unit. At this point, Captain Thomas Corbet said he could not put his name to it because he believed Sweeny had not taken the oath, and encouraged others not to. This split the Irish officers and those who supported Sweeny signed their own document saying that he had taken the oath. It was when news reached Sweeny of Corbet's part in this affair that he strode out to confront him as all the other Irish soldiers stood in line on the parade ground. Sweeny walked up to Captain Corbet and punched him in the face so hard that Corbet fell to the ground. Sweeny carried on kicking and punching Corbet, despite the intervention of fellow officers, including Corbet's brother, William. Eventually, Adjutant Commander MacSheehy placed Sweeny and both Corbet brothers under arrest and escorted them off the parade ground. But moments later William Corbet came back and shouted at the rest of the officers: 'We are among a pack of assassins.'

'You lie, you rascal,' replied Dublin-born Captain Patrick Gallagher. This so infuriated Corbet that he lunged at Gallagher with the brass butt of a musket. Another officer tried to shield Gallagher from the blow and was struck on the arm. Gallagher wrenched the gun away from Corbet and threw it on the ground, telling him, 'It would be beneath my dignity to use this musket against you!'

MacSheehy was furious with Corbet. 'How dare you strike an officer!' he told him. 'I could have you shot for such an act!'

In the subsequent investigation of the incident, Thomas Corbet insisted that both Sweeny and Gallagher, supporters of Emmet, be removed from the regiment. Sweeny explained his assault on Thomas Corbet by saying: 'I only did that which is the custom in my country towards one who does not conform to the ways of an honourable man.' He also condemned the 'vile intrigues' of Corbet that had disrupted the functioning of the Irish Legion since its foundation.

MacSheehy kept Sweeny and the two Corbets under arrest throughout the summer until a decision was made by the French authorities on their fate. It seemed likely that all three would be expelled from the Legion, but come September, it was MacSheehy who was removed from his position as commander and replaced by an Italian, Chef de Bataillon Antoine Petrezzoli. Shortly afterwards, Sweeny and the Corbets were released from arrest pending a further decision on what should happen to them. Thomas Corbet seized the opportunity to challenge Sweeny to a duel.

The duel took place on the afternoon of 20 September 1804 in Lesneven, fifteen miles north-east of Brest. In the exchange of shots, Sweeny was wounded in the arm. Corbet refused to accept this as satisfaction and wanted another shot. This time, it was Corbet that was wounded but he claimed he was able to continue. In the final exchange of bullets, Corbet was hit in the stomach and could not carry on. He was carried to a hospital and later died from his wounds. The unseemly parade-ground brawl and the subsequent duel confirmed the splits among the Irish contingent in Napoleon's army and in their attitude to French military service. The scandal damaged the reputation of General O'Connor and his influence with the French authorities waned after it. Many Irishmen left the Legion. John Sweeny emigrated to the United States, while Corbet's brother William resumed his position as an English teacher.

By the spring of 1805, Napoleon's failure to win naval control of the English Channel meant that his projected invasion of England and Ireland was cancelled, so the Irish Legion never would join with the French in liberating their homeland. But as Napoleon turned back towards Continental affairs, those Irishmen that remained in his army were under no illusions of serving their own national interests but chose to stay because they wished to become professional soldiers. Before leaving for America, Emmet had already anticipated the transformation of his freedom-fighting Irishmen into imperial warriors, saying: 'When you went down you intended to be Irishmen, and as such to fight under the French banners in your own country, and for its freedom. Have you all determined now to become subjects of the French empire, and to follow a military life?' Their positive answer was demonstrated by several years of hard fighting for the emperor. The republican idealism embraced by Wolfe Tone and Emmet had long passed.

*

Miles Byrne was twenty-three years old when he fled to Paris in 1803 to join Napoleon's Irish Legion, the son of a County Wexford farmer. He had joined the Society of United Irishmen in their rising of 1798 and fought in several battles against the British, but when the rising was crushed he escaped to Dublin, where he kept a low profile, working as a book-keeper. In 1803, he met Robert Emmet, younger brother of Thomas Addis Emmet, and helped him launch an assault against Dublin Castle. When this failed, he had little choice but to join the other rebel émigrés in France. Being educated and having some military experience, Byrne was commissioned as a second lieutenant into the Irish Legion in France in December 1803.

For the next few years, after the abandonment of Napoleon's invasion of England and Ireland, the Irish Legion was relegated to a minor garrison unit and Byrne languished in Paris. In 1807, the Legion received a fresh influx of Irishmen captured from the king of Prussia's army, where they had been exiled as political prisoners by the British, along with some Poles. A year after the commencement of action in the Peninsular War, a battalion of Irishmen was detached from the Legion and sent south. Again, they performed only garrison duties, but did come to the personal attention of Napoleon when they had the honour of guarding him at Burgos in Spain in January 1809.

'It was the first time I had seen [Napoleon] since 1803, when he was First Consul, and he appeared to have become stouter,' remembered Byrne. 'We were gratified to have been the only troops on guard during his short stay, and being conspicuously placed, and our uniforms tolerably good, we appeared to advantage.'

The Irish Legion was then strengthened to four battalions, partly, thought Byrne, thanks to the good impression they made on Napoleon at Burgos. Byrne was also promoted to captain and hungered for some action against the British, but their first clashes came against Spanish guerrillas as the Irishmen were tasked with escorting the mail that came from France to Madrid. During one of their escort missions, Byrne fell into conversation with a Spanish priest who had got to know several Irishmen at the ecclesiastical college at Salamanca. The priest pointed out the similarity between Irish rebels fighting for freedom in their own country and the Spanish wanting liberation from the invading French. It was a valid comparison that could have embarrassed Byrne, but he refused to see any parallel between the two oppressed peoples. In Spain, Byrne argued, 'the inhabitants were not persecuted and deprived of their civil rights on account of the religion they professed … whilst in poor Ireland the millions of unemancipated Catholic serfs were kept in bondage by a Protestant ascendancy of a few hundred thousand individuals, acting there the part of the cruel task masters of England'.

The Spanish priest was unimpressed with this line of argument, saying the Spanish had a just cause for fighting Napoleon's army: 'It is because we want to remain a Spanish nation independent of foreigners, and we hope it will never cease till the last French soldier is driven from our country.' This passion struck a bell with Byrne, reminding him of the 'virtuous clergymen who suffered torture and death, as martyrs, both in the fields and on the scaffold, in Ireland in 1798, endeavouring to set their country free from the cruel foreign yoke'. However Byrne presented it, alongside his veteran United Irishmen, who were drawn together by anger against British injustice, he was now in the contradictory position of fighting to support the tyranny of Napoleon in Spain and Portugal.

In February 1810, the Irish Legion was incorporated into the French 2nd Division that marched out of Burgos to the Spanish city of Astorga and helped lay siege to it. For three weeks, the Irishmen held their positions in the trenches as French guns pounded the walls. When the time came to attack a breach in the walls, 150 men from the 2nd Battalion of the Irish Legion were selected to lead the assault under the command of Captain John Allen, who had distinguished himself in a number of clashes with Spanish soldiers. Their attack began at five o'clock in the afternoon on 21 April.

When the signal was given, the Irishmen ran across 200 yards of open ground, carrying ladders, exposed to the fire of 2,000 defending Spanish troops. Allen led his men through the storm of musket fire and cannonballs to clamber up through the breach and on to the top of the wall, where, in a bravura gesture, he turned round and saluted the French army.

Having surmounted the wall, Allen and his Irishmen took possession of a house near the rampart. They piled up their backpacks to create a barrier from behind which they could shoot at the enemy troops on their flank and provide covering fire for the rest of their own men, who continued to surge up through the breach. It was desperately hard fighting. An Irish drummer had both his legs broken by musket fire as he mounted the breach, but he kept hold of his drum, sat down and beat the charge until the rest of the battalion joined him. For that act of valour, he was later awarded the Légion d'honneur, the highest military decoration in France.

Allen and his men defended their position all night and the French commander, General Jean-Andoche Junot, doubted whether they could survive to the morning, but one of Allen's aides emerged out of the breach in the darkness and asked him to send the beleaguered soldiers something to drink. A handful of men were ordered back into the breach to take Allen the supplies he needed. Many of them were killed or wounded on the way. One of these Irishmen was taken to the French field hospital, but sat silently, allowing other men to be treated before him. When news of this forbearance got back to Junot, he declared, 'What a pity such men have not a country of their own to fight for!'

The next day, when the Spanish garrison saw that the Irishmen were still in possession of the breach, they knew the game was up and promptly surrendered. The Irish escorted 5,000 Spanish troops out of the city. As an honour, Allen and his surviving soldiers, only 150 still standing out of the total battalion strength of 900, were instructed to return to the breach where they were reviewed by Junot and all the French generals present. Each one of them embraced Allen – the only senior officer in his unit to have escaped death or injury.

None of the Irish or French was allowed to plunder the conquered city of Astorga: Junot had one French looter shot as an example to the rest. 'What a striking contrast compared to the conduct of the English at Badajoz,' commented Byrne, 'where Wellington allowed his army during twenty four hours to commit all kinds of horrors on the innocent inhabitants … Though indeed I should not have been surprised at the want of English discipline, from the knowledge I have had of the cruelties committed by the regiment of ancient Britons in my own unfortunate country.' Of course, the truth was that many fellow Irishmen were among the plundering redcoats at Badajoz.

*

The Irish Legion was at the battle of Bussaco in 1810, where Wellington's Connaught Rangers and other redcoat Irish units clashed with the French, but were kept in reserve and so never fought their own countrymen on the battlefield. Connaught Ranger William Grattan heard rumours of their presence, but when his regiment advanced against the defeated French army, 'we could not discover one Irishman amongst them'. Nevertheless, the campaign was tough and the Irish Legion suffered from the assaults of Spanish and Portuguese guerrillas, with Captain Allen being wounded and captured by them. This was to be the final contribution of the Irish Legion to the Peninsular War. In August 1811, the Legion was renamed the 3rd Foreign Regiment and lost its Irish identity, with many Austrians joining its ranks.

Captain Miles Byrne continued to serve in the 3rd Foreign Regiment, and with several of his fellow Irish officers petitioned the French Minister of War to serve in the front line in Napoleon's campaign in Central Europe. Following the disaster of the retreat from Russia in 1812, the Irishmen were welcomed into the Grande Armée in February 1813. This was a different kind of fighting to the counter-insurgency experience in Spain in which hundreds of thousands of troops from many nations clashed in large-scale bloody battles. Byrne and his Irishmen were outnumbered by German and Hungarian troops in their regiment.

In May 1813, the 3rd Foreign Regiment proved itself in Germany at the battle of Bautzen, near Dresden, by driving off a Prussian cavalry attack, and when the emperor heard that Captain John Allen was back in the unit, he asked the Irishmen to guard him in camp outside the town of Liegnitz. On that same day, Marshal Michel Ney reprimanded an Irish sergeant named Costello for not responding to a trumpet call to withdraw to his unit during earlier fighting. A Cossack had fired at him twice, explained Costello, and he wanted to kill him before quitting the battlefield.

'And did you kill him?' asked Ney.

'I hope so,' said Costello. 'I saw him fall from his horse.'

The Marshal was impressed and let the Irishman go.

The final phase of the 1813 campaign proved to be a brutal affair for Napoleon's Irish soldiers, who had become part of the Vth Corps commanded by Count Lauriston and took the full brunt of an attack launched by Prussian Field Marshal Gebhard Leberecht von Blücher near the town of Lowenberg on 19 August. The Irishmen formed a hollow square to withstand a cavalry charge, but then the Prussians brought up an artillery battery to pound the vulnerable lines of men. Grapeshot and cannonballs took away whole ranks of Irishmen, but they stood their ground, filled the gaps, and the Prussian cavalry never broke their square.

'The Irish regiment suffered much in this day's fighting,' recalled Byrne.

Three hundred men were killed or wounded; four officers were killed and eight wounded. Their commander Tennant was among them. 'Cut completely in two,' noted Byrne, 'the cannon ball striking a belt in which he carried his money and served as a knife to separate the body.' When his soldiers buried him, several gold coins fell out of his entrails. Sergeant Costello, so bold in front of Marshal Ney, lost his arm. 'The officers who escaped being wounded in this action', wrote Byrne, 'had their uniforms bespattered with the blood and brains of the men killed beside them, by the grape-shot from the enemy's artillery.'

Just two days later, the Irishmen had to lick their wounds and lead a French counter-attack across the River Bober under fire. In the midst of the combat, their colonel, William Lawless, saluted Napoleon, who was watching the assault, but then Lawless had his leg shattered by enemy shot and had to be carried off the battlefield. Napoleon sent the surgeon of his Imperial Guard to perform the amputation.

In subsequent fighting, the gains of the Irishmen were lost and the French army was forced into a general retreat that led them to the rain-swollen River Bober. All the bridges crossing the river had been swept away and the Irish halted in Lowenberg to wait for the waters to subside, but the pursuing Prussians and their Russian allies were on their heels. The French and the Irish were trapped as the water rose behind them. Fighting to their last cartridge, they had little choice but to surrender or throw themselves into the raging river. Hundreds attempted to swim across, but were swept away and died. Only 150 soldiers of the French division escaped, Byrne among them, and he recorded the tragedy.

> Eight officers and thirty men of the Irish regiment with
> commandant Ware, and the ensign who saved the Eagle
> of the regiment, had the good fortune to get out of the bed
> of the river, but had to walk through a sheet of water which
> covered the other side for more than half a mile under the
> fire of the enemy, and many were wounded in this passage.

Had the enemy not been distracted by the temptations of looting their prisoners, Byrne believed that none of them would have escaped. General Puthod and the rest of his division who remained behind were taken by the Russians and sent to Siberia.

The Irish survivors of this slaughter limped back through Germany to their base in Holland. The remnants of the unit were reorganized into a 1st Battalion that was ordered to defend the Lowlands against an allied invasion in 1814. They held out in Antwerp until Napoleon was forced to abdicate. They had a new colonel, Jean Mahony, but in the peace that followed, Irish tensions rose again and he fought a duel with Major Ware, survivor of the German debacle.

With Napoleon in exile, the new French government selected three foreign regiments to defend it, and such was the reputation of the Irish for their courage and loyalty that they were chosen as one of them. That trust was misplaced, because as soon as Napoleon returned from Elba in 1815, the Irish declared for their old master, the emperor. However, once all the non-Irish troops were reallocated to other foreign regiments in Napoleon's army, the Irish contingent was not strong enough to join him for his final battle at Waterloo. With Napoleon defeated, all his foreign units were disbanded by the restored French monarchy.

While most of the men who had served in Napoleon's Irish Legion returned home, a few stayed on to enlist in the Royal Foreign Legion, the precursor of the more famous Foreign Legion formed in 1831. As a renowned Bonapartist, Miles Byrne was dismissed from the French army, but his reputation as a professional soldier was such that in 1828 he was recalled at the age of forty-eight to serve in an expedition to southern Greece. He was promoted to chef de bataillon in 1830, becoming commander of the 96th Regiment, and retired two years later. He never returned to Ireland and spent the rest of his life in Paris, where he wrote his memoir chronicling the sacrifices of the Irish Legion.

Chapter 5
Latin American Adventures

The liberation of South America from the crumbling Spanish Empire offered just the kind of adventure that appealed to Irishmen looking for a new life in a faraway land. The reality of what this meant was illustrated by the extraordinary career of Peter Campbell. Born in western Ireland in 1780, Campbell grew into a tall and well-built teenager who gravitated towards physically demanding work. He was apprenticed as a tanner, a harsh and stinking job that involved soaking animal skins in urine and then scraping off the flesh and hair with blades. The skills he learned in handling knives inside the tannery stayed with him for the rest of his life and would enhance his reputation as a mean street fighter.

As soon as he was old enough, Campbell ran away to join the British Army. He ended up in the 1st Battalion of the 71st Highland Regiment garrisoned at Ballinasloe and Loughrea in County Galway. Having been posted abroad on tough missions in India and Ceylon, the Scottish regiment, like many in the British Army, couldn't find enough of its own countrymen to replenish its ranks and turned to young Irishmen keen for travel abroad. Campbell was just the kind of hardy recruit they were looking for and his commanding character was quickly rewarded when they made him a sergeant.

It was the height of the Napoleonic wars when Campbell joined the Highlanders and in June 1806 the British government seized an opportunity to weaken Spain – then an ally of Napoleon – by attacking one of its overseas colonies in South America. They dispatched an expeditionary force of 2,000 redcoats to occupy Buenos Aires and Peter Campbell's 71st Highlanders set sail from Cork with them. At first, the British were welcomed as liberators and Campbell and his fellow Irishmen enjoyed the sensation of being local heroes, feeling very much at home among the Catholic men and women of the city.

The more relaxed Latin American lifestyle was in stark contrast to the harsh discipline of the British Army. 'The males seem to have no pursuit', noted one of the Irish soldiers, 'and no visible means of existence but from rapine and the lasso. The liquor shops are many, and thither the multitude repair upon Sundays to carouse after worship...' Campbell rather liked this new world and at some stage made up his mind, along with several other Irish soldiers, to desert.

In the meantime, several prominent businessmen in Buenos Aires turned against the intervention of the British and their demands to open up their markets to free trade. With local militiamen, they re-took the city and made the remaining 71st Highlanders prisoners. It would take a second expedition by the British in the following year, including Irish Fusiliers and Connaught Rangers, to release the captives. But by then the population of Buenos Aires had had enough of the invaders and after bitter street fighting the British were forced to evacuate their troops and sail home. It had been a complete disaster and the Viceroyalty of the Rio de la Plata, with its capital at Buenos Aires, remained within the Spanish Empire. By this time, Campbell and his deserters had disappeared into the Latin American hinterland.

Escaping the political turmoil, the Irish sergeant made his way to Corrientes, the capital of a province 600 miles to the north of Buenos Aires, laying on the eastern shore of the Parana River, close to the border with present-day Paraguay. There, in a region dominated by vast herds of cattle, Campbell returned to his first career, gaining employment in a large tannery. For some time, he kept his head down and led a quiet life, enlivened by regular drinking bouts with gauchos, the local cowboys. He learned to hold his own in their rough company and gained a formidable reputation as a brawler.

Campbell's speciality was to fight with a large carving knife as his sword and a poncho wrapped round his left arm as a shield. 'I did not hear that in any of his single combats he had killed his opponent,' said a contemporary, 'but he had maimed, wounded, and disabled so many, that none dared at length to engage him.'

Three years later, the mayhem that had engulfed Buenos Aires came to Corrientes, thanks to events in faraway Europe. Spain had broken away from its alliance with Napoleon and been invaded by the French as a result. This meant the British were now allies of the Spanish, but could do little to help the country and its king was deposed. The collapse of Spanish control over its colonial empire led to the May Revolution in Buenos Aires in 1810, with the Viceroy being replaced by a local junta or assembly.

Local military commanders rallied to the cause of independence from Spain and one of them was José Artigas, who volunteered to help Buenos Aires keep its freedom from Spanish loyalists based in Montevideo in modern-day Uruguay. Marching north to Corrientes, he recruited an army from the hard-living gauchos. Among them was Peter Campbell. A Scots cattle farmer living in the area described the Irishman's appearance after living on the pampas for several years: a 'tall, raw boned, ferocious looking man' with two cavalry pistols stuck in his waistband and a sabre in a rusty steel scabbard hanging from his belt.

> His face was not only burnt almost to blackness by the sun, but it was also blistered to the eyes; while large pieces of shrivelled skin stood ready to fall from his parched lips. He wore a pair of plain ear-rings, a foraging cap, a tattered poncho, blue jacket, with tarnished red facings; a large knife in a leather sheath …

Artigas had fought against the British in the streets of Buenos Aires when their venture had turned sour and had a certain respect for them. As soon as he heard of the presence of the former Highland sergeant in his ranks, he asked Campbell to help train his men. These included Guarani Indians who Campbell armed with European muskets and taught how to charge forward on horseback, then, if initially unsuccessful, to fall back and disperse, dismounting to attack as infantry. British Army discipline helped transform Artigas's motley recruits into a war-winning machine and in 1811 they defeated Spanish loyalists at the battle of Las Piedras and laid siege to Montevideo.

As Artigas's fame spread and he was acclaimed liberator of what would become an independent Uruguay, with its capital at Montevideo, so Campbell shared in his good fortune and became a prominent personality in his own right. He further assisted Artigas by turning a collection of river craft into a twenty-three-boat squadron that patrolled the Parana River as far as the River Plate estuary and for this reason the Irishman enjoyed the honour of being dubbed naval commander-in-chief and founder of the Uruguayan navy.

Once the fighting was over, Campbell had to make a living but his newly won prestige meant he could no longer go back to tanning. Instead, he made the most of his military reputation by offering protection to wealthy landowners. One evening in 1815, he rode on to an estate owned by a Scots immigrant in Corrientes called John Parish Robertson.

At first, Robertson feared the red-haired rider and his followers might be bandits come to loot his farm, but once the fierce-looking man opened his mouth, he spoke in a mangled Spanish with a strong Irish accent. Surprised, Robertson wondered whom he had the honour of addressing.

'"Por Dios!" said the Irishman. "Don't you know Peter Campbell? Pedro Campbell as the Gauchers calls me?" He pronounced Pedro as "Paythro". "You're the only gentleman in the who'al country as has not."'

It was true. As soon as Campbell said his name then it rang a bell for Robertson, and when the local governor turned up at the ranch that evening for a drink, the Scotsman gathered the full importance of the man in their midst. The governor immediately recognized Campbell and embraced him. Later, after they had drunk their beer and Campbell had left, the governor turned to Robertson and told him: 'Next to the Protector [Artigas], there is no man can be of such service to you in this province as Don Pedro Campbell.'

The next time he saw Campbell, he was clean-shaven and wearing a smart blue frock coat and large straw hat. The Irishman had a proposition for Robertson and his brother. He realized that like so many other managers of vast cattle-raising estates in the region, plagued by banditry, they wanted to realize quickly the value of their investment and move to somewhere more civilized, like Buenos Aires. He could help with that, or, as he put it:

There is not an *estanceiro* [estate owner] that has the liver
to go to his own estate; peep out of his own window; slaughter
one of his own animals; carry ten dollars in his pocket, take
time to sip a *mate* [a tea-like drink], or venture to light a
cigar after dusk, unless he knows I am out in the camp to
protect him.

Campbell was offering muscle for hire. 'If he heard of a quarrel
or a fight among these gambling and drunken Gauchos,' noted
Robertson, 'he would rush into the midst of the knives which all of
them were brandishing. He designated the combatants with all the
energy of an Irish accent … [and] he would lay about them with
stick, knife, or sabre, whichever came first to hand.' After such a
scrap, he would lean on the counter of the bar and 'burst into a
hoarse laugh'.

The Robertson brothers agreed to pay Campbell 1,200 dollars,
and for that the Irishman recruited a gang of ex-soldiers and
gauchos and commanded them to gather all the cattle and horses
on the territory. After a year's work, he presented the Robertsons
with 150,000 hides, which were then bundled into carts and given
an armed escort to Buenos Aires where the brothers could hand-
somely realize their assets.

Protection deals such as this proved a profitable line of business
for Campbell and soon he was ensconced in a fine house on the
pampas. In 1819, he was appointed deputy governor of Corrientes
province. It had been a long and strange journey for the Irish tanner,
but he had made it purely through his fighting skills. As William
Robertson put it:

His physical strength – his undaunted, if not ferocious,
courage when roused – his dexterity with his knife, and
his ever ready appeal to that, or to his gleaming sabre,
cowed all spirits less daring than his own, and left him
undisputed master of the field.

Eventually, however, as Campbell's fortunes had risen with those
of José Artigas, so they would fall with him. Having liberated
Montevideo, Artigas oversaw the creation of a new federation of
provinces that included Corrientes and would become the future

Uruguay. This brought him into conflict with the rulers of Buenos Aires, who wanted to keep hold of their northern territories. In the following fighting, Artigas was defeated and withdrew into Paraguay, with the loyal Campbell following him into exile.

Little is known about Campbell's last years, although some say he returned to his old trade of tanning. It is thought he died in Pilar, possibly murdered, in 1832, but befitting the memory of a national liberator his remains were removed from Paraguay and reburied in Montevideo.

*

Several other Irishmen made notable contributions to South American independence at the beginning of the nineteenth century. Bernardo O'Higgins has the most Irish of names and was the liberator of Chile, but his links with Ireland are only through his name. Born in Chile, he was the illegitimate son of Ambrose O'Higgins, a Spanish officer born in County Sligo, who then spent most of his life in Chile as a governor of the country. Despite this lack of Irishness, there are plaques in honour of him in both Sligo and Dublin

More genuinely Irish was John Devereux. Coming from County Wexford, he was just the kind of revolutionary figure to be swept up in the romance of Latin American liberation, but he turned out to be more of a scoundrel than a patriot. Taking part in the failed Irish rebellion of 1798, he had fled abroad with like-minded rebels to continue the war against Britain by joining Napoleon's Irish Legion in France. When that came to nothing, he sailed to America to seek his fortune, where he gained experience as a trader in coffee and weapons.

By pure chance, Devereux arrived in Cartagena, on the northern coast of present-day Colombia, just as Simón Bolívar was planning to liberate his homeland of Venezuela from its Spanish rulers. Elaborating his military background in revolutionary France and his business contacts in Britain, Devereux offered to raise an Irish Legion to help Bolívar in his fight against the Spanish Empire.

Devereux fixed a price of $175 for every Irish soldier he delivered to Venezuela. By December 1819, the first contingent had landed on Margarita Island. On the 14th of that month, an official proclamation was made by Simón Bolívar, which later appeared in the London *Times*.

> Irishmen! Having left your own country, in order to follow the generous sentiments which have always distinguished you among the illustrious of Europe, I have the glory now to number you among the adopted children of Venezuela, and to esteem you as the defenders of the liberty of Colombia.

Pitched at restless Irishmen looking for a cause to pin their hopes for fame and fortune, Bolívar seemed to understand them very well. In reality, the appeal was perfectly directed at wandering Irishmen because the message was, in fact, a fake composed by Devereux himself, who knew only too well the desires of frustrated Irish rebels. In the same advert, Devereux restyled himself as the 'virtuous and brave General D'Evereux'.

It was all part of an elaborate confidence scheme to line Devereux's own pockets. By using a forged letter from Bolívar, he returned to Ireland with the intention of selling commissions in his Latin American Irish Legion. The announcement in *The Times* furthered his plan to recruit Irishmen throughout Britain. Tragically, the scam worked and many adventurers and ex-soldiers joined up on the promise of rewards in Venezuela as part of Bolívar's liberating army. The reality was horrendously different. When they arrived on the mosquito-infested coast, they were faced with meagre rations and no pay. Mutiny, sickness and losses in battle followed, with most of the Irishmen begging to be evacuated to Jamaica.

Fearing death or injury from these irate Irishmen, Devereux fled back to Venezuela, where he managed to shift the blame for this failure to the local authorities for not preparing a better reception for his recruits. Bolívar appeared to be convinced by this and kept the Irishman in his entourage, promoting him to the rank of major general in 1821. Bolívar could afford to be generous as his armies had liberated an enormous swathe of Spanish America, including Venezuela, Colombia, Panama and Ecuador. Having a certain talent for talking his way out of trouble, Devereux simply rode on Bolívar's coat-tails and was appointed his ambassador to the courts of northern Europe.

Back in London in 1824, Devereux wrote a letter to a Dublin-based friend, Daniel O'Connell, in which he tried to excuse his own role in what had turned out to be a disaster for many of the Irishmen caught up in his money-spinning enterprises.

> I cherished the delightful hope of coupling the glories
> of the country of my birth with the new-born liberties of
> the country of my adoption: but to no man did I ever hold
> out a delusive prospect, or lure him forward with promises
> which I could not realize. To each and all who joined my
> standard, I frankly explained the hardships which awaited
> them, and that our way to success must be fought through
> sickness, perils and fatigue.

In an earlier letter from another military associate, O'Connell was told that Devereux must be worth at least £150,000 – a vast sum at the time. The next year, Devereux's past crimes caught up with him as he travelled through Europe discussing access to Colombian gold mines, when he was imprisoned in Venice by the Austrians. Eventually released, he travelled to the United States where he lived on a Venezuelan pension awarded in thanks for his dubious contribution to their liberty.

Despite the perils of fighting in Latin America, Irishmen continued to volunteer their services to the newly liberated counties, but sometimes they proved to be more of a hindrance than a help. In Brazil, freed from Portugal in 1822, Irish soldiers were recruited alongside Germans to form an army to fight a war against Argentina. Many of the 2,000 Irishmen were raised by William Cotter from County Cork with the promise of land after five years of service. Sadly, the presence of so many foreign troops in the Brazilian capital Rio de Janeiro did not go as planned, and on 9 June 1828 a major mutiny broke out.

The spark that set it off was an incident involving a German grenadier. He failed to lift his cap in salute to a superior officer and was arrested, being sentenced to 500 lashes. The soldier, of otherwise good record, was nearly dead when other officers intervened to stop the punishment and release him, which caused a crowd of German soldiers to appeal to the Brazilian Emperor Pedro I against the unfairness of the flogging. At that moment, the Germans were joined by a group of Irish soldiers on the booze. 'These furious and desperate ruffians,' declared a contemporary report, 'who were already intoxicated, inflamed the Germans by their vociferations.' The situation rapidly deteriorated.

A military magazine was broken open, and, armed with these weapons, the German and Irish mutineers stormed and looted the houses of the commanding officers. Musketry echoed throughout the night as the plundering soldiers broke into shops. The Brazilian emperor ordered his own private guard to protect his palace. Loyal officers trying to stop the riot were killed and others fled, leaving the mutineers to embark on two days and nights of orgiastic destruction. Eventually, it was the Germans who tired of the mutiny and turned on the Irish, expelling them from their part of the city. However, a native regiment, the 28th Cacadores, just returned to the city, saw the disorder as an opportunity to avenge themselves against their regimental major, who had refused them allowances in the past. They were going to drag him before the emperor to plead their case, when the Irish intervened and killed him.

The shock of this death brought the mutiny to an abrupt halt and the Irish and German troops were confined to their barracks. But stories abounded that the foreign troops were going to rise again and this time plunder the entire city. The Irish hadn't finished either and broke out of their quarters into the local police station where they armed themselves. 'They proceeded to rob some shops, taverns and houses,' said a newspaper report. 'They drank to such excess, that they conducted themselves like madmen. They fired on the negroes, and on every person that passed.' They then linked up with some of the poorer African-Brazilians and went on a rampage with them.

The Rio militia were finally called out, along with some cavalry and three artillery pieces. A volley of musketry was fired, with powder only, at the Irish barracks but the Irishmen were far from intimidated. It was only when the guns were loaded with bullets that the Irish stayed inside their quarters and slept off their terrible night of destruction. When they awoke, the Irish soldiers surrendered to the militia and were escorted to ships that took most of them back to Ireland. Some, however, stayed on and formed a colony in the province of Bahia. The mutineers among the Germans were also punished, but Emperor Pedro I and his fellow Brazilians swore never again to trust their national security to the Irish.

*

John Riley was a strapping young man, over six feet tall with blue eyes, dark hair and a ruddy complexion. He was born in County Galway and like many young Irishmen chose a military career as his pathway to adventure, but little did he know it would bring him close to the hangman's noose. He joined the British Army, becoming a non-commissioned officer, and was posted across the Atlantic to Canada. He didn't quite fit in and deserted, crossing the border southwards into Michigan to work as a labourer for a fellow Irishman from County Mayo. At the age of twenty-eight, Riley enlisted in the United States Army in 1845. As a private in the 5th Regiment of Infantry, he was dispatched to Texas, sailing along the Mississippi to New Orleans and then on to Corpus Christi, where his regiment became part of General Zachary Taylor's Army of Occupation.

At that time, the United States had just annexed Texas from Mexico and was keen to absorb large chunks of California Territory too. When the proposal of American President James Polk to buy this land was ignored by the new anti-American government in Mexico City, General Taylor was ordered to take his soldiers further south to the Rio Grande in March 1846 to confront the Mexicans. John Riley marched with his comrades the 170 miles through the desolate plain until they set up camp on the banks of the border river, opposite the Mexican town of Matamoros. On Sunday, 12 April 1846, Riley asked permission to attend a Catholic mass held by a Mexican priest on the Texan side of the river. Given a pass, he went off, never again to return to his unit. He was reported as a deserter.

Riley later gave his own explanation of what happened. As he attended the religious service, he was captured by Mexican soldiers who took him across the river to Matamoros. There, he was brought before General Pedro de Ampudia, who interrogated him about the numbers of General Taylor's army. The Mexican then invited Riley to join his own force as a lieutenant.

The answer that I made him, that in case that I took arms against the United States, that I was taking them against my brothers and countrymen. He has told me, that as being an alien to the United States and Mexico both, I should suffer death; [he] brought me out on the plaza, with my hands tied behind my back as a prisoner and sentenced me to be shot in 25 minutes …

At that moment, another Mexican general rode up and declared that no such execution should take place as long as he was commander of the army in the region. He then questioned Riley again about the American army across the river and offered him the same deal. He gave him four days to make up his mind about joining his army or he would be sentenced to death. 'No consul belonging to Great Britain being in that part of the country at the time,' reasoned Riley, 'I thought fit to accept of the commission for fear of being immediately shot.' Riley was given a sword and became a first lieutenant in the Mexican artillery on a higher monthly rate of pay than in the US army. A month later, the United States and Mexico were at war – and Riley was on the wrong side as far as his personal future was concerned.

In Matamoros, Riley gathered together a company of forty-eight Irishmen in a similar situation to himself. A year later, this unit had grown to over 200 and was called the San Patricio or St Patrick's battalion and was essentially a volunteer militia artillery unit, although Riley would have contested the term 'volunteer'. His second-in-command was Patrick Dalton, born in County Mayo, who had deserted from the US 2nd Regiment of Infantry when they were based the other side of the Rio Grande. Not all the San Patricios were Irish or Roman Catholic, with several coming from England, Germany, France and Poland, and some being born in the USA, but Riley ensured the battalion had an overall Irish identity: their flag was later described by a New Orleans war correspondent as being of green silk with a harp on one side and the motto 'Erin go Bragh' – 'Ireland for Ever' – and on the other side an image of St Patrick.

The first significant battle for the San Patricios was at Monterrey on 21 September 1846, where they defended the city with their artillery against several US assaults. In the end, their Mexican com-

mander decided to give up the city on condition they were allowed
to withdraw fully armed. With their flags held high, the Mexicans
marched proudly past the assembled US soldiers, but William S.
Henry was one of several scowling Americans who spotted the
Irish among them.

> Several of our deserters were recognized in the ranks
> of the enemy, the most conspicuous of whom was an
> Irishman by the name of Riley, who has been appointed
> a captain in the artillery of the enemy. He was
> recognized by his old mess-mates, and passed them amid
> hisses and a broadside of reproaches. The dastard's cheek
> blanched, and it was with difficulty he retained his
> position on his gun.

After Monterrey, the San Patricio battalion were incorporated into
the larger Mexican army commanded by Antonio Lopez de Santa-
Anna that marched north to fight US forces at the battle of Buena
Vista in February 1847. There were put in charge of a battery of
heavy cannon and destroyed the US artillery opposite them. A
group of the Irishmen even managed to charge a US battery, bayoneting their crew and dragging back two cannons. The Irish were
proving to be a thorn in the side of the Americans and could expect
little mercy in the future. The battle turned into a defeat for the
Mexicans, however, and as the San Patricios covered their retreat,
US guns were turned on them and they suffered heavy casualties,
up to a third of their total number.

In April, matters only got worse at the battle of Cerro Gordo.
Realizing they faced harsh punishment if they were captured by
the US army, the San Patricios threatened wavering Mexicans with
their artillery fire if they retreated, but such was the hard fighting
that the Irishmen were too busy defending themselves to halt the
disintegrating units around them.

By the summer of 1847, the fighting reputation of the San Patricios was such that Santa-Anna personally encouraged the creation
of a larger infantry battalion, dubbed the Foreign Legion of Patricios, in which volunteers from all European countries were
welcome. This was commanded by Colonel Francisco Rosendo
Moreno, with Riley heading the first company. Such was the Irish-

man's fame now that the newly promoted Major Riley's name appeared on the draft of a printed appeal, encouraging deserters from the US army.

'My countrymen, Irishmen!' said the circular. 'For whom are you contending? For a people who, in the face of a whole world, trampled upon the holy altars of our religion, set the firebrand upon a sanctuary devoted to the blessed Virgin, and boasting of civil and religious liberties, trampled in contemptuous indifference all appertaining to the dearest feelings of our country.'

If Riley was involved with the drafting of this open letter it certainly revealed a religious bitterness towards the US forces that perhaps explained the reason for so many Irish Catholics joining the Mexican ranks. The notice concluded with Riley saying he had received nothing but kind hospitality from the Mexicans and promised the same warm welcome for any army deserters. It was perhaps lucky for Riley that this was never printed.

As the US army, under the command of General Winfield Scott, advanced on Mexico City, the San Patricios were holed up in the fortified convent of Churubusco. General Santa-Anna ordered the Irishmen and the other Mexican troops ensconced behind its high walls to hold the position whatever the cost. Around midday on 20 August 1847, an American division pushed through fields of maize towards the convent.

The defenders waited until the US troops were within musket range and then let loose a devastating volley, compounded by the artillery of the San Patricios. Blue-coated soldiers fell in waves before the fire. The survivors withdrew, but then came back at the convent and threw themselves at the walls of the building for three hours. This fearless assault, accompanied by a continuous artillery bombardment, began to wear down the resistance of the Mexicans and their Irish comrades. Running short of ammunition, the defenders retreated inside the convent as the Americans climbed over its walls.

Some Mexicans began to raise white flags in hope of surrender, but the desperate San Patricios tore them down, intent on fighting to the last man. Instead, with guns empty of bullets, there was little they could do but stand impotently as the Americans surrounded them and claimed the convent. 'It was with much difficulty that the American soldiers could be prevented from bayoneting these miscreants on the spot,' remembered one US officer, 'so deep was their indignation against them.' In the chaos, some San Patricios did manage to escape, but many were dead or wounded and some eighty-five were taken prisoner, among them an injured Major John Riley. It was a moment of great satisfaction for the Americans as the existence of the battalion of traitors had severely embarrassed them. When Santa-Anna heard of the end of the Irishmen, he declared: 'Give me a few hundred more like Riley's and I would have won the victory.'

Just three days after their capture, the first of the San Patricios were put on trial. Three days after that, a second court martial dealt with the rest. Special attention was given to Riley, deemed the ring-leader of the deserters, and he made his case strongly, claiming he was forced into Mexican service and even calling on four character witnesses. He argued that he had come to the aid of fellow Americans he came across in Mexico, but the judges were having none of it and he was found guilty of desertion and sentenced to death. The same punishment was passed on all the other San Patricio prisoners, bar two. The method of execution was to be by hanging, not the usual firing squad, as it appeared the military authorities wanted to underline their disgust at the activities of the Irishmen.

Mass hangings took place from 10 September onwards and Patrick Dalton, Riley's early second-in-command, was among the first. On 13 September, with the taking of the fortress of Chapultepec, the last obstacle before the capture of Mexico City, General Scott decided on a symbolic moment for the next set of executions. At the precise moment that the Stars and Stripes replaced the Mexican flag on the battlements of the fortress, thirty San Patricios were hanged in full view of both armies, but they voiced their defiance to the last by cheering the fluttering Mexican flag before they dropped.

It seemed that Riley would be next for execution, but General Scott softened his attitude, declaring that the remaining prisoners would not be hanged as they had deserted before the USA was at war with Mexico. Instead, Riley and the rest were to be given fifty lashes on their bare backs and branded with a 'D' for deserter on their right cheeks. Days later, US soldiers marched victoriously through the gates of Mexico City. The war was won and California, New Mexico and Texas were incorporated as US territories.

Riley stayed in prison as long as US soldiers occupied Mexican territory. From behind bars, he wrote a letter to his Irish employer in Michigan saying how proud he was to fight for Mexico against the Americans and attain the rank of major, the highest received by a foreign soldier. He appreciated their hospitality towards him as an Irishman and a Catholic. 'It grieves me to have to inform you', he concluded, 'of the death of fifty-one of my best and bravest men who has [sic] been hung by the Americans for no other reason than fighting manfully against them ...'

On their release in 1848, Riley and the surviving San Patricios were taken back into the Mexican army to form the basis of a new battalion of foreign fighters. While stationed in Puebla de los Angeles, a passing American observed that Riley 'wore his hair long, to hide the [branding] marks on his cheek and ear. He stands over six feet in height, is quite social, but a miserable, dissipated fellow.' He served his last eighteen months in the army in Puebla and then, on his discharge, became embroiled in a financial squabble with the Mexican government regarding outstanding back pay. Playing up his British citizenship, he begged the British consul for money, which was not forthcoming. He finally received a military pension and lived the rest of his life in Veracruz. It has been suggested that he may have sailed from the Mexican port to return to Ireland, but a death record in the cathedral at Veracruz confirms that he died there at the age of forty-five 'as a result of drunkenness, without sacraments'.

Reviled by the Americans as traitors, Riley and the San Patricios live on in the memories of Mexicans as national heroes. A century after they fought for their cause, their names were inscribed on a memorial in 1959 in San Jacinto Plaza in Mexico City, the place where the first captured Irishmen were hanged. In 2004, the Mexican government presented a bronze statue to Ireland in memory of the San Patricios, which now stands in Riley's hometown of Clifden in County Galway.

Chapter 6
Queen Victoria's Invisible Army

At the beginning of the nineteenth century, there were as many Irishmen as Englishmen in the British Army. Some 42 per cent of the soldiers were Irish, according to some estimates, as opposed to 41 per cent English, and the rest Scots and Welsh. Thus, Queen Victoria's Empire was being extended and defended by a vast contingent of Irishmen, but their presence was downplayed and even hidden by their incorporation into red-coated 'English' regiments. This fact was picked up in an article written for the Dublin newspaper *The Nation* in May 1843. The commentator argued that many English regiments were largely Irish – as Irish as the Connaught Rangers or Inniskilling Dragoons – and that this should be recognized with a change in uniform from the familiar scarlet jackets.

As an example, he focused on the 28th Regiment of Foot. 'Though the 28th bears an English name – "North Gloucestershire" – it was, when in Egypt, and has since been a thoroughly Irish regiment,' he explained. 'Why have they not green uniforms, the colour of their country, the colour they love?'

> We have been asked these questions, and our answer is, because the Saxon government are afraid to show their strength to the Irish soldiery ... While there are 42,000 Irishmen (even by the Horse Guards and Ordnance returns) in the so-called *English* army of about 100,000, it would

be hazardous to let the Irish see their strength, as they would
if separately regimented.

It was a good point, but *The Nation* had a strongly nationalist agenda
and therefore refused to acknowledge the reality that many Irishmen considered themselves very much part of a United Kingdom.
Whether they lived in Dublin, Cork, Liverpool or London, they
were happy to serve the interests of the British Empire and their
Irish identity became subsumed in that enterprise. Ireland was
their home but they fought and died under the Union flag.

The reason why so many young Irishmen joined the British Army
was the same reason that explained the mass emigration of Irish
people to the New World or the massive shift of Irish labour to
England in the nineteenth century. Victorian Ireland was princi-
pally an agricultural economy with few opportunities for jobs or
careers outside farming. In contrast, the great industrial cities of
England and America needed armies of labourers to work in factories and build roads, canals and railways.

Agricultural economies are vulnerable to crop failures and subsequent famines, and these increased the urge to take a job that
offered a regular meal. For those men that didn't fancy hard labour
and didn't mind the discomfort of campaigning, the army was the
better choice. The British imperial army also offered free travel
abroad and for a young man familiar only with his local village,
this was a passport to adventure and the opportunity to come back
and impress his family and friends with tales of strange lands.

Above all, Irishmen shared the English tongue with their British
military comrades and this common language meant they could fit
more easily than other foreign soldiers into the red-coated ranks.
Like Highlanders and other Celtic fringe warriors, Irishmen had an
age-old reputation as fearless, relentless fighters. Harsh landscapes
and rural poverty toughened up men. All this meant that British
regiments, after long stints in imperial outposts, came to replenish
their numbers in Ireland, where steady streams of young men were
always keen to join up.

This was true of the 61st (South Gloucestershire) Regiment of
Foot. By the middle of the nineteenth century so many of the soldiers were Irish – 600 out of a total strength of 700 – that the 61st
was referred to as the 'banner Fenian Regiment'. George Alexander

Bace was just such a soldier in this Irish-English regiment. His father had served in the 61st and married his mother during a stopover in Malta. It seems likely that George was born to them while they were garrisoned in Ireland and he considered Dublin his home where he lived with his parents.

Bace's military career began in July 1844, when he was gazetted as an ensign in the 61st and joined them at their headquarters in Cork. As part of their duties in Ireland, Bace and the 61st had to support the local police as they removed poor tenants from their homes on the orders of rich landowners wanting to change the use of their property. The Irish soldiers regarded the task as 'disagreeable' and 'barbarous' and it came as a relief when they were posted abroad to India. They sailed from Cork on 3 July 1845 and arrived in Calcutta five months later.

The British business of empire in India in the 1840s consisted of extending their authority over native regimes. Friction between the British and the Sikhs of the Punjab culminated in a Sikh invasion of British territory in December 1845. Even though they were already stationed in India, the Irish of the 61st were not involved in the first war between the two powers. Bace's journal during this period records mainly the death of fellow officers from illness. It was not until the Second Sikh War of 1848 that the South Glosters marched into the Punjab to confront the fierce warriors.

They were greeted by a terrible dust storm and forty-eight hours of rain that transformed the land into a sheet of water and flooded their encampment. By November, they had made contact with the enemy around the Sikh town of Ramnagar, but the fighting was inconclusive. In addition, the 61st were told by their divisional commander, Brigadier General Sir Colin Campbell, not to fire randomly at the enemy and preserve their ammunition. 'Such a precaution was needless,' noted Bace. 'Each man had 60 rounds in his pouch and a musket would become hot after firing half or less than half that quantity.'

On 13 January 1849, the Irish of the 61st were advancing through thick jungle towards an entrenched Sikh position at Chillianwallah. Bace climbed up a tree to get a view of the enemy, but it was impossible to see far through the forest. Back on the ground, Bace cocked his pistol, ready to shoot any Sikhs that appeared out of the dense foliage. Once they entered a clearing, they picked up the pace.

'The 61st advanced in double quick time, yelling and firing,'
recalled Bace. 'Soon we passed guns, which our rapid advance and
destructive fire had caused the enemy to abandon; these were
spiked. At length we halted, the foe having fled before us.' Or so
they thought. Suddenly, out of nowhere, Sikh cavalry attacked the
Irish from all angles, sometimes getting behind them and forcing
the Glosters to face about and give them a volley of musket fire.
Their civilian-clothed paymaster, Captain Toole, a veteran Peninsular War officer, was observed flinging his walking stick and then
a scimitar, which his servant had taken off a dead Sikh. Another
soldier of the 61st, Sergeant Ford, gives a vivid description of the
combat.

> The Sikhs were fierce and desperate fighters and
> splendid swordsmen. They did not show a sign of
> defeat until they recognised that the position which
> they had considered impregnable had been stormed
> and taken by British and native troops.

At Chillianwallah, the Irish of the 61st had achieved a notable
victory against a tough opposition and the Duke of Wellington
later praised their performance as one of the most brilliant exploits
of the British Army. But it is noticeable here, as in virtually every
other account of Victorian Irish soldiers in battle they are referred
to as British, and not by their native nationality. It was this that
contributed to their apparent invisibility in Queen Victoria's army
despite their making up almost half of its manpower.

After the battle of Chillianwallah was over, rain fell in torrents
and Bace celebrated with a bottle of beer and a slice of cold meat
and bread. After resting a few days, the Irish 61st resumed their
pursuit of the Sikhs and cornered them at Gujrat a month later.
Over 2,000 Sikh warriors were slaughtered and their leaders surrendered. The Punjab was annexed to the British Empire soon
afterwards. With the war over, the 61st were based in Peshawar
and deployed on punitive raids against local tribesmen, some of
which proved to be costly in lives. An earthquake wrecked their
accommodation.

Bace stayed on in India for another six years and rose to the rank
of captain, but he endured the life so typical of many Irishmen

posted to the tropics – not so much a battle against foreign warriors, but against sickness. Around him, dozens of officers died of disease. Captain Toole, the bold paymaster at Chillianwallah, suffered from illness for several months before finally succumbing. Bace read out the news to him from the *Calcutta Englishman* on the day he died in his armchair: 'The poor man's constitution was completely broken.'

Bace escaped the stifling heat of the Indian plains by visiting the foothills of the Himalayas at Simlah. It was a brief respite and he complained bitterly of suffering from repeated attacks of fever.

> Although I myself chose the Army as my profession;
> yet it was much against my will that I ever came to
> India, and still more against my will has it been that I
> have struggled on so long in a country which I detest
> beyond measure and which is not in any way suited
> to me.

After ten years' service in India, George Bace finally stepped on a ship destined for Ireland in December 1855, but he died from illness during the voyage.

Bace was probably buried at sea, but, in the meantime, Bace's father had also died and been interred in Mount Jerome Cemetery in Dublin, an exclusively Protestant burial place. Bace and his father were Protestant Irish officers and, although most of the rank and file of the 61st were Irish Catholics, it was unusual for a Catholic to serve as an officer. Queen Victoria's army mirrored the hierarchy of life in nineteenth-century Ireland in which the Protestant Ascendancy – the name given to the Anglo-Irish Protestant land-owning establishment – lorded it over the poorer Catholic majority. John Patrick Redmond was an exception to this rule.

Coming from a long and distinguished military Catholic family from County Wexford, Redmond could have continued their tradition of serving abroad for other nations, including France, but instead he enrolled in the British Army and the 61st. He fought alongside Bace at the battle of Chillianwallah. Unlike Bace, he rather liked India and stayed on, getting caught up in the Indian Mutiny of 1857. During the traumatic events of that uprising, the Irish of the 61st were stationed at Ferozepore and had to stand their ground against mutinous sepoys. Redmond was wounded in the conflict but recovered to take part in the capture of the rebel stronghold at Delhi. He had the honour of being a member of the British court that put on trial the last Mughul emperor of India.

Despite his Catholicism, Redmond was promoted to lieutenant colonel and continued to serve with the Glosters when they returned to Ireland. It was at this time that the 61st were suspected of harbouring as many as 600 Fenians in their ranks and Redmond took part in the courts martial to root them out. Fearing for their continued loyalty, the 61st were deployed abroad to the West Indies and Canada with Redmond as their commander. A loyal servant of the Empire to the day he died, Redmond donated money to a national monument to Queen Victoria in 1901.

*

The Glosters were just one of many British regiments full of Irishmen in the nineteenth century. You could not find a more English unit than the 44th (East Essex) Regiment but when they came back from the disastrous First Afghan War in 1843, in which their battalion was virtually annihilated during a gruelling withdrawal from Kabul, they were sent to Ireland to replenish their ranks.

During their time stationed in Dublin, Newry, Fermoy and Cork, an additional 1,200 Irishmen were recruited. So many, in fact, that when the Essex Regiment returned to England a second reserve battalion was formed. The rush of enlistments was due in part to the desperate situation created by the Great Famine of the 1840s, in which the potato crop failed and thousands of Irish families died from starvation. Thousands more left the country for America. For those that escaped to the British Army, they were keen to prove their worth but whether they would be regarded as Irishmen or British soldiers when it came to the ultimate accolade of courage was exemplified by the story of one of the first Victoria Cross winners in the Essex Regiment.

Robert Montresor Rogers was born in Dublin in 1834 and joined the 44th in 1855 at the age of twenty-one. Soon after, he was commissioned as a lieutenant and sailed with the Essex Regiment to the Crimea, where he was present at the taking of Sevastopol. Five years later, he was part of a British imperial force sent to China to investigate why the emperor of China was refusing to ratify the Treaty of Tientsin. This agreement had been imposed on China in the wake of the Second Opium War, which insisted that the Chinese open more of their ports to Western traders. British ships had tried to force their way up the Peiho River, but had been repulsed with heavy losses at the Taku Forts. It was up to the Essex Regiment and their Irish troops to return in strength and take the fortifications. It was no easy task.

The ground leading to the Chinese entrenchments at Sinho, protecting the rear of the Taku Forts, was a network of broad canals used for making salt and the soil was heavy going. The Chinese could call upon ferocious Tatar cavalry to protect them, armed with bows, swords and old-style muskets, but the British had new Armstrong guns – rifled, breech-loaded artillery with increased range and accuracy. With their superior firepower, the British quickly took the Sinho trenches and captured the town of Tangku.

On 21 August, having built a road across the muddy land, the British made their first attempt on the most northerly of the Taku Forts. The 44th were accompanied by the 67th (South Hampshire) Regiment. Royal Marines carried pontoon bridges for crossing the wet ditches. Armstrong artillery and gunboats provided covering fire that ignited enemy gunpowder stores, but still the Chinese resisted the main assault on their fort. Essex soldiers swam or waded across two filthy water-filled ditches and then clambered up a bank studded with sharp bamboo stakes.

Dubliner Lieutenant Rogers fearlessly led the way, accompanied by a Scotsman, Lieutenant M'Dougall of the 44th, and an Englishman, Lieutenant Lenon of the 67th. They stabbed their bayonets into the muddy walls of the fort and used these as steps to climb up into the stockade, becoming the first of the British to enter it. For this heroic achievement, all three won the Victoria Cross.

> For distinguished gallantry in swimming the ditches
> and entering the North Taku Fort by an embrasure
> during the assault. They were the first of the English
> established on the walls of the Fort, which they entered
> in the order in which their names are here recorded.

This was the official citation of the award published in the *London Gazette* in 1861 and it is worth emphasizing that all three men, including the Irishman Rogers and the Scotsman M'Dougall, are labelled as Englishmen. Even in an official history of the Essex Regiment published in 1923, there is no mention of Rogers being an Irishman. His Irishness, like that of so many of his comrades, was invisible in the British Army. Worst of all, he was not even described as British but as an Englishman!

The Taku Forts were taken and this honour added to the colours of the Essex Regiment. Rogers went on to have an illustrious military career. Promoted soon after to Captain, he transferred to the 90th Perthshire Light Infantry. In the Anglo-Zulu War of 1879, Colonel Rogers commanded the 90th at the battles of Zunyin Nek and Kambula. Made a CB – a Companion of the Order of the Bath – in 1886, he ended his life as a major-general, dying in Maidenhead in 1895.

Rogers was not the only Irishman to win a Victoria Cross for the Essex Regiment. The very first VC awarded to the 44th was earned by Sergeant William McWheeney from Bangor, County Down. Serving with the 44th during the Crimean War, he volunteered as a sharp-shooter at the beginning of the siege of Sevastopol in October 1854. When one of his unit was badly wounded, McWheeney took the soldier on his back and carried him to safety under heavy fire. Two months later, he repeated his bravery by bringing back another wounded comrade under fire. This time, he dug a small mound with his bayonet behind which the two sheltered until darkness came. The Irishness of McWheeney is not mentioned either in the 1923 regimental history of the 44th.

Thirty Irish-born soldiers in the British Army won the Victoria Cross in the Crimean War. Two years later, fifty-eight Irishmen won Victoria Crosses fighting in British regiments during the bitter fighting of the Indian Mutiny. Further Victoria Crosses were won by Irish-born British soldiers in the Opium Wars in China, New Zealand Colonial Wars, the Andaman Islands Expedition in the Bay of Bengal, in Abyssinia, in South Africa against both Boers and native tribesmen, Afghanistan, Burma, in fact in every corner of Queen Victoria's globe-spanning empire.

In the Zulu War, there were six Irish-born recipients of the Victoria Cross. One of the most celebrated incidents of the Zulu War occurred after the slaughter at Isandlwana in 1879, when twenty-six-year-old Nevill Coghill, born in the Dublin suburb of

Drumcondra and a lieutenant in the 24th Regiment of Foot, tried to save the Queen's Colour from falling into the hands of the Zulus. Along with fellow officer Teignmouth Melvill, they rode off with a band of warriors in hot pursuit. Plunging into the Buffalo River, Melvill lost his horse and Coghill rescued him. Struggling on with the flag, they fought hand to hand with the Zulus until they were overcome and killed. It was an heroic moment after a disastrous battle and was reproduced in many imperial images. Coghill and Melvill were the first posthumous recipients of the medal.

William Beresford was born in Mullaghbrack, County Armagh, the son of the 4th Marquess of Waterford. Not only did he win a VC, but he ensured that a fellow Irishman did too. A thirty-one-year-old captain in the 9th Queen's Royal Lancers, Beresford rode to the assistance of Sergeant Fitzmaurice at the battle of Ulundi, when his horse rolled on top of him. Beresford hauled the sergeant up onto his own horse. Sergeant Edmund O'Toole of the Frontier Light Horse provided cover for Beresford by firing his carbine at the advancing Zulus, but the wounded Sergeant Fitzmaurice was in danger of falling off his rescuer's mount and so O'Toole dropped his carbine to ride beside him, keeping him on the horse.

At first, the Victoria Cross was awarded only to Beresford but as Queen Victoria pinned the medal on his chest, the captain said he could not have saved the sergeant had it not been for the bravery of Sergeant O'Toole and could not receive the award unless he too was honoured. The Queen recognized this and the Irish-born South African was also awarded the VC.

*

The Victorian British Army befitted enormously from the influx of Irish manpower and raw courage, but the high proportion of Catholic Irishmen within its ranks was seen by a few as a chance to cause political mayhem. One of these plotters was John Devoy. Born in County Kildare, he served abroad in the French Foreign Legion for a year before coming back to Ireland to rally to the cause of the Fenian Brotherhood, an Irish-American group devoted to ending British rule in Ireland and the creation of an Irish Republic. They were successors to the United Irishmen who had risen in rebellion in 1798, but been crushed by the British authorities.

The trauma of the Great Famine and the failure of the British to ameliorate its effects had encouraged an armed uprising in County Tipperary in 1848 called the Young Irelander Rebellion, but this had failed too. Several Irishmen involved in that uprising took their anger abroad and in the USA founded the Fenian Brotherhood in 1858. When John Devoy returned to Ireland, he was appointed chief organizer of Fenian sympathizers within the British Army.

In his later *Recollections of an Irish Rebel*, Devoy claimed that out of the 26,000 British troops stationed in Ireland in 1865, no less than 60 per cent of them were Irish and one third of them were sworn Fenians devoted to fighting for an Ireland independent from Britain. He overestimated the number of Fenians within the army, but there were enough of them to encourage him to turn them to armed resistance.

'One of the most intelligent and best educated of the Fenian soldiers was Corporal Thomas Chambers,' recalled Devoy, 'who was Centre [a secret agent] of the 61st [South Gloucestershire]. It was supposed to be an English regiment, but there were not a hundred men in it were not Irish, and there were 600 Fenians. It was the banner Fenian Regiment.'

Devoy helped frame a plan for an uprising of Fenian-supporting soldiers early in 1866, including 900 sympathizers from within the 61st Glosters and 60th Rifles based in Richmond Barracks in Dublin. Having obtained a key to the rear gate of the barrack gates facing a canal, the rebel soldiers were to make their move on a moonless night. Tom Chambers, according to Devoy, 'would pick out a small number of the best men of the regiment to remain out of barracks and form the vanguard of the attacking party. They would know every man of the guard and would serve as guides.'

With the confidence of the other soldiers, the Fenians would swiftly march through the gate inside the barracks and make prisoner any opposing Irish officers, alongside the smaller number of English soldiers. 'We could have probably captured Richmond without firing a shot,' boasted Devoy. 'If there was any fighting it would speedily be over.'

With rifles taken out of the barracks to arm their other supporters, the Fenians planned to capture the Island Bridge Barracks next, which was held only by 400 troopers of the 10th Hussars. Finally, Devoy and his redcoat Fenians would square up to the soldiers in the Royal Barracks. An impressive fortress of a building, it housed regiments of foot and cavalry as well as a battery of artillery. But Devoy calculated that Fenians stood within their ranks too. 'In the 8th Foot we had 200 men', he wrote, 'and in the 5th Dragoon Guards, 300.' With them, the Fenians would outnumber any loyal soldiers and 'chances would all be in our favor'. Unfortunately for the Fenians, informers told the authorities about the insurrection before it ever happened.

A Dublin correspondent for the London *Times* reported the moment when the conspirators were arrested on 22 February 1866, an act which 'reveals the fact that the Fenians have corrupted the military to a greater extent than had been imagined'. That night, a unit of policemen were called to a meeting at a pub in James Street. Held in a large back room, it was crowded with a mixture of soldiers and civilians, some of whom were armed with loaded pistols. One of them pointed his revolver as a policeman burst in, but was swiftly disarmed. The rest were arrested and among them was Corporal Thomas Chambers, who had deserted from his regiment nine months earlier. Six other soldiers from the 61st Glosters were also taken into custody, along with soldiers from the 60th and 5th Dragoons. The police were edgy that night as one of their number had recently been shot by an Irish-American Fenian in County Limerick.

A general court martial commenced on 28 May 1866 at the Royal Barracks in Dublin, with Colonel Brett of the 61st presiding over the trial of several soldiers accused of fomenting a Fenian-inspired mutiny in January. Kilkenny-born Corporal Chambers admitted to desertion, but refused to enter a plea regarding the accusation of failing to inform his commanding officer of an intended mutiny because it was 'vague, uncertain, and indefinite'. Private James Meara of the 8th Foot was called to give evidence against Chambers. He said that he had witnessed Chambers swear in Fenians and say that the Irish in the army would not be expected to rise by themselves but would be joined by 60,000 Fenians coming over from America in the autumn.

Meara later said that upwards of twenty-five soldiers from various regiments came together regularly for Fenian meetings. A civilian witness called Baines said he had met Chambers in a pub and he had introduced him to an American officer. Chambers then told the soldiers present in the pub – from both the 61st and the 5th Dragoons – that they should 'make away with all the ammunition of the soldiers who were not Fenians'.

An editorial in *The Times* during the trial reflected the level of concern within the British establishment. 'What is really serious', it said, 'is the undoubted fact that not only privates but non-commissioned officers of our army are Fenians in disguise.' A comparison was drawn with the Indian Mutiny in which once-loyal native troops had turned on their British commanders. 'Were disaffection to spread among our troops in Ireland, it would entail a cost of bloodshed and devastation which several generations might fail to repair.'

In a concurrent trial, a Private Abraham of the 61st said that another soldier, Private Cranston, had told him that if they had to confront any Fenian uprising, the Fenian soldiers in the 61st were to fire over the heads of the rebels and then join them. Cranston had also declared his intention to sabotage non-Fenian rifles by placing bits of sponge over the firing nipples of the weapons. Cranston defended himself by saying that Abraham was a Protestant and biased against him, but that wasn't convincing enough to save him. Another soldier, Private Hassett, was put on trial for making the following statement: 'Bad luck to traitors! If it were not for them we would have the Irish Republic long before now. Ireland would be taken without firing three shots ...'

At the end of his trial, Chambers was found guilty and sentenced to death, but this was later commuted to penal servitude for life. He was eventually released and sailed away to America. In total, twelve Irish soldiers serving in the British Army were convicted of crimes relating to mutiny and a Fenian conspiracy. They received various sentences from life imprisonment to ten years' penal servitude. Dressed in convict clothes, they were sent to Mountjoy Prison. John Devoy had also been put on trial for treason and was sentenced to fifteen years' penal servitude. In 1871, after organizing several prison strikes, he was exiled to America, where he became a prominent fundraiser for the republican movement.

In October 1866, with a big question mark hanging over their loyalty, the 61st Glosters were removed from Dublin and sent to Bermuda. It was a punishment and humiliation that was completely left out of the official history of the Gloucester regiment, *Cap of Honour*, published nearly a century later. In the 1881 reforms of the British Army, the 28th and 61st were combined to form the 1st and 2nd Battalions of the Gloucestershire Regiment. Queen Victoria's Irish army had become invisible again.

Chapter 7
The Emerald Flag

'Every day here is as good as Christmas day in Ireland,' wrote one Irish immigrant to the United States in 1850. 'Here the meanest labourer has beef and mutton, with bread, bacon, tea, coffee, sugar and even pies, the whole year round.' The year before, he had left Limerick for Wisconsin, where he purchased 120 acres of land at $5 an acre. He had cleared fifty acres of it and had a beautiful farmhouse with a spring well nearby. It made him proud to know he owned the land outright, with no rent paid to any landlord. Above all, the soil was fertile, bringing forth bumper crops of Indian corn. 'I shudder when I think that starvation prevails to such an extent in poor Ireland,' he said. In Wisconsin, the potato crop never failed.

The Great Famine had forced millions of Irish to flee across the Atlantic to America. Between 1840 and 1860, nearly half of all immigrants to the United States came from Ireland and two-thirds of these were Catholic. Just one of these immigrants was William McCarter. Born in Derry in northern Ireland around 1840, he came to Philadelphia where he traded as a currier, a man who prepares tanned hides for use by soaking or colouring them. He married a woman called Annie and had several children.

By the time civil war broke out in 1861, McCarter had no hesitation about volunteering for service with the Federal army. He did so because he believed he owed a debt of gratitude to his new home. McCarter had a bad stammer, but when he wrote his thoughts flowed effortlessly. He stepped up because of 'my love for my whole adopted country, not the North, nor the South, but the

Union, one and inseparable, its form of government, its institutions, its Stars and Stripes, its noble, brave and intelligent people ever ready to welcome, and to extend the hand of friendship to the downtrodden and oppressed'.

The Irish currier joined Company 'A' of the 116th Pennsylvania Infantry on 23 August 1862. Under the command of Colonel Dennis Heenan, a local Irish-born militia leader, they mustered in the woods near Hestonville until rail transportation was ready to take them to Washington DC. On 2 September, they huddled in dirty cattle cars that took them to the nation's capital via Baltimore. The journey was slow and uncomfortable and they were given nothing to eat, but just as they were grumbling among themselves as they waited in an empty tobacco warehouse, they were invited to a feast hosted by the citizens of Baltimore. 'The table was actually loaded with large dishes full of corned beef sliced, sliced ham and tongue and cold roast beef, besides a good supply of butter, and any quantity of hot coffee and bread,' recalled McCarter. 'To all these luxuries, we did ample justice.'

In Washington, McCarter and his comrades learned the basics of military life, drilling and digging trenches. The 116th Pennsylvania was incorporated into the Second Brigade of the First Division of the Second Corps of the Army of the Potomac. The unit was better known as the Irish Brigade and was commanded by Thomas Francis Meagher, a New York lawyer who had a bitter hatred for Britain. Born in Waterford in 1823, Meagher intended to join the Austrian army as many Wild Geese had before him, but instead he became involved in the 'Young Irelanders' group, which wanted to repeal the Act of Union of Ireland with Great Britain passed in 1801.

This led Meagher into revolutionary politics and in 1848 he travelled to France, caught up in its own political turmoil. He returned with a new flag for an independent Ireland, a tricolour of green, white and orange. A key member of the Young Irelander rebellion in County Tipperary that year, Meagher was arrested by the British authorities and sentenced to death. In the wake of an international public outcry, the punishment was commuted to exile in Tasmania. After three years there, Meagher escaped to America, where he studied law and founded his own newspaper, the *Irish News*. He also became a captain in the New York State militia.

Following the failed rebellion of 1848, the New York militia became a refuge for many exiled rebel Irishmen, who hoped to turn these military companies into units that, one day, might fight the British. One of these was the 69th Regiment, which later became known as the Fighting 69th – the most famous of Irish-American military units – its official date of organization being given as 21 December 1849. It later absorbed two other Irish New York regiments. However, tension grew in New York between the Irish militias and the American Nativists, American-born nationalists who formed their own regiment, the 71st, called the American Guard, to counter-balance the influence of the immigrants. Following the murder of the Nativist leader, 'Bill the Butcher', and subsequent riots, Irish militias were banned from marching in St Patrick's Day parades.

On the outbreak of the civil war, Meagher, like many Irishmen, was ambivalent about which side to serve on. He had great sympathy for the southern Secessionists and many ordinary Irishmen disliked the idea of fighting for the liberation of black slaves: they feared the freed slaves would come north and steal their jobs.

In the end, Meagher put his full backing behind the North and recruited actively for the 69th Regiment. After the disaster of the first battle of Bull Run in July 1861, Meagher was asked to form an Irish Brigade, which would consist of the 63rd, 69th and 88th New York volunteers, the 116th Pennsylvania and the 28th Massachusetts infantry, a Boston Irish volunteer outfit.

A committee of prominent Irish New Yorkers came together to assist in the task of raising and funding the Irish Brigade. Joseph Stuart, chairman of the committee, made it clear that Irishmen fought best when they fought together. The English and the French knew that, he argued in an appeal published in the *New York Times*, and the American army should recognize this.

> Aggregated together, the exploits of their countrymen
> at Fontenoy, Ramillies, Cremona, and Badajos, and
> through all the battlefields of Europe, appeal to the
> heart, and nerve the arm of every man to an Irish
> regiment whenever the cry of battle swells upon his ear;
> he feels instinctively that the honor of his native land,
> and the military traditions of his race are committed to
> his personal keeping …

There was no shortage of money for this enterprise and the colours for the Irish Brigade were manufactured at Tiffany's in Broadway, where they went on display to the public. 'They are of the costliest material, splendid design and the most artistic workmanship,' said a contemporary report. The motto of the Brigade – 'They shall never retreat from the charge of lances', taken from the fake Celtic epic by Ossian – was embroidered in gold thread on an emerald background, while a Celtic harp was emblazoned beneath a sunburst. There is no truth, however, in the assertion that the Irish Brigade wore their own version of the Union blue uniform with green cuffs and collars. They wore regulation dark blue uniforms throughout the war, apart from a green waist sash worn briefly by Meagher's Zouave unit at the battle of Bull Run.

The new recruits to the Irish Brigade did not always live up to the honourable expectations of their sponsors, and the *New York Times* described an incident in which the 63rd Regiment provoked a bloody riot. The fresh soldiers were embarking from the southern tip of Manhattan onto a ferry at the start of their journey to Washington DC when they attracted the attention of some women eager to follow them on board. The women were turned back by sentries on the boat and the embarkation was temporarily halted. Kept hanging around on the pier, some of the Irishmen broke ranks and headed for the saloons around Battery Park. Treated to drinks by well-wishers who had come to see them off, the soldiers got rapidly drunk.

When the order came through to resume embarking on the ferry, the soldiers rushed forward with their friends and took exception to the civilians being held back from joining them on the pier. As the officers tried to prevent this, fighting broke out. 'Bayonets, knives, and other weapons were then freely used,' noted the report, with several serious casualties. The mass brawl went on for about an hour until the local police force intervened to help the officers restore order. The most seriously wounded was a soldier cut on the head by an officer's sword. The rest of the recruits were bundled onto the steam ferry, but two of them later died on board, it was claimed, from intoxication.

From 3 February 1862, Meagher was appointed commander of the Irish Brigade with the rank of brigadier general. He continued to actively promote the recruitment programme and the style of his rousing speech-making was recorded during one gathering at the 7th Regiment Armory. In a drill hall packed with Irish New Yorkers, he declared it was the 'intense ambition of every Irishman, who has one chord within him that vibrates to the traditions of that old lyric and martial land of his, not to permit its flag, so vividly emblematic of the verdure of its soil and the immortality of its faith, to be compromised in any just struggle in which it is displayed'. Greeted by cheers, he went on to compare the Irish Brigade colours to the flag that flew in defiance of the Protestant English at Limerick in 1691 and the flag held by doomed revolutionary Robert Emmet in 1803. For Meagher and his rebel supporters, the Irish Brigade was just a necessary diversion in their ongoing struggle against Britain.

*

Before Private McCarter and his 116th Pennsylvanians joined the Irish Brigade, the New York regiments saw hard fighting throughout the summer of 1862. In June, at the battle of Fair Oaks, the Irish Brigade caught the attention of the printmakers Currier & Ives, who portrayed Meagher on horseback leading a bayonet charge of Irishmen. A month later, it was at the battle of Malvern Hill that the 69th forced the retreat of the celebrated Confederate Louisiana Tigers and reputedly provoked the Confederate General Robert E. Lee to call them the 'Fighting 69th'. In action again during the Peninsular Campaign – a major Union operation in south east Virginia – the Irish suffered heavy losses at Antietam, Maryland in September. Meagher was wounded and 540 men fell to volleys of musket fire as the Irish led an assault on a position later called the Bloody Lane.

When McCarter joined this brigade of hardened veterans in October 1862, he wondered how he would shape up when tested in battle. His talent as a writer had endeared him to his fellow Irishmen, for whom he wrote letters home. This skill also drew him to the attention of General Meagher and he served the legendary Irish leader as an adjutant, executing crisply written orders for him. At close hand, McCarter was impressed by his commander. 'In polished, gentlemanly manners and bearing (when himself), he was head and shoulders above any other man occupying a similar position in the army,' noted McCarter. 'He spoke fluently not only English, but also Greek, Hebrew, French, German, Welsh, and the native Irish language.' The caveat 'when himself' was important because Meagher suffered from one weakness. 'It was the besetting sin of so many Irish then and now – intemperance.'

One night, McCarter recalled being on guard duty outside his commander's tent when he saw General Meagher staring at the camp fire. On closer inspection, he could see Meagher was 'very drunk, looked strangely wild and only prevented himself from falling down by his grasp of the center pole [at the tent's entrance]'. McCarter was concerned because if Meagher let go of the pole he would fall directly into the fire. He watched over him for a few minutes and then the inevitable happened – Meagher let go of the pole and toppled towards the flames. McCarter quickly thrust his musket in front of the general, diverting him from the fire. The gun went off and officers ran out of the tent to attend to the now uncon-scious Meagher. The next morning, McCarter was presented with a brand new musket to replace his old one that got singed in the fire, and swore never to tell any of his comrades about the embarrassing episode.

The Irish Brigade marched south in late October as part of General Ambrose Burnside's Army of the Potomac in pursuit of General Lee. Pushing towards the Confederate capital of Rich-mond, Virginia, Burnside crossed the Rappahannock River to enter Fredericksburg. On 13 December, his troops pushed through the streets of artillery-battered buildings to advance upon the main Confederate force entrenched on high ground known as Marye's Heights, overlooking the south-west side of the town.

The night before, McCarter and his fellow Irish soldiers had barely slept. At four o'clock in the morning he was jolted awake by the sound of Confederate artillery shells bursting over the river in an attempt to destroy the Union guns. Two hours later, they were cooking their breakfast when they were told to expect to move off shortly after daybreak. The Irish Brigade was barely half a mile away from the Confederate lines and when the first Union assault went up the hill, they could smell the burning gunpowder wafting across the battlefield.

Dug in behind strong fieldworks, the storm of fire from the Con-federate soldiers shattered the Union attack and they slunk back into the town. McCarter's officers now ordered the Irishmen to take up their weapons and move into their regimental lines.

'Be ready, be firm', instructed one of the lieutenants. 'Keep cool and do your duty when brought face to face with the enemy.'

It was nine o'clock and the bright morning sky had suddenly darkened as thick clouds rolled above them. General Meagher appeared on horseback and shouted to his men to 'Fall in'. It was the sign that their part of the battle was about to begin, but before they advanced up the hill, Meagher instructed two orderlies to distribute sprigs of green boxwood among his Irishmen. They were to put the green foliage in their caps to distinguish them from the other Union troops and proclaim their Irishness in front of the enemy. That, in combination with their green flags flapping in the wind, would bring terror to the Confederates who feared the Irish as tough, stubborn fighters. Ten minutes later came the order: 'Shoulder arms. Left face. Forward, march.'

Some 1,200 soldiers of the Irish Brigade, alongside two other brigades, advanced through the streets of Fredericksburg raked by Confederate artillery fire. Smoke from a burning cotton factory blew in their faces. For half an hour, the 116th Pennsylvanians paused beside the damaged factory wall, fearing it might fall on top of them but determined not to shift their position without orders. Hearing the conflict ahead of them, but unable to see the enemy, stretched their nerves nearly to breaking point, as did the sight of the wounded from the first attack being brought back in to the town. Around them the civilian population was panicking at the bombardment and McCarter saw one poor woman cut in half by a cannonball on a street corner.

At last, General Meagher appeared and, waving his sword above his head, ordered the Irish to follow him. Shortly afterwards, a Confederate shell smashed into a factory chimney not far away from the Irish column, knocking it down onto the street near McCarter. Shrapnel slashed through the air, wounding eight Irishmen, including McCarter. 'A piece of it hit me in the calf of the left leg,' he remembered, 'drawing blood quite freely.' The more seriously wounded were sent back to their camp across the river, but McCarter stayed in line. In total, even before seeing a single Rebel soldier, seventeen Irishmen had been killed and twenty-six wounded.

From the streets of Fredericksburg, the Irish Brigade advanced double-quick towards the Confederate trenches on Marye's Heights. Union artillery gave them cover by sending shells roaring above their heads towards the enemy. At the bottom of the hill, the brigade halted to gather their breath. Although closer to the opposing lines, they were briefly shielded from their direct fire by the slope. They were then ordered to move up the hill across a railway track in full view of the enemy.

McCarter wondered at the wisdom of this exposure to such terrible enemy fire, but he had no choice but go along with it. Winding their way up the hill, past the bodies of dead and mutilated Union soldiers, the Irish re-formed, ready for the final surge towards the enemy lines. The Confederates held their fire until the Union soldiers came nearer to their guns. The Irish Brigade was ordered to 'Fix Bayonets'.

> This was done amid the yells and cheers of the men,
> resounding from one end of the valley to the other.
> The enemy undoubtedly must have heard. And as the
> clink, clink, clink of the cold, glittering steel being
> placed in position sounded down the long rows of
> soldiers … Well did the men realize that in preparing
> to use their favourite weapons of war, so dreaded by
> the enemy, especially when accompanied by the green
> flag, that a fearful, bloody struggle laid before them.

One Irishman next to McCarter placed the bayonet on the muzzle of his gun and said in a broad Irish accent, 'Damn them. That's the thing to fetch the sons of bitches.' Moments later, he was killed.

Reaching the crest of the hill, the Irish came to within 200 yards of the Confederate trenches when the enemy unleashed their first volley of musketry. The hail of shot made the Irish line stagger. A bullet cut off the peak on the front of McCarter's cap. But the Irish Brigade pressed on until they were within fifty yards of their target, a long low stone wall. At that point, 2,400 more Rebel infantrymen sprang up and poured their gunfire at the Irish. This concentrated storm of bullets halted the Irish. 'It was simply madness to advance as far as we did', recalled McCarter, 'and an utter impossibility to go further.'

General Meagher noted the slaughter around him and ordered the Irish to fire at will. A cannonball then struck him in the thigh and he had to be carried off the field. For McCarter, the gunfire was deafening as both sides blasted away at each other. The Rebels had the benefit of firing from behind cover, whereas every third man among the Irish fell, rising to every second in some parts of their ragged line. Nearly all the officers were killed or wounded. Bullets sang around McCarter, tearing at his uniform, cutting open his cartridge box. Having discharged some half dozen shots, he was raising his right arm to ram his next cartridge into the barrel of his musket when he was hit in the arm near the shoulder and the limb suddenly dropped powerless at his side. At first, McCarter thought he had been struck accidentally by one of his own men loading their own gun.

'A stream of warm blood now came rushing down the inside and outside sleeve of my uniform,' remembered McCarter, 'then down the side of my pants into my right foot shoe until it overflowed.' The bullet had severed an artery and the sudden loss of blood made McCarter faint. He slumped to the ground, the body of his neighbour, killed shortly after he was hit, shielding his body from absorbing any more bullets. When he recovered consciousness, soldiers were still blazing away, but the Irish had lost half their men. McCarter made a prayer, reconciling himself to death.

Eventually, around two o'clock, the call came: 'Fall back, men. Every man for himself!' The Irish had had enough, turned their backs and fled back down the hill. McCarter couldn't move and was left behind. He pulled over a blanket roll to absorb the bullets that kept digging up the dirt around him. McCarter lay on the ground for the entire afternoon and witnessed yet more waves of Union soldiers sent fruitlessly against the wall of Confederate fire.

At one stage, a Rebel horse broke out from behind the stone wall, dragging its dead rider behind it. 'Snorting so loud that I distinctly heard the noise, with nostrils extended and like to burst, the horse darted to and fro, its mane standing stiff on end.' McCarter feared it might trample over him, but a multitude of bullets riddled the animal until it fell dead.

Gathering what little remained of his strength during a lull in the firing, McCarter turned towards a little house in the middle of the battlefield, on top of which flew a red flag signifying it was a field hospital. Honourably, the Confederates avoided firing on the building with their artillery, allowing wounded Union soldiers to huddle behind its pockmarked walls. Unable to reach the shelter, McCarter screamed out for a drink of water and one soldier tried to throw him a canteen, but he was forced back by enemy fire.

Even when darkness fell, around four o'clock that winter afternoon, the Union army tried one more assault, which again ended in failure. The battle of Fredericksburg was finally over and the Irish Brigade had lost 545 men killed or wounded, a casualty rate of 45 per cent. Three of its five regimental commanders were wounded, along with General Meagher.

Many Irish fought for the Confederates and some of them were at the battle of Fredericksburg. They were moved when they saw the Irish Brigade hold aloft their emerald green flag, but still considered they were on the wrong side. 'The traditions of their country should have warned them to take the side of the oppressed,' reasoned one. Another, John Edward Dooley, revealed a bizarre twist to the bloody struggle for Marye's Heights. The field at the bottom of the hill was owned by Colonel Morton Marye, a Confederate officer. 'In 1848 or '49,' explained Dooley, 'when famine was inflicting such distress in Ireland, the whole crop of corn raised upon this identical field had been sent in contribution for the relief of that starving and oppressed people.' Dooley cursed the Irish Brigade for trampling over this land and attacking the people who had done so much to help the Irish.

Another Confederate soldier was even more critical and accused the Irish Brigade of being drunk when they ran up the hill. 'It must be said in credit of their valour, or liquor possibly', he admitted, 'that a few of them came nearer than any others to our batteries, some lay within fifty yards of our lines ... [but] Their liquor had led them into the "slaughter pen".'

Some of the surviving Union soldiers were very aware of how lucky they were to get away without any injury. 'Our men were mown down like grass before the scythe of the reaper,' noted William H. McCleland of the 88th New Yorkers. Also from the 88th was Captain William J. Nagle, who wrote to this father saying: 'Irish blood and Irish bones cover that terrible field today ... We are slaughtered like sheep, and no result but defeat.'

The high casualties caused by the Union frontal assault on an entrenched position – a total of nearly 1,300 killed and 9,600 wounded – caused a scandal and an investigation followed into the conduct of the generals involved. As a result, General Burnside lost the respect of his subordinates and was later removed from command of the army. McCarter held him personally responsible for the slaughter. 'No doubt General Burnside was only carrying out the instructions of his government in assaulting the place,' he wrote. 'Yet at the same time I think he was to blame for … rushing his men into the jaws of death.' McCarter wasn't the only Irishman to have doubts about the wisdom of his military superiors.

In the spring of 1863, the Irish Brigade was engaged at the battle of Chancellorsville. It was another savage encounter in which the Union army was again defeated by the Confederates. Just 300 Irishmen survived the battle. Having just recovered from his own serious wound at Fredericksburg, General Meagher had, three days before Chancellorsville, taken active command of his brigade again, but he was disgusted at the waste of lives and sent a letter of resignation to his superiors, stating the 'brigade no longer exists'. In his letter, he revealed that, surveying his sick and wounded soldiers after the battle at Fredericksburg, he had very reasonably made a request for his damaged brigade to be temporarily relieved from field service so it could rebuild its strength, but this request was ignored.

'The depression caused by this ungenerous and inconsiderate treatment of a gallant remnant of a brigade', wrote Meagher, 'that had never once failed to do its duty most liberally and heroically, almost unfitted me to remain in command.' Meagher stayed on in command, but as he led his reduced Irish Brigade to Chancellorsville, he believed he was proceeding towards a 'sacrifice rather than to a victory'. When he viewed the bodies of yet more Irishmen killed to little effect, he felt he could no longer command them. 'To do so any longer would be to perpetuate a public deception in which the hard won honors of good soldiers, and in them the military reputation of a brave old race would inevitably be involved and compromised. I cannot be a party to this wrong.' It was a strong condemnation of the Union military leadership. Meagher was no longer prepared to lead his fellow countrymen to certain death and destruction.

Meagher was called back to the war in September 1864, but was given a duty in the western theatre, far away from his Irish troops. After more administrative work, he resigned from the US army in May 1865 on the conclusion of hostilities. He was appointed acting governor of Montana, but always kept an eye out for fellow Irishmen. He angered many when he reprieved an Irishman from punishment for manslaughter. Involved in campaigning against Native American tribes, he was travelling to Fort Benton to organize a shipment of guns when he became ill and, on the evening of 1 July 1867, fell overboard from a steamboat on the Missouri. His body was never found and some suspected he had been murdered by political enemies; others presumed he was drunk. In 2004, a statue of Meagher on horseback, sword raised, was erected in his home town of Waterford, Ireland.

It took five months for Private William McCarter to recover from his serious arm wound at Fredericksburg. It left him permanently crippled and when he was discharged from the Union army in 1863 he was given a Federal pension for the rest of his life. His wife died six years later. He married for a second time and it was his new wife that encouraged him to write down his memoirs of army life, the only record of an enlisted man in the Irish Brigade. He died in 1911.

The Congressional Medal of Honor is the highest military decoration presented by the US government to a member of their armed forces. It is awarded to those who distinguish themselves 'conspicuously by gallantry and intrepidity at the risk of his life above and beyond the call of duty'. It was first instituted by President Abraham Lincoln in December 1861 and eighty-nine Irish-born Union soldiers won the medal during the American Civil War. In 1975, the Congressional Medal of Honor Society presented a plaque to Irish President Cearbhall Ó Dálaigh, commemorating the fact that the Irish are the largest group of servicemen born outside the USA to be given their highest medal of valour. It is a unique achievement.

Chapter 8
Frontier Fighting

The end of the American Civil War meant that Captain John O'Neill could return to his civilian occupation of selling land in the untamed western territory of the USA. He worked as a land claims agent and steadily amassed a fortune of $50,000. He got married in Nashville, Tennessee, and had three children, each born in a different state, but like several of those Irish-born officers who had turned their immigrant militia companies into regiments for the Union army, he had a separate political agenda that centred on the still unresolved struggle in his homeland.

'I could not, while fighting in the armies of the United States,' he later told a US court, 'when face to face with those who would haul and trample beneath their feet the flag of freedom, and baring my bosom to their bullets – I could not forget that I was born in another land – a land oppressed and tyrannized over … and while I have tried to be a faithful citizen of America, I am still an Irishman, with all the instincts of an Irishman.' It was an attitude that would bring him into conflict with the laws of the United States and see him launch an invasion of another country from its soil.

O'Neill was born in Drumgallon, County Monaghan, to a farming family. His mother and two of his siblings emigrated and went to America. At the age of fourteen, in 1848, he joined them and worked as a travelling salesman for a Catholic publishing company. He opened a bookstore in Richmond, Virginia, and established links with fellow Irish nationalists by joining the Emmet Monument

Association, devoted to the memory of the martyred Irish revolutionary Robert Emmet.

In 1857, yearning for adventure on the frontier of the American West, O'Neill joined the US Cavalry, serving in the 2nd Dragoons during a campaign against rebellious Mormons. Disillusioned with the campaign, he deserted and fled to San Francisco, where he joined a group of radical Irish exiles; but they did more talking than doing and, tiring of a life on the run, O'Neill turned himself in to the US army. He was reassigned to his old cavalry regiment.

On the outbreak of the American Civil War, O'Neill volunteered for combat and joined the 1st US Cavalry when it took part in the 1862 campaign to capture the Confederate capital at Richmond, his old East Coast home. He was a courageous soldier and promoted for his gallantry in several battles. 'It gives me great pleasure to state that from personal observation', testified Brigadier General H. M. Judah, 'I deem Lieutenant John O'Neill, of the 5th Indiana Cavalry, one of the most gallant and efficient officers it has been my duty to command. His daring and services have been conspicuous and I trust he may receive what he was so ably merited – his promotion.'

In 1864, O'Neill was given the rank of captain and transferred out of the cavalry to command a US Colored Infantry regiment. Dogged by a wound he received in fighting around Nashville the previous year, he was forced to resign from the US army later that year. He retuned to Nashville, married his long-term girlfriend, Mary Ann Crowe, an Irish Australian, and began his land claims agency business. Two years later, he joined the Irish-American Fenian Brotherhood, devoted to the establishment of an independent Irish Republic. Wishing to deliver a major blow against their imperial oppressors, they came up with a sensational plan to realize this: they would invade British Canada.

*

'Canada is a province of Great Britain,' John O'Neill argued, 'the English flag floats over it and English soldiers protect it, and, I think, wherever the English flag and English soldiers are found, Irishmen have a right to attack.' In striking at England through Canada, he claimed, the Fenians were attempting no more than was done by the American Republic in their War of Independence.

The direct invasion of Ireland was impossible, but

> Canada once gained, would serve as an excellent base of opera-
> tions against the enemy; and its acquisition did not seem too
> great an undertaking, from the number, strength, and resources
> of our people on the American Continent. There was, too, an
> army of veteran Irish soldiers but just disbanded by the close of
> civil conflict in the United States, that were ready and anxious
> to be led to battle for their country.

Once victorious on Canadian soil, O'Neill felt sure that thousands
of Irish-Canadians would join their cause.

With his extensive military experience, O'Neill was quickly
selected to lead the enterprise. Another prominent Fenian was
General Thomas William Sweeny. A Cork-born, one-armed veteran
of the Mexican-American War of 1846–48 and the civil war, Sweeny
helped organize the military expedition. On 27 May 1866, O'Neill
rode out with 115 men from Nashville. At Louisville, Kentucky, the
column was joined by 144 men and at Indianapolis by 100 more. In
Cleveland, Ohio, orders arrived from Sweeny in New York to travel
to Buffalo where they arrived on the 29th. By now, they had a force of
around 600 men, which was known as the Irish Republican Army –
the IRA. The Fenians had no distinct uniforms of their own, although
one contemporary newspaper account says that some of them were
dressed in old Confederate uniforms. It has been suggested that the
US government turned a blind eye to the activities of the Irishmen
because many senior Americans had still not forgiven the British for
giving help to the Confederacy during the civil war.

Before sunrise, on 1 June, the Irish soldiers, with all their arms
and ammunition, were towed across the Niagara River in four
canal boats. Once they stepped onto Canadian soil, they planted
the Irish flag in to the ground in defiance of the British. More practical measures were taken by O'Neill who had the local telegraph
wires cut and a nearby railroad bridge destroyed. They then occupied Fort Erie, hoisting their flag over the settlement, with O'Neill
reassuring the locals that they had come to drive out British authority and not pillage them.

The possession of Fort Erie sounded impressive but a letter published in *The Times* of London reassured worried Britons. 'It may

relieve the anxiety of people to know that Fort Erie, which belongs to me,' wrote the Kensington-based correspondent, James M'Cullam, 'consists of a corn mill with a dwelling house and a few acres of land on the Canadian side of the Niagara. The corn mill was burnt a few years ago and the whole … is worthless as a post for the Fenians or for any other belligerent.'

Early that evening, news came through to the Fenians that local Canadian forces were advancing towards them in two columns and, most worryingly, numbered some 5,000 troops. O'Neill was in a difficult situation as about a hundred of his men had already deserted him, thinking better of their day out in Canada and going back across the border to Buffalo. He had weapons for 800 soldiers but only 500 men to fire them, so he destroyed 300 of the guns.

Instead of panicking, O'Neill went on the offensive and marched towards Ridgeway to intercept one of the Canadian columns, composed of the Queen's Own Rifles, the York Rifle Company, the 13th Hamilton Battalion and the Caledonia Rifle Company. Around seven o'clock on the morning of the 2nd, the Irish made a temporary defensive line for themselves out of railway lines. From behind this fence, they engaged the Canadian militia skirmishers for over half an hour. The Queen's Own were armed with highly effective Spencer repeating rifles and when they sensed they faced only a small force, they began to outflank the Irish. O'Neill ordered his men to fall back a few hundred yards and form another line.

The Irish kept their nerve and gave the Canadians a volley of musket fire. At this point, the Fenians were helped by some Canadians suddenly fearing they were being attacked by cavalry, when in reality they saw only a handful of Irishmen on horseback. Panicking, the Queen's Own sounded the retreat and fell back to form a square. This gave the impression to the rest of the Canadians that they were withdrawing from the battlefield.

The Irish seized their opportunity and with one more volley followed up in the confusion with a blood-curdling bayonet charge. It was enough to scatter the 1,400 unprofessional militiamen, who left behind eight dead and thirty-nine wounded. The Irish pursued them for three miles through the town of Ridgeway as the Canadians threw down their arms and knapsacks. A Toronto reporter was sitting in a nearby tavern when the militiamen fled past the building. Some Fenians burst into the bar.

> They were the most cut-throat-looking set of ruffians
> that could well be imagined. Supposing me to be the
> landlord, they immediately demanded liquor. In vain
> I urged that I was as much a stranger as themselves.
> Their leader presented a revolver at me, and ordered
> me behind the bar.

Every jar he looked at was empty, but when he discovered a small keg of rye whiskey, he hastily distributed it to about fifty of the men in the tavern. They downed this and resumed chasing the Canadian militiamen.

Captain J. A. Macdonald was an officer in the Canadian Army during the Fenian invasion and took some grim satisfaction in describing a bizarre incident that occurred during the pursuit. A Private Hines of the Queen's Own was taken prisoner by the Fenians when one of the Irish officers grabbed his gun and smashed the stock against a rock, saying it would never shoot another Fenian. 'The Canadian gun, being loaded and at full cock,' noted Macdonald, 'went off with the concussion, and the bullet passed through the Fenian's body, killing him instantly.'

'Although we had met and defeated the enemy', recalled O'Neill, 'yet our position was still a very critical one.' He decided to withdraw back to Fort Erie and await news from the rest of the Fenian forces. He sent a message back to his comrades in Buffalo, explaining that they were heavily outnumbered, but if there were to be Fenian attacks elsewhere along the border, he would hold out in Fort Erie to the last man. In the meantime, his men were hungry and tired.

When news finally reached him that there were to be no more Fenian attacks, O'Neill had no choice but to re-cross the Niagara River back to Buffalo. At that point, the US government intervened, sending a gunboat, the USS *Michigan*, to arrest O'Neill and his men. She fired a 12-pounder gun across the bows of the Irish boats and threatened to use it on them unless they surrendered. O'Neill and 317 men laid down their arms. The expedition had been a complete waste of time and lives. In the fighting at Ridgeway and a subsequent skirmish, the Fenians lost eight dead and fifteen wounded.

The blame for the Fenian failure rested mainly on Sweeny, who was in charge of the overall strategy, but O'Neill received his share of criticism and, after his brief arrest, he returned to Nashville. There, he bided his time until he became president of the Fenian Brotherhood in 1868 and started planning another assault on Canada. It took him two years and although many fellow Fenians pledged their support, he realized too late that they had their private doubts about the viability of the whole project. This time, on 25 May 1870, some 400 Fenians gathered near Franklin, Vermont, on the Canadian border, but the Canadian militia had been given prior warning and they engaged the invading Irishmen before all of them had crossed over.

Many of the Fenians were not the military veterans who had triumphed at Ridgeway, but were inexperienced young men, and they faltered under the fire of the Canadian militia. O'Neill had to give them a stiff talking to. 'Men of Ireland, I am ashamed of you!' he shouted at them. 'We dare not go back with the stain of cowardice on us. Comrades, I will lead you again, and if you will not follow me, I will go with my officers and die in your front!' The brave words did him no good and the Irishmen broke before a determined Canadian advance.

One of the Irish soldiers, a Major Daniel Murphy, made his own report on the fiasco amid dark rumours of financial corruption and disunity among the leading Fenians.

> In conclusion, I have only a few words to say … Never
> go to Canada on a hostile mission, for, just as sure as you
> do, you will fail if Uncle Sam is not at your back. Never
> join an organization of Irish Nationalists (so called) if
> they are not united; you are only helping to prolong the
> quarrel and indefinitely postpone the freedom of Ireland.

O'Neill was equally bitter. Put on trial on 30 July 1870, he took the opportunity to apologize to the US court for his illegal actions, 'as a man who has fought and bled to preserve those laws'. He argued that the Irish had always been loyal supporters of the American Republic, refusing to support King George when he wanted money and soldiers to put down their revolution and then committing thousands of fellow countrymen to the cause of the North in the civil war. He saved his anger for those Irishmen who conceived the plot to invade Canada, 'who urged myself and others to take part in the endeavor, [but] basely and deliberately deserted us at the critical moment and left us to our fate'. He admitted it had been a 'ridiculous farce'.

The US judge was unmoved by his arguments, despite his good service to the US army. 'The more you are exalted by the exhibition of courage, of military skill and successful achievement in the past,' said Judge Woodruff, 'the greater is the crime when you prostitute that skill and courage … to engage in hostility towards a nation with which we are at peace.' Mindful that the US government had been too lenient with O'Neill the first time around, a stiffer sentence was required for repeating the crime. The Fenian leader was sentenced to two years in prison. O'Neill was lucky – he feared being sent to the gallows.

For all his passionate words during his day in court, denouncing fellow Fenians for the failure of his 'ridiculous farce', as soon as O'Neill was released from prison, after serving just a few months behind bars, he seemed to have learned little and organized yet another attempt to invade Canada in 1871. Other Fenians, however, were tired of O'Neill's posturing and, on this occasion, he had the support of only thirty-five men. His plan was to link up with the French Canadian rebel Louis Riel and his Métis tribesmen, but they had already settled with the British and O'Neill and his handful of men were taken prisoner by US soldiers near Pembina in North Dakota. Released almost immediately, O'Neill seems to have finally got the message that the Irish would never liberate British Canada. Instead, he moved to Nebraska and spent the rest of his life convincing Irishmen to settle in this part of the American West. In this he succeeded and an Irish settlement in Nebraska still bears his name today. He died in 1878.

*

Twenty-two-year-old Captain Myles Keogh had a lucky escape at the battle of Fredericksburg in 1862. Unlike his infantry countrymen of the Irish Brigade, he would not be thrown in a relentless wave against the artillery of the Confederacy on Marye's Heights. His Union cavalry unit was held back to exploit the breakthrough that never came. The US army had other plans for him, which would include his presence at the most famous battle fought on the American frontier – the battle of Little Bighorn.

Born in Leighlinbridge, County Carlow, Keogh was hungry for adventure and could think of no nobler cause than to fight to defend the Roman Catholic Pope in his war against Piedmont and Giuseppe Garibaldi's nationalists. Stepping on a train at the newly built Carlow station, he set off for Italy with 1,400 other Irishmen. Their boats and trains had to avoid both Britain and France, who had lent their support to Garibaldi, but that just added to the thrill for the excited Irishmen.

In Rome, Keogh and his comrades were organized into a battalion of St Patrick, but they had no training, no uniforms and poor weapons. Fortunately, the war was soon over, but wherever the Irish were posted they saw stiff fighting and between seventy and a hundred were killed or wounded. Keogh stayed on as a member of an Irish Zouave company that served the Papacy, but there was little future in it and he decided to embark for America in early 1862 via the port of Liverpool. Both his parents were dead and he appears to have felt little need to see his brothers and sisters in Ireland.

Keogh arrived in New York in April 1862 and joined the Union forces as a captain of cavalry. Within days, he was on the battlefront in Virginia serving as an aide-de-camp to an Irish brigadier. The fighting was on a much larger scale than in Italy and, at the beginning, Confederate forces seemed to be having the best of it. Keogh survived Antietam, Fredericksburg and Brandy Station. The latter combat was the biggest cavalry battle of the war and Keogh proved himself a skilled horseman. He rode in many cavalry raids and was one of the first to gallop into Gettysburg at the beginning of the epic battle. It was during that fight that another ambitious cavalryman, George Armstrong Custer, commanded a brigade. The two would have known each other at this stage and their futures would be closely linked.

More and more Irishmen arrived in America, willing to volunteer their services to the Northern side, and two of them were cousins of Keogh. He did his best to use his influence to get them commissions, but it was not as easy as it had been at the beginning of the war and Keogh struggled to support them financially. New Yorker General Wesley Merritt was impressed by the eager young men, commenting: 'They are dashing officers; you Irish can fight like devils. I often wonder why the hell you didn't kick the English out of Ireland.'

In 1864, Keogh was promoted to major and was transferred to the western theatre of the war, fighting in the advance on Atlanta. It was during this campaign that he was captured by the Confederates, but he was so highly regarded by his comrades that he was soon after released in a prisoner exchange. Keogh loved being a professional soldier and by the time the civil war came to an end, his greatest fear was that he would be thrown out of the army as it radically downsized.

Keogh frantically appealed to his superiors for letters of recommendation. His curriculum vitae was impressive and listed Custer among those commanders who personally requested him to serve at their side during the last cavalry campaign of the war. Eventually, his persistence paid off and he was commissioned as a second lieutenant in the 4th Cavalry of the regular US army. Later, in July 1866, he was promoted to captain and joined the 7th Cavalry, of which Custer was lieutenant colonel. Keogh was delighted.

'I have had unequalled promotion', he told his brother, 'and now when all the great volunteer army is scattered to the winds I am one among the few selected to be retained in the regular army.' It was a proud moment for him and, remarkably, considering he was just twenty-six years old, he was the fourth senior captain in his regiment. He felt as though he was one of the rising stars of the US cavalry, just like Custer, who was only three months older than him.

Keogh was put in command of Troop I and stationed at Fort Wallace in Kansas. He had ninety-eight soldiers under his command and they came from a variety of backgrounds. A good many of them were German immigrants, but around a quarter were Irish, at least one of whom had served with him in Italy.

Born to Irish parents, Lieutenant Henry J. Nowlan was a Sandhurst graduate who had served in the British Army in the 41st Welch Regiment during the Crimean War, before coming to America. Sergeant Jeremiah Finley was a veteran of the civil war, but he came with baggage – the rumour that he was on the run after having killed a man in Ireland. Finley was a talented tailor and made the buckskin jacket that became part of Custer's famous frontier garb. The soldiers were armed with sabres, Remington revolvers and Spencer repeating carbines. Keogh was an excellent shot with a Spencer and could hit a bottle at 150 yards.

The primary task of the 7th Cavalry was to secure the western frontier of the United States and this involved them in several campaigns against the Native American tribesmen, including the Cheyenne and Sioux. The terrain was tough and dangerous, but Keogh was happy in his life on the frontier. He had no wish to settle down. 'My great weakness is the love I have for the fair sex and pretty much all my trouble comes [from] or can be traced to that charming source,' he revealed in a letter home. His lack of money always bothered him and this was another excuse for not marrying. 'I am too proud to marry and have my wife support herself,' he said, but 'I fancy if I had an economical wife I might get on gloriously.'

In 1867, Keogh was promoted to the brevet rank of Lieutenant Colonel for his gallantry during the civil war. It was an honorary rank that did not impact on his day-to-day service as a captain, but it satisfied his ambition and he wondered whether it was the time to return to Ireland to see his family. He planned the trip, but just as he had secured replacements for his two Papal medals lost in a fire, he broke his leg. The recovery was long and painful and he became depressed over his lack of money. He thought he might be better off serving as a soldier of fortune in South America. Keogh eventually made it home to Ireland in 1869, but the visit was perhaps a disappointment for him and he came back to Kansas. Keogh resigned himself to his fate as a frontier soldier and in 1876 that career reached its climax.

*

Fighting had broken out on the Northern Plains when the Sioux and Cheyenne retaliated against the invasion of their land in the Black Hills of Dakota by gold miners. Crazy Horse was chief of the Oglala Sioux and gathered an alliance of 10,000 tribes-people in an encampment near the Little Bighorn River in Montana.

Lieutenant Colonel Custer had a reputation for leading brutal pre-emptive attacks against Indian settlements and in June 1876 he saw little reason to change his tactics, but he could also be recklessly overconfident and on that occasion it proved his undoing. Captain Myles Keogh had a bad feeling about the June venture. 'This month has never passed since I left home', he had said years earlier, 'without something very unpleasant occurring for me.' He gave his will to Lieutenant Nowlan to send on to his sister if anything happened to him.

After a three-day ride into Indian territory, Custer set up camp early on the morning of 25 June near the Little Bighorn River. Keogh's Troop I had been acting as a rearguard, keeping an eye on the straying mules of the baggage train, but this duty was passed to another troop and the Irishman was free to join in the action. Indian scouts reported to them a large number of ponies in the river valley and this encouraged Custer to launch a surprise assault on the encamped tribesmen, although it has also been suggested that Keogh's dumping of packs from the slow mule train had alerted the Indians and also spurred on Custer's decision to attack.

Just after noon, Custer divided his modest force of 700 US cavalrymen into three battalions at the beginning of his advance into the Little Bighorn valley, in the hope that he could squeeze the Indian encampment between a two-pronged attack. But he had badly underestimated the number of Sioux and Cheyenne he faced.

Captain Frederick Benteen took three companies to scout bluffs nearby, while three companies under Major Marcus Reno rode to the far bank of the Little Bighorn River towards the Indian tents. Custer led the main battalion force of five companies towards the north end of the encampment, hoping to catch the panicked tribesmen between himself and Reno. Captain Keogh, riding as second-in-command of Custer's wing of the attack, led Troop I and possibly also Troops L and C.

Hearing the white men charge towards them, the Sioux and Cheyenne quickly grabbed their weapons and mounted their horses. Reno's 130 or so men were easily repulsed with heavy casualties by the hundreds of tribesmen who next turned their anger on Custer's paltry force. Crazy Horse led the attack as the US cavalrymen scrambled back up the hill away from the hordes streaming across the river. It all happened very quickly. Indian warriors claimed the final phase of the fighting lasted little more than twenty minutes. 'It took about as long', said Cheyenne Chief Two Moons, 'as it takes a hungry man to eat his dinner.'

The US cavalrymen under Custer's command fought a desperate running battle up the slope. It has been suggested that Custer was killed early on and that Keogh took over command, falling back alongside his men towards the ridge overlooking the valley before the overwhelming numbers of Sioux and Cheyenne. Out of bullets, they would have ended their lives in a desperate hand-to-hand struggle. All five companies, some 225 men, were killed.

Reno and Benteen could do little to help Custer. Reno was later criticized for this but he was occupied defending his own position against tribesmen throughout the night and on into the next day, until they were relieved by a rescue column. Crazy Horse and his warriors had won a famous victory, even though they could never hope to win the war. Major General John Gibbon, who last saw Custer three days earlier, recorded the appearance of the battlefield shortly after the fighting was over.

> Dead men and horses were scattered along [the slope]. These became more numerous as the terminating knoll was reached, and on the south-western slope of that lay brave Custer surrounded by the bodies of several of his officers and forty or fifty of his men, whilst horses were scattered about in every direction. All were stripped, and most of the bodies were scalped and mutilated …

Keogh's body was stripped of his buckskin jacket – similar to that worn by Custer – but was not mutilated. His left leg and knee had been smashed by a bullet as he rode his horse and a final shot to his temple had finished him off. According to a trapper called Ridgely, who claimed he witnessed the battle before being made a prisoner, Captains Keogh and Yates were the last to die. The account of the Indian warrior Wooden Leg may also refer to Keogh's last moments.

> It appeared that all of the white men were dead. But there was one of them who raised himself on his left elbow. He turned and looked over his left shoulder, and then I got a good view of him. His expression was wild, as if his mind was all tangled up and he was wondering what was going on here. In his right hand he held his six-shooter. Many of the Indians near him were scared by what seemed to have been a return from death to life. But a Sioux warrior jumped forward, grabbed the six-shooter and turned it on the white man, and he was shot through the head.

At least thirty other Irish-born US cavalrymen perished on that afternoon. The tough Sergeant Finley was found pierced with arrows, lying alongside his horse. Private Thomas Downing in Keogh's Troop I was barely twenty years old when he died withdrawing along the top of the ridge. Private Richard Farrell died in the ravine leading up from the river, near to where Custer went down. Sergeant Robert Hughes carried Custer's personal pennant and fell early on.

Only one horse belonging to the 7th Cavalry survived the slaughter and that was, remarkably, Keogh's mount called Comanche – the horse he had ridden for most of the previous decade. Other wounded horses were put out of their misery on the battlefield, but, according to a report in the *St Paul Pioneer Press*, 'there were those present who felt a great tenderness for anything nearly associated with Keogh', and despite his many wounds, the animal was saved. As the only survivor of Custer's Last Stand, Comanche became very famous and lived on until 1891.

Three months after the battle of Little Bighorn, a pair of gauntlets marked with Keogh's name and the pennant of his Troop I were retrieved from an Indian warrior. Parts of his dress uniform and his sword were sent back to his family in Ireland. In 1877, a US army fort was built near the Yellowstone River in Montana and named after Keogh. In the same year, Keogh's body was exhumed from the battlefield and reburied in Auburn cemetery, New York State. A marble marker commemorates the place where Keogh fell on the battlefield.

Chapter 9
South African Irish

At four o'clock on the morning of 13 September 1896, a British detective burst into a hotel bedroom in the port of Boulogne, France, and held a revolver against the head of an Irishman. If he made the least resistance, the Scotland Yard detective threatened, he would shoot him dead. The sleeping man was Patrick J. P. Tynan and a large amount of money and incriminating papers were found on him. He was accused of meeting with fellow Irish plotters in Paris intent on taking bombs to England to blow up the Prince of Wales. As an American citizen, naturalized in 1888, Tynan appealed to the American ambassador to France and reminded the French of how the Irish had fought for them at the battle of the Fontenoy. The French government refused to extradite him to England and released him a month later. Tynan promptly got on a ship back to New York.

Tynan was the so-called 'No. 1' of the Irish National Invincibles, a radical splinter group of the Irish Republican Brotherhood (IRB) that had caused a political sensation by assassinating Lord Frederick Cavendish in the Phoenix Park murders in 1882. Cavendish was the chief secretary for Ireland and he was stabbed to death in the Dublin park along with a senior Irish civil servant. The assassins also plunged a dagger into the more moderate movement for Irish Home Rule, postponing its introduction for three decades. While his fellow conspirators were arrested and hanged, Tynan had fled to America. A year later, he had been interviewed in Brooklyn, where the reporter was a little disappointed by his mild-mannered appearance: 'Altogether "Number One" looks more like a Professor of a Western college than the Executive of Irish Invincibles.'

After his narrow escape in France, Tynan sought other ways to strike back at England and his gaze turned to South Africa. There, the semi-independent Boer Republic of Transvaal was engaged in a struggle against British authority. To Tynan, the Boers were natural allies and he wrote to their leaders from New York in 1897. He warned them that the British could be expected to recruit Cape colonists and Sikh soldiers to put down any Boer rebellion, just as they did the American War of Independence, 'when they employed the red man to scalp our women and children'. But Tynan had little regard for the regular British Army. 'Your people could whip them three to one. It is composed of the off-scouring of British poverty and rascality. Boys from the purlieus of the cities and immature youths compose 90 per cent of the British Regular Service.'

During his recent trip to Europe, Tynan had visited the British military base at Gibraltar and seen Highland soldiers whose legs were 'not thicker than the wrist of a healthy man'. But what the British feared most, he explained, was the intervention of a major foreign power, such as Germany, in favour of the Boers. 'God grant it', he wrote, 'and then we'll see a smash up of the brutal and bloody British Empire.'

A facsimile of Tynan's letter was published in *The Great Transvaal Irish Conspiracy*, an anonymously authored pamphlet distributed in Cape Town in 1899, the year in which war broke out between Britain and the Transvaal republic. It was printed alongside other scurrilous accounts of Irish collusion with the Boers. One report pointed the finger at Solomon Gillingham, a highly successful Irish trader whose mansion in the capital of Pretoria became a centre for Irish–Boer secret diplomacy: the Irish green flag with harp and the Boer *Vierkleur* ('four colours') flew outside. Gillingham had grown rich on food concessions granted by the Boer government and was happy to return the favours in whichever way he could. The author of the pamphlet ventured into a bakery shop run by Gillingham in Pretoria and found more Irish conspirators there than buns being sold.

'This little den was always in semi-darkness,' noted the informer. 'The walls were adorned with blood-curdling pictures of England's perfidy and cruelty, and the *Irish Freeman* was lying usually scattered around.' A hunchback Irishman stood behind the counter and if he gave you the nod you passed into the back room, which was Gillingham's inner sanctum. 'Here Volksraad members and secret service agents met, over coffee and kookies, spinning out visionary pictures of the fall of the British Empire, [and] a free and united South Africa.'

According to the *Conspiracy* pamphlet, Irish agents were travelling around the world, raising support for the Transvaal republic. In America, Fenians were keen on recruiting 10,000 Irish-Americans to set sail to join the Boer cause, but the plan was scuppered when the Federal government learned of the involvement of the notorious Patrick J. P. Tynan. It now turns out that the anonymous author of *The Great Transvaal Irish Conspiracy* may well have been Tynan himself. His purpose in penning this leaflet was to fan the flames of British antagonism towards the Irish in South Africa and thus drive the latter closer to the Boers.

In the booklet, Tynan reproduced a notice distributed in Johannesburg entitled *A Call to Arms to Irishmen in South Africa*. It came from the Transvaal Irish Volunteers and compared the situation in South Africa to the English conquest of Ireland. 'With the story of Ireland's wrongs and sufferings before them,' said the Transvaal Irish Volunteers, 'no wonder the Boer people refused to surrender their cherished independence to the hateful sway of Britain.' They called upon Irishmen living in South Africa to step forward and join in the defence of Boer freedom and thus strike a blow against their hated enemy. 'England has been the vampire that drained Ireland's life-blood for centuries, and now her difficulty is Ireland's opportunity.'

*

One of the leaders of the Transvaal Irish was John MacBride. Born in Westport, County Mayo in 1865, he was an apprentice draper when he first became involved with the Irish Republican Brotherhood, the Irish counterpart to the American Fenian Brotherhood, both determined to turn Ireland into an independent republic. By the age of thirty, MacBride had joined the Irish National Brotherhood, which had split away from the IRB and was more active in the USA. He went to Chicago for a convention as their Dublin representative. All this political activity drew him to the attention of the police, who kept a report on him.

In 1896, MacBride decided to leave Ireland for good and seek his fortune in South Africa, where he hoped to work in the Transvaal gold mines as an assayer. He arrived in turbulent times. Early that year, the Jameson Raid had been planned as a coup d'etat against the Transvaal government by British colonists wanting to take over the Afrikaner state. It failed, but it exposed the weaknesses of the Boer government and they quickly stockpiled weapons against any further threats. MacBride was firmly on the side of the Boers resisting British authority, and criticized those Irish colonists who rode in the Jameson Raid. 'The number of those Irish "Heroes" did not exceed thirty', he noted sourly, 'and their "loyalty" to the Crown and constitution had been purchased ... for the gift of a rifle and pound a day for their valuable services.'

As soon as MacBride arrived in the gold fields of Transvaal, he set about organizing like-minded Irishmen into a political group. He made contact with the well-connected Irish trader Solomon Gillingham, and when war came, he volunteered his services to the Boer President, Paul Kruger, offering to bring over thousands of Irishmen from Ireland and America. Kruger believed the foreign army wouldn't be necessary, but was happy to have MacBride organize his own unit of Transvaal Irishmen. In truth, Kruger and the Boers were always fearful of *uitlanders* – outsiders – and it was their wish to exclude them from their own government that was one of the bones of contention with the British.

MacBride was offered command of the Transvaal Irish Brigade, but declined due to a lack of military experience. That role went to the Missouri-born Colonel J. Y. F. Blake, a veteran of the 6th US Cavalry, who had fought in the Indian Wars. MacBride was given the rank of major. Gillingham organized the weapons and logistics. The Boer War started on 11 October 1899 when the Transvaal Boers crossed the border with Natal into British-ruled territory. The Transvaal Irish Brigade joined the advance. The majority of their troops were Irish-born but there were some American-Irish and French as well. They carried a green flag designed for use in an abortive Fenian uprising in Ireland in 1867. MacBride wanted it known that this action in South Africa was simply a continuation of the long struggle against British rule.

On 20 October, a Boer force, including the Transvaal Irish Brigade, entered the coal-mining town of Dundee, occupied by nearly 4,000 British troops with 18 field guns. At first, MacBride and his compatriots feared the British artillery, but their marksmanship was poor and many of the shells didn't even explode. The British claimed to have fought them off, but the Boers returned, and rather than enduring a siege, the British decided to evacuate the town. Forty of them failed to withdraw in time and were captured by the triumphant Boers, who then looted the town. Among the British prisoners were soldiers belonging to regiments raised in Ireland.

'Colonel Moller and forty of his Dublin Fusiliers and Irish Fusiliers were driven into a cattle pen and forced to surrender,' recalled MacBride. 'A number of the Irish Brigade had been at school with some of the captured men – a humiliating position all round.'

*

The number of Irish settlers in South Africa was never as great as it was in America or other parts of the British Empire. A census of 1891 in Cape Colony noted there were only 14,000 Irish-born immigrants out of a British population of 130,000, less then 11 per cent. The activities of MacBride's Irish volunteers grabbed newspaper headlines in Ireland but they barely numbered 500 in total. By far, the largest group of Irish fighting in the Boer War was in the British Army, with one estimate putting this at 28,000 Irish soldiers. The Irish (5th) Brigade was led by Major General Arthur Fitzroy Hart and consisted of four distinguished regiments: the 1st Royal Inniskilling Fusiliers, the 2nd Royal Irish Rifles, the 1st Connaught Rangers and the 1st Royal Dublin Fusiliers.

The war began badly for the British, with the Boers capturing Dundee and laying siege to Ladysmith, Kimberley and Mafeking. Then came the infamous Black Week in December 1899 in which the British were defeated in three battles. The might of the British Empire was truly being tested by an irregular force of Boer farmers – but the farmers were armed with excellent high-velocity rifles and had an instinctive talent for guerrilla warfare. In January 1900, a new British commander-in-chief, Lord Roberts, was dispatched to South Africa, and along with his chief of staff, Lord Kitchener, took a grip of the situation. With substantial reinforcements, Roberts went on the offensive. In Natal, the British marched to the relief of Ladysmith.

Daniel Auchinleck came from an Omagh family in County Tyrone and was a lieutenant in the 1st Battalion of the Royal Inniskilling Fusiliers. The Inniskillings had suffered badly in earlier defeats of the war, but their spirits were raised when they started to taste victory on their advance towards Ladysmith in February 1900. The Boers withdrew before them rather then engaging in a costly battle. 'We amused ourselves all morning examining the enemy's trenches and picking up odds and ends as trophies,' noted Auchinleck in his diary. 'Found any amount of cartridges and other things the enemy had left behind in their hurry to get off.' But this hasty evacuation was offering the British a false hope, as the Boers took up a stronger defensive position on the high ground overlooking the Tugela River, barring the British move towards Ladysmith.

General Redvers Buller was in charge of the British forces at Tugela and he was hungry to avenge earlier humiliating defeats. He used his artillery skilfully to pin down the Boers as his troops crossed the river. From the heights overlooking the river, Major MacBride and his Transvaal Irish Brigade watched the advance of Buller's troops on the morning of 21 February until the British artillery shells started exploding around them.

> Suddenly the roar of Buller's seventy guns broke the
> serenity of that beautiful summer morning and lyditte
> and shrapnel came shrieking and tearing in every
> direction. The English gunners concentrated fire on
> one Kopje [hill], for a time moving from the base to the
> top. The accuracy was remarkable but all the Kopje
> which were hit did not have any Boers there ...

MacBride and his Irishmen kept their heads down as the British artillery expertly raked the hillside, but as the ranks of khaki-clad British soldiers crossed the river and moved closer, the Boers opened up with deadly fire from their Mauser rifles. MacBride's Irishmen stripped off their coats and carried shells to the Boer artillery. MacBride delighted in seeing the shells explode among the advancing British, cutting down his fellow countrymen alongside

English and Scots. 'The Anglo-Irish mercenaries with the fighting courage of their race make a desperate effort to make their way forward,' he observed, 'but as for the others, one would imagine that some terrifying volcanic eruption had taken place in their midst.'

It was the turn of Major General Hart's Irish (5th) Brigade to march into action at Tugela Heights on 23 February. Just after daybreak, and almost immediately as they commenced their advance, they came under fire from the Boer artillery. They sheltered beneath the high banks of the river, but as they moved in single file along a railway line they were forced into the open, running across a railway bridge, which they dubbed Pom-Pom bridge after the rapid one-pounder shell fire from Maxim-Nordenfelt Pom-Pom guns. During this race, Lieutenant Auchinleck and his Inniskillings lost between twenty and thirty men. On the other side of the river, the steep slope of the high ground gave them some shelter from the artillery fire and two regiments of the Irish Brigade re-formed, with the 1st Royal Inniskillings on the left, the 1st Connaught Rangers in the centre, and the Imperial Light Infantry, a colonial unit, on the right.

Under covering fire from their own artillery, the Irish regiments reached the summit of one of the hills on the Tugela Heights in the afternoon, but then their artillery had to cease fire for fear of hitting their own men. This left the Irish regiments exposed to the fire of the Boers in trenches just 150 yards ahead of them. The rifle fire took a heavy toll of the Irishmen, but they re-formed on the ridge of the captured hill and made the brave decision to rush the Boer position. Auchinleck recorded what happened next.

> Then the Regt charged and men and officers fell in
> dozens; after going some way the Regt rallied and
> charged again and this time got to within 50 yards of
> the enemy's trenches. Here the fire was awful coming
> from four different directions and it is marvellous how
> the men faced it.

The survivors of the slaughter huddled behind a low stone wall and slugged away at the Boers, with neither side willing to give way. Both sides stayed there all night. The fighting carried on the next day and it is not surprising that the position became known as Inniskilling Hill in honour of their dogged resistance. Major C. J. Lloyd Davidson was one of the soldiers trapped behind the stone wall, and at one stage, heavy rain fell. 'I remember opening my mouth to catch what I could,' recalled Davidson, 'being very thirsty. Then the sun came out, burning hot. The firing never ceased throughout this long day ... the Boer rifle fire hitting the rocks all around us; if anyone moved or helmet showed, a dozen bullets came at us.'

A truce came on the following day, Sunday 25th, and both sides took away their wounded and dead from the hill. They had been fighting for forty-eight hours without food and water. Davidson was carried out to a dressing station beside the River Tugela. 'I'll never forget the relief it was to be away from the sound of the whistling bullets,' he said.

Auchinleck had lost many of his good friends in the regiment. Only eight officers were left in his battalion. Their commanding officer, Lieutenant Colonel T. M. G. Thackery, and their second-in-command had both been killed. Auchinleck took the belongings of the dead men back to the supply wagons. At eight o'clock that evening the truce came to an end and the shooting started again.

The next day, British artillery chipped away at the Boer positions. It was beginning to have an effect and on the 27th, General Buller, the British commander, ordered one final massive advance, which included the other Irish (5th) Brigade regiments, the 2nd Royal Irish Fusiliers and 1st Royal Dublin Fusiliers. The Boers had had enough and many of them jumped out for their trenches waving white flags, but many of the British had had enough too and were in no mood for mercy, shooting them down.

It was a great victory for Buller, and Auchinleck called it the 'most eventful day of my life'. It occurred, satisfyingly, on the anniversary of the battle of Majuba, the dreadful loss inflicted on the British by the Boers in 1881, and was soon followed by the relief of Ladysmith. But it had all come at a tremendous cost to the Irish (5th) Brigade. Five officers were killed and 21 wounded; 86 other ranks killed, with 340 wounded and 59 missing. The Royal Inniskilling Fusiliers had lost 72 per cent of its officer strength and 37 per cent of its enlisted men, in just one battle. For the Inniskillings, the fighting was over and they were withdrawn from the Irish

Brigade, performing garrison duty at Ladysmith until their strength could be built up again.

When news got back to Britain of the great victory won by Buller and the part played in it by his Irish regiments, Queen Victoria was so impressed that she commanded that the wearing of the shamrock be officially instituted for all Irish regiments on St Patrick's Day.

In addition to this, on 1 April 1900, an Army Order was issued declaring: 'Her Majesty the Queen, having deemed it desirable to commemorate the bravery shown by the Irish regiments in the recent operations in South Africa, has been graciously pleased to command that an Irish regiment of Foot Guards be formed. This regiment will be designated the Irish Guards.' The Guards Division is the premier infantry unit in the British Army, the first two English Guards regiments being established in the 1660s and the Scots Guards in 1686. Finally, after over 200 years of hard, frequently unacknowledged, military service, the Irish had joined the ranks of the British fighting elite. The Welsh Guards followed in 1915.

On 17 March, the Inniskillings celebrated St Patrick's Day in Ladysmith with plenty of beer. 'In the evening,' recorded Auchinleck, 'after an enormous dinner, soup, curry with rice, potatoes and French beans, Roly Poly pudding followed by pineapples, oranges, cakes and marsala, we had a sing-song. Bed pretty late.'

*

Irishmen living around the world in British colonies rallied to the cause of the British Empire during the Boer War. Many of them believed the red-coloured imperial map of the Victorian schoolroom was as much their achievement as anyone else's and they wanted to protect it. Daniel Patrick Driscoll was born to Irish parents in Burma and had his earliest military training in the Far East, but he kept a noticeably strong Irish brogue. At the age of thirty-seven, he was outraged by the news of early Boer victories over the British, especially their Irish regiments, and paid his own passage to the Cape where he volunteered his services.

Driscoll's sentiments were shared by many other Irish living in South Africa and on St Patrick's Day in 1900 in Cape Town a number of Irishmen rode through the town demonstrating their loyalty to the Empire and their willingness to fight for it. At first, Driscoll was made a captain in the Border Horse, a Cape Colony raised unit, but soon he formed his own band of soldiers, called Driscoll's Scouts, in March 1900. It consisted of sixty volunteers from Cape Colony who agreed to ride into Boer territory in the Orange Free State.

By the summer of 1900, the war was entering a new stage. Most of the set battles were over and major Boer cities had been captured. The Boer President Paul Kruger had fled abroad to France, but Boer resistance carried on in the form of guerrilla warfare. This state of affairs suited Major Driscoll just fine and his Scouts thrived in the irregular fighting. Driscoll quickly won a reputation for his daring exploits. One of his Scouts, R. W. Glyn, kept a diary and recorded a typical incident involving his commander.

Driscoll was out scouting by himself when he came upon a farm-house. Chatting to the farmer, he discovered that the family was pro-British and he was welcomed inside for a cup of coffee. As they talked, the door burst open and four armed Boers walked into the room. Never far from his rifle, Driscoll reacted quickly, grabbed his gun and told the Boers to drop their weapons and put up their hands. In the darkened interior, the Boers could not reckon how many of the enemy they faced and by the time they realized it was Driscoll alone, he had them bound up and took them back to camp as his prisoners.

'It gained him many recruits,' reported Glyn, but it was also his natural charisma that earned him a following. 'He was a real warrior,' wrote Glyn. 'When he was in a temper, his language was a real "education" and made everyone jump. He did not know what fear meant, but strange to say was still full of life when the war ended. He drank well, fought well, played well and was as straight as a die. We were very proud to serve under him.'

It was irregular forces like Driscoll's Scouts that helped Britain meet the challenge of Boer guerrilla warfare and heralded a new flexibility in British military thinking that would lead to the forma-tion of commando units in later wars. Driscoll was a new kind of military hero and his exploits began to be featured in *Boy's Own* fiction. He even starred in his own adventure story, *Driscoll – King of Scouts*, published in 1901, an elaborated version of his actions in South Africa. The author, A. G. Hales, delighted in contrasting his rough appearance with the parade-ground style of a traditional British officer.

> There wasn't a solitary inch of Driscoll's [uniform] that had not got a stain ... Driscoll was as dark as a Sioux Indian ... His mouth was hard and firm; his glance proud and almost defiant, as if he challenged all creation to better what Ireland had produced when it produced him.

This new phase of the war did not suit Major John MacBride at all and his Transvaal Irish Brigade was disbanded. A steamship was charted to take many of them to Trieste, as it was not thought safe for them to remain behind in South Africa. Many went on to the USA, but MacBride went to Paris to meet the exiled President Kruger. There, he was formally thanked for his contribution to the war.

'I shall never forget,' said Kruger, 'and my countrymen will never forget, how the Irish Brigade stood by the men of the Transvaal in their hour of need.'

'To fight for the liberty of any land', replied MacBride, 'could only be a happiness and honour for an Irishman, but to fight for the liberty of a land whose enemy is also our own is the birthright of an Irish Brigade.'

The press asked MacBride what he planned to do next.

'I believe more in the efficacy of one well-directed bullet', he replied, 'than in that of a hundred appeals to the foreign Parliament that has its seat at Westminster, but I may give some lectures in America.'

In fact, in Paris MacBride married Maud Gonne, a founder of Sinn Féin, and they returned to live in Dublin, where he got a job as the city water bailiff. Of course, MacBride had achieved very little practically in South Africa, but he did strike a chord with republicans in Ireland. The Irish Transvaal Committee in Dublin had matched his harassment of British forces by distributing thousands of leaflets. Written by a Catholic priest, the leaflets told potential Irish recruits to the British Army that the fighting in South Africa was an unjust war that imperilled the salvation of their souls.

Such appeals did little to dissuade the many Irishmen who joined the Imperial Yeomanry Force – mainly middle class volunteer cavalry units that supplemented the regular British Army. Two contingents were raised in Dublin and three in Belfast. They wore a slouch-hat, typical of the more irregular warfare demanded of them, except for the Belfast 60th, who wore sun helmets adorned with a badge featuring the Red Hand of Ulster on a white shield. The Dublin 61st were granted the privilege of being the first Irish Imperial troops to wear a brass shamrock on their hats. The 60th and 61st squadrons set sail for South Africa from Southampton in April 1900.

The horse-mounted Yeomanry were the perfect troops to pursue the swift-moving Boer commandos. On St Patrick's Day in 1901, the Irish Yeomanry took a leading role in an attack on a Boer position at Magermansberg. They had ridden through the night, during a thunderstorm and continuous rain. 'It was so dark', wrote Trooper Earl of the 61st Squadron, 'that I could not see the head of the horse I was riding … The only time I could see before me was when the lightning flashed.'

The 100 Yeomanry rode alongside 300 regular British soldiers. At two o'clock in the morning, they halted, spread out oiled sheets and rolled themselves up in their horse blankets for three hours' rest. They resumed their march, had breakfast, and then spotted the Boers at ten o'clock. The Yeomanry were given the very simple orders of directly attacking the Boer hillside position, which they were to do in an old-fashioned cavalry charge. Bearing in mind they faced Boer marksmen armed with high-velocity rifles, this was an almost suicidal task. Trooper Earl reckoned the distance they had to gallop across was three-quarters of a mile and there were about 200 Boers in the hill.

Ordered to give a good account of themselves by their commanding colonel, the 60th and 61st Yeomanry set off in extended order with about thirty yards between each man. The fire of two 12-pounders and a rapid-fire Pom-Pom gun covered their swift advance, although this probably did more to alert the Boers than shield them. Across two dry riverbeds they dashed 'as hard as our horses could go'.

> The noise was awful … Bullets whistling around, guns roaring, and we were galloping like devils over the plain and up the hill. It is a day I shall never forget. All thoughts

of being hit never entered my head. All I thought of was
the top of the hill.

Miraculously, Earl and the Irishmen made the summit of the hill
without one of them being hit. The Boers had bolted and the Yeomanry dismounted to fire at their backs. For the next few hours,
they engaged in a fire-fight. The cover on top of the hill was sparse
and Earl hid behind a little pile of stones. One explosive bullet blew
the stones away and hit him in the shoulder. Despite the bravery of
their charge against the hill – named 'Paddy's Kop' by them – the
Yeomanry engagement was indecisive and the Boers withdrew to
fight another day. Such was the frustrating nature of guerrilla
warfare.

In the end, it was the less heroic but more effective use of barbed
wire, blockhouses and concentration camps by the British that
brought the Boers to the negotiating table. The 1st Battalion of the
Royal Inniskilling Fusiliers was deployed in the mundane work of
constructing these blockhouses. These were built along railway
lines and linked to each other by barbed wire fences, thus restrict-
ing the open areas over which the Boer commandos could ride.

'A party of 20 men have to build one Blockhouse per day',
remembered Private L. J. Bryant, 'and one man gets one shilling for
every Blockhouse he builds.' Boer snipers took pot shots at the
builders and skirmishes frequently erupted around them. The
Inniskillings got adept at creating trip wires between the blockhouses to alert them to night-time attempts by the Boers to cross the
wires.

> We have two rifles loaded pointing down on each side
> of the wire, and we have a wire leading right into the
> roof of the blockhouse and tin attached to it, so that
> when it is touched it makes a noise and so gives us
> the alarm and all the sentry has to do is to fire each
> rifle down the wire.

A further refinement was to have trip wire attached to the triggers
of the rifles so they would fire automatically when sprung. Such
methods hemmed in the Boers so they could no longer carry out
their hit-and-run raids.

The Boer War ended in May 1902. It had been an exhausting and devastating conflict for both sides and, in many ways, heralded the brutal modern warfare of the First World War. Some of the Irish soldiers who fought in South Africa would next find themselves on the battlefields of the Western Front.

At the age of thirty-seven, Daniel Auchinleck served as a captain with the 2nd Battalion of the Royal Inniskilling Fusiliers in 1914 and was killed within a few months of the beginning of the war in Belgium near Ypres. Lieutenant Colonel Daniel Driscoll volunteered the service of his unit of a hundred Frontiersmen, envisaging their employment on the Western Front as behind-the-lines raiders. The offer was rejected and Driscoll took his Frontiersmen to fight the Germans in their East Africa colony where they distinguished themselves in bush fighting. After the war, Driscoll retired to Kenya, where he died in 1934.

John MacBride joined the Easter Rising in Dublin in 1916 and was captured by the British. His role leading the Transvaal Irish Brigade compounded his crimes and he was one of the first rebels to be executed by firing squad. Offered a blindfold, he refused, saying: 'I have looked down the muzzles of too many guns in the South African war to fear death and now please carry out your sentence.'

Chapter 10
Great War Irish

At four o'clock in the afternoon on Saturday, 15 July 1915, a large crowd of Londoners, several thousand strong, gathered in Hyde Park. A military band entered the north-east corner of the park near Marble Arch, followed by a horse-drawn carriage bearing Thomas Power O'Connor, the celebrated Athlone-born journalist and MP for Liverpool. Next to him sat a twenty-five-year-old khaki-clad soldier beaming broadly at the sea of faces around him. When the carriage reached a wooden platform in the middle of the crowd, O'Connor and the soldier from County Cork stepped up onto the stage to a mighty roar. Dozens of women surged forward to reach out their hands to the soldier as he tossed flowers at them. Who was this fighting man? Why did he deserve such a welcome? O'Connor addressed the crowd, telling them that no general or king could expect such a warm reception.

'I am but a man of words,' said O'Connor, 'and words are vain, empty, futile things. I stand by the side of a man of deeds. Our military history is crowded with records of Irish valour, and bright and luminous as its pages are there is no page brighter than that which records the deeds of Michael O'Leary.'

The crowd roared its approval as O'Connor handed O'Leary a cheque raised from the subscriptions of fellow Irishmen keen to show their thanks. It was now time for the Londoners to hear from the soldier himself and Sergeant O'Leary saluted them before saying a few words.

'I thank you for your kindness,' he said. 'This is more than I expected from the people of London.'

'Why?' shouted a man in the crowd. 'We are Irish!'

'Well, it is far more, for I have done nothing more than other men at the front have done. I don't like fuss. I don't like handshaking about it. I did my duty as a soldier and a man, as a soldier should.'

The London Irish cheered.

'There are many others who have fought and are fighting,' continued O'Leary, 'who have attempted and have done more than I for King and Country. I have had the luck. I thank you all very much for your kindness, and I say to all who are fit to serve – don't be content with looking on … Join – give us a helping hand.'

The recruiting officers were busy that day as hundreds of young Irish Londoners stepped forward to serve their country, for they all wanted to be like Michael O'Leary – the first Irish Guardsman to win the Victoria Cross.

*

Fifteen years earlier, at the height of the Boer War, a letter had appeared in *The Times*, arguing that the valour of Irishmen fighting for Britain had not been sufficiently recognized. Far from home, hundreds of Irishmen had just lain down their lives for the Empire in South Africa, among them soldiers from the Inniskilling Fusiliers, Dublin Fusiliers and Connaught Rangers. 'Is there not one mark of distinction and honour that can be conferred upon them and their country which belongs to Scotchmen [*sic*] and Englishmen, but is withheld from them?' asked Cumming Macdona, MP for Southwark. 'There are Scotch Guards and English Guards, why not add to the roll of glory a regiment of Irish Guards?'

Events moved quickly after this appeal, matching the mood in the royal household and the British government, and by 1 April 1900, the Irish Guards had come into existence with a proclamation from Queen Victoria. Field Marshal Lord Roberts, from an Anglo-Irish family, became its first colonel, and Major R. J. Cooper, from the Grenadier Guards, was appointed its first commanding officer. Some 200 Irishmen, also from the Grenadier Guards, became the nucleus around which the regiment grew. Wearing a ceremonial uniform similar to the other Foot Guards, including a bearskin and scarlet tunic, the Irish Guards added a St Patrick's blue plume, a shamrock emblem on each end of their collar and tunic buttons arranged four, four and two. A mascot was donated by the Irish Wolfhound Club and was named Brian Boru, after the ancient Irish hero.

Twenty years old, Michael O'Leary was attracted by the glamour of this new Irish regiment and joined them in 1910. Brought up on a farm near Macroom in County Cork, he had wanted more out of life and joined the Royal Navy at the age of sixteen. Still restless, he served three years in the Irish Guards before leaving to sail across the Atlantic to Canada join the Royal North West Mounted Police. His fearless character demonstrated itself during a two-hour gun battle in which he arrested two outlaws. With the outbreak of the Great War, O'Leary got permission to re-join his old regiment as the Irish Guards became part of the British Expeditionary Force in Flanders in November 1914.

By this time, the opening months of manoeuvre warfare had bogged down into the grim reality of trench fighting. The Irish Guards Regimental Diary recorded the non-stop battle against the elements during that winter.

> No sooner is a trench dug than it fills with water …
> The soil is clay, and so keeps the water from draining away
> even if that were possible. In order to keep the men at all
> dry, they have to stand on planks rested on logs in the
> trenches, and in the less wet places bundles of straw and
> short fascines are put down. Pumping has been tried, but
> not with much success.

Soldiers went down with trench-foot and a variety of other illnesses – fifty Guardsmen went to hospital in just one forty-eight-hour period.

To keep their spirits up, one young subaltern started a trench newspaper for the 2nd Irish Guards called *The Morning Rire*. In it, he lampooned his superior officers, one of them, taking over as mess president, making the following statement: 'I am here for two purposes. To do as much damage to the whiskey as possible and to hold my part at all costs.' A mock advert claimed: 'Most of us enjoy shellfire. The hissing sound is an invigorating tonic, but there are still some who do not. Buy our "What is to be" ear lobes, and dream that you hear your friend's best girl ask you to have a drink all day and all night.' A parody of a Sherlock Holmes detective tale was entitled 'The Adventure of the Haunted Latrine'.

> There seems little doubt that the Officer's Latrine in the Ducks Bill is haunted: instead of the usual sounds such as groans and sighs, ghastly enough we admit, but sounds such as one would associate with such a locality, there is heard at frequent intervals during the night, sounds of gurgling and snatches of laughter. The mystery remains unsolved and we look to Major Holmes to unfathom it.

Lance Corporal Michael O'Leary was in the 1st Battalion Irish Guards when they advanced towards the Flanders Front in late January 1915. The weather was appalling but they were assured that their new trenches would be not too wet. They moved along the line of a canal from Bethune towards Cuinchy. The Germans were relentlessly shelling the canal, hoping to breach its walls and flood the area. The 140-strong Irish Guards were accompanied by the 2nd Coldstream Guards. They took a position to the west of the Railway Triangle, where three railroad tracks joined. The land was flat except for large mounds of abandoned bricks with trenches running between them. Early on the morning of 1 February, the Germans launched an attack along a trench towards the Coldstream Guards. The Irish were called in to help them.

Initially, the Germans had the best of it, but then the British artillery opened up and shelled the hollow where some of them lay, killing them outright. Fifty Coldstream Guards and thirty Irish Guards counter-attacked, surging across the open ground towards an enemy trench.

O'Leary was an orderly that day, which meant he was not on active duty and carried no bayonet for his rifle. He watched the British artillery shell the Germans, throwing up geysers of mud and earth, and something told him to get involved. Despite the bombardment, the Germans were showing strong resistance, their fire stalling the advance of the Coldstream Guards. The Irish ran to their support and O'Leary joined them, rushing ahead of the other men so he alone faced the enemy guns.

Suddenly, the ground gave way and he stood on the edge of a pit. The sight of a German with a grenade made him spring back, but he lowered his rifle and shot the soldier dead. He ran up to a junction in the enemy trenches that allowed him to approach it from the side. Inside, he saw five enemy solders. One of them fired at him but missed, and with five careful shots he dispatched them all.

To his side, O'Leary saw Irish Guardsmen using their bayonets against the enemy, but left them to that and moved on. This time, he approached a German machine-gun nest. He made the rapid calculation that the Germans would have removed the gun from the position during the bombardment – and if only he could get to it before they re-mounted the gun, he could knock out the crew. He pressed five more cartridges into the ten-bullet magazine, with one in the breech, and, avoiding the swampy ground between him and the machine-gun nest, ran sixty yards along the firmer ground beside a railway embankment.

Inside the protected position, the Germans were indeed re-mounting their machine gun when O'Leary appeared to their side on the rim of the sandbags. The German officer was about to press the button of his machine gun when O'Leary emptied his rifle, killing three of the crew. The other two threw up their hands and the Irish Guardsman made them his prisoners. Company Quarter-master-Sergeant J. G. Lowry of the Irish Guards witnessed the action.

> O'Leary came back from his killing as cool as if he
> had been for a walk in the park and accompanied by
> two prisoners he had taken. He probably saved the lives
> of the whole company. If the machine gun had got slewed
> round No 1 Company might have been nearly wiped out.
> We all quickly appreciated the value of O'Leary's sprinting
> and crack shooting and when we were relieved that night,
> dog-tired as we were, O'Leary nearly had his hand shaken
> off by his comrades.

For that act of valour, O'Leary was promoted to sergeant and won the first Victoria Cross awarded to his regiment. He carried on serving alongside his comrades in the trenches of the Western Front for the next few months but, as news of his VC-winning action spread, the British High Command realized he could be more useful as a morale-raising recruiter. In May, it seemed that this realization had come too late for O'Leary as an artilleryman reported back that the Irish Guardsman had been killed in battle. The news spread quickly round the world, with a headline appearing in the *New York Times* declaring him killed in battle. Fortunately, it was a false rumour and a reassuring postcard to his parents arrived later that month.

O'Leary arrived back in Ireland in June 1915 to a rousing welcome. He was given a banquet in his honour in County Cork, where he declined the offer of wine with his dinner, preferring just lemonade because, he said, he had to 'keep fit'. He signed so many autographs and shook so many hands that he joked to a journalist, 'looking at his bruised right hand, that he must get back to the trenches to rest!'

'He is quiet, soft-voice, intelligent above the average,' noted an Irish journalist, 'speaks well with an accent rather inclined to English than to the brogue. But he can talk Irish, too, fluently though he admitted he hadn't much practice in it since he left home ten years ago.'

The only person who not so impressed by O'Leary's achievements was his father: 'I am surprised he didn't do more,' said Daniel O'Leary to a local newspaper. 'I often laid out 20 men myself with a stick coming from Macroom Fair, and it is a bad trial of Mick that he could kill only eight, and he having a rifle and bayonet.'

After his recruitment drive came to an end, O'Leary was commissioned as a second lieutenant and transferred from the Irish Guards to the Connaught Rangers for service in the Balkans from 1916 until the end of the war. There, he caught malaria, which dogged him for the rest of his life. In 1921, O'Leary returned to Canada and joined the Ontario police force. His health took a turn for the worse in the 1930s and the British Legion brought him back to Britain where he lived in North London and worked in their poppy factory before becoming a commissionaire at the Mayfair Hotel.

With the outbreak of the Second World War in 1939, O'Leary joined the British Expeditionary Force as a captain of the Middlesex Regiment, but had to be invalided out of the army soon after because of his malaria. Two of his sons served as pilots and both won the Distinguished Flying Cross. Such was the celebrity still attached to this Irishman that his place at the centenary review of VC-winners in 1957 was taken by an impostor in a bath chair. O'Leary died in Islington in 1961.

*

It has been estimated that over 200,000 Irishmen took part in the Great War. Some claim figures as high as 400,000, but this includes all those Irishmen living abroad and volunteering for service in armies outside Britain, including that of the United States. Without doubt, it was the greatest deployment of Irish soldiers in the country's military history. For many of them, service in the Great War began with a letter from King George V. David Campbell was a student at Trinity College Dublin when he received his. He had joined Trinity's Officers Training Corps in March 1914, so it was no surprise when he received his commission into the British Army as a second lieutenant a few months later in August. The royal letter arrived just as he was studying a Greek textbook and he kicked the volume high in the air saying, 'I'll never open you again!'

After a month's training, Campbell was posted to the 6th Royal Irish Rifles at Fermoy, County Cork, where he was put in charge of a platoon of reservists who were mainly middle aged and used to only one month's military service every year. They hated physical exercise and were difficult to control, but as they got fitter, they soon took a pride in their appearance and became efficient soldiers. Twenty-mile route marches, carrying iron weights in their ammunition pouches, and mock battles in Phoenix Park in Dublin completed their preparation for battle.

Early in the New Year, Campbell was promoted to lieutenant and his company commander, J. F. Martyr, was made captain. Martyr had been waiting for this for ten years and, with the increase in money that came with it, he seized the opportunity to marry his long-time fiancée. 'I don't think I ever saw such a devoted and happy pair,' noted Campbell.

In May 1915, Campbell and his battalion of the Royal Irish Rifles were transferred to Basingstoke, England, as part of the 10th (Irish) Division. Composed exclusively of Irish battalions, it included among its ranks Connaught Rangers, Royal Munster Fusiliers, Royal Dublin Fusiliers, Royal Inniskilling Fusiliers, Royal Irish Fusiliers and one battalion from the Leinster Regiment. Among the many volunteers in this division was a 'Pals' company raised from Dublin's rugby clubs.

Training continued in England, but Campbell managed to grab a few days' leave in Brighton where he visited the smart hotels and tasted crème de menthe for the first time. 'May and June went by pleasantly enough', recalled Campbell, 'and we almost began to think we'd never get away.' In July, the 10th (Irish) Division got orders to embark for the Dardanelles.

The Dardanelles campaign was intended as a blow against the Ottoman Turkish Empire, the weaker ally of Germany. It began as a naval operation to force a passage through the Dardanelles Straits towards the Turkish capital of Istanbul, but the battleships failed to make the breakthrough and a land assault was needed at Gallipoli to knock out Turkish resistance. The 10th (Irish) Division was to join the British, Indian and Anzac troops tasked with storming the beaches and silencing the Turkish guns. General Sir Ian Hamilton was commander-in-chief of the 75,000-strong army.

Lieutenant Campbell and his Irish Riflemen set sail for a voyage through the Mediterranean via Malta and Alexandria. They were excited by the prospect of all the new sights that awaited them, but on 21 July 1915, when they disembarked at the Aegean harbour of Mudros on the volcanic island of Lemnos, the prospect was less than appealing. 'There was no visible sign of vegetation,' remembered Campbell. 'All was dull and monotonous, sickly yellow.'

The Royal Irish Rifles were taken ashore in little fishing boats that held up to twenty men. The sea was choppy and the soldiers were told to loosen their shoulder straps in case they were pitched over into the water and had to jettison their backpacks. Once ashore, the locals sold them tomatoes and melons. The Irishmen set up their camp on the island, but they had no tents and lay in the open under the night sky. At last, they had a vision worthy of the long journey: 'Stars crowded the sky and winked and glowed ... the Milky Way was a belt of star dust stretching from horizon to horizon, brilliant, beautiful.'

The hardness of the ground meant that not only was it difficult to raise tents or any kind of construction, but also, crucially, the army

(*top*) King William III leads his Protestant army to victory over the Irish Catholics at the battle of the Boyne, 1690. Illustration by R. Caton Woodville.

(*above*) The Wild Geese – Jacobite Irish soldiers leave Limerick for France in 1691.

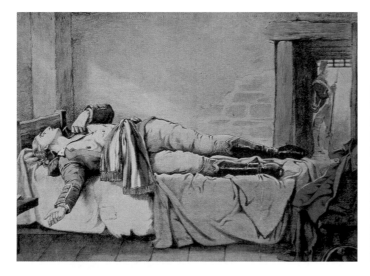

(*left*) Theobald Wolfe Tone, founder member of the Society of the United Irishmen, commits suicide, rather than be hanged by the British for his part in a projected French invasion of Ireland in 1798.

(*right*) British soldiers – many of them Irishmen – storm the ramparts of Badajoz in 1812.

(*left*) American Civil War recruiting poster for the Fighting 69th in 1861.

Royal Munster Fusiliers form a square for a photograph during the Boer War *c.* 1900.

(*right*) Irish recruiting poster of World War One, printed in Dublin in 1914.

FOR THE GLORY OF IRELAND

BELGIUM

'WILL YOU GO OR MUST I'?

(*left*) Michael O'Leary, Irish Guardsman and Victoria Cross winner, near his home in County Cork, 1915.

(*left*) Statue to Father Francis Patrick Duffy in Times Square, New York, inspirational military chaplain to the Fighting 69th in World War One.

(*right*) The band and wolfhound mascot of the Irish Guards wearing the shamrock on St Patrick's Day. Painting by Douglas Macpherson.

(*above*) 2nd Battalion London Irish Rifles, part of the 38th (Irish) Infantry Brigade in World War Two, advance towards River Reno in 'Kangaroo' armoured carriers, Italy 1945.

(*right*) Statue to Sean Russell in Fairview Park, Dublin, defaced by swastika graffiti. Russell was an IRA chief who secretly worked with Nazi Germany during World War Two. A controversial figure, an earlier stone statue of Russell in the same place had an arm and head knocked off before being replaced with this bronze version.

(*left*) Seventeen-year-old Private John Gorman in the Congo, shortly after the battle of Jadotville in 1961, in which Irish United Nations peacekeepers fought off an attack by hundreds of Katangan soldiers.

(*below*) The Lexington Avenue Armory, New York headquarters of the Fighting 69th, used as a help centre following the terrorist attack of 9/11 in 2001.

(*above*) Royal Irish soldiers in Afghanistan in 2008 as part of an operation training the Afghan National Army. Company Sergeant Major Dominic 'Brummie' Hagans in the centre, Sergeant Boyle, right, Major Armstrong, left.

(*below*) Remains of Royal Irish Land Rover after it was blown up by a Taliban roadside bomb in September 2008. Hagans and his crew all survived the blast.

latrines were not dug deep enough. Clouds of flies buzzed around them and dysentery spread rapidly among the battalion. Campbell developed a way of eating in which he covered his plate with a cloth and then raised the corner to quickly withdraw a forkful of food before putting the cloth down again.

> The flies had strong allies in the ants, small black ones.
> They invaded our valises, they penetrated the food baskets
> and got mixed with the bread and the raw meat. They were
> particularly partial to bully beef and simply wallowed in
> Nestlé's Condensed Milk if they got the chance …

Bathing in the warm Aegean Sea made up for some of this misery and a little wooden pier was reserved for the use of the officers first thing in the morning and in the early evening. Lieutenant General Sir Bryan T. Mahon, from County Galway, was the commanding officer of the 10th (Irish) Division and he joined his men for a swim. Some of the other officers took this as a chance to show off. One saluted Sir Bryan and executed a perfect dive into the sparkling water. He was disappointed when his prowess was rewarded with everyone laughing at him as he emerged out of the waves. It was only then that he realized that he'd forgotten to take off his valuable wristwatch.

On 5 August 1915, Campbell, the Royal Irish and the rest of the 10th (Irish) Division embarked for Suvla Bay on the Gallipoli peninsula. Alongside the 11th (Northern), 13th (Western), 53rd (Welsh) and 54th (East Anglian) Divisions, their mission was to relieve the pressure on the British and Anzac troops that had landed earlier on Gallipoli but were pinned down by tougher than expected Turkish resistance.

That night, the 10th Division sailed along the Gallipoli coast, seeing it dimly to the east of them. They heard the sound of artillery fire and saw the flash of flames from the mouths of the big guns. Star shells burst in the night sky, draping ribbons of red, green and white light over the blasted landscape. One Turkish shell crashed into the sea near their ship, sending up a column of water, but they were spared any further bombardment.

As they drew closer to Anzac Cove, just to the south of Suvla Bay, Campbell and his comrades heard the rattle of machine guns and rifle fire. They saw little lights sparkling in the hillside above the beach, belonging to Australian and New Zealand dugouts. Then, just half a mile away from their destination, the breeze brought a terrible odour: 'It was the smell of decaying animal matter … of dead men's rotting flesh and bones.'

At eleven o'clock barges came alongside the troop ships and the Irish scrambled into them, any sense of dread being forgotten in the business of landing. Guides helped them find their way in the darkness across the beach. They advanced up a gully, the steepness of the ground overlooking the cove protecting them from the direct fire of the Turks.

Marching for about two or three hours, they got near to the brow of the hill where they rested where they could, grabbing a few hours of sleep before they were awoken by the sound of gunfire and occasional shells screaming over their heads. It was dawn on 6 August and the Irish dug in. The ground was as hard as on Lemnos and they had to use pickaxes to chip away at it. At eleven in the morning enemy shelling began in earnest.

It was their first time under fire, but they noted that the Australians across the gully from them were unfazed by the assault and so they tried to act as coolly as them.

The bombardment lasted all day and the Irish grabbed a little rest during the hot afternoon. Towards evening, the Irish were each issued with a square of white cotton material and told to sew it on their jackets. This indicated a night attack was imminent and they would need the square of white to identify friend from foe.

An hour before midnight , they moved off, relieved to be marching away from the constant shelling. Their pockets were stuffed with sugar, tea and biscuits in case they lost touch with their base. They spent most of the night advancing through gullies, losing their sense of direction, and catching the occasional smells of decomposition.

For two days, Campbell and the Royal Irish Rifles clung to the hillside above Anzac Cove. The entire mission of the 10th (Irish) Division, intended to catch the Turks by surprise and outflank them, thus helping the other British and Anzac troops, had stalled badly. Two brigades of the Irish Division were landed to the north of Campbell in Suvla Bay but on the wrong beaches, causing much confusion and delay. To top it off, there was dissension among the generals as Lieutenant General Mahon refused to serve under another general who was technically inferior to him in ranking but who had just been appointed commander of the operation. Appallingly, Mahon departed from the area, leaving his Irish division behind.

On 9 August came orders for a general attack. British artillery bombarded the crest of the hill above Campbell and the Royal Irish Rifles. A battleship joined in and huge slabs of earth were thrown up in the air. The Irish climbed up the slope through dense patches of holly and laurel. As the scrub ended, they came to the edge of a wheat field. It was then they got orders to attack the enemy trenches.

Bullets buzzed around Lieutenant Campbell as he led a charge into the field. He had got about fifty yards when he turned round to see who had followed him – only about half his platoon. At that moment, a bullet cut through the calf of his leg. It slashed the band of his puttee which got tangled around his legs. As he tried to untangle it, his fingers were covered in blood from his wound. Followed by few of his men, Campbell headed for a patch of scrub that gave him some cover from the fusillade of Turkish bullets.

As he rested, a soldier from a previous attack crawled over, gave him a swig from his water-bottle and dressed his wound. When that helpful soldier was struck by a bullet in the foot, Campbell helped him apply a dressing to his wound. There was little Campbell could do, pinned down as he was by gunfire all around him. He felt he should go back across the field to check on the rest of his men but the Turks had him covered. To go ahead by himself would be useless. 'I felt miserable and utterly ashamed of myself,' recalled Campbell. The decision was made for him when a second bullet slammed into his foot. 'I was satisfied that I was properly knocked out this time, for the bullet had driven a hole though my foot.' Bandaging his wounds with his puttees, he took off his equipment and piled it in front of him. He then lay flat on his back and lit a cigarette.

As Campbell lay in the frontline with Turkish snipers' bullets exploding around him, his blood loss made him feel sleepy and he dreamed of the paddock in front of his family house in Crinstown in County Kildare. He was ten years old and making daisy chains with his friends. As his comrades gazed across the wheat field at the body of their platoon commander, they were sure he was dead.

So was he. In his dream, the paddock was reality and he hovered above the battlefield below.

When Campbell awoke, he decided to drag himself back to his own lines. The assault had failed and he crawled on his hands and feet along the edge of the scrub, avoiding the deadly wheat field. It meant he constantly knocked into other wounded soldiers who swore at him, telling him not to attract enemy fire. Some were badly wounded and he wanted to help but knew he could not. Eventually, he got to the edge of the scrub just fifty yards away from his trenches.

The ground was exposed, but Campbell was determined to get back. He raised himself on to one foot and hopped the final distance. In the trench were dozens of seriously wounded Irishmen. Campbell's fellow officers smiled grimly at him and called him a 'lucky dog'. He'd got what was called a 'Blighty one' – a non-serious wound that was a ticket out of the frontline. Company commander Captain J. F. Martyr, so recently and happily married, was not so lucky; he had been shot dead in the first attack that day.

The wounded Irish waited in Suvla Bay for evacuation by hospital ships. Artillery and sniper fire tormented them as they lay in the sun. Campbell had lost his pith helmet on the way down from the hill.

> Fearing I should get sunstroke, I took off my jacket
> and put it over my head. This was but poor protection,
> the burning rays seemed to penetrate to one's very soul.
> Anyway they penetrated my right shin from which I had
> removed my puttee to use it to protect my wounded limb.
> My shin was scorched most unmercifully and for days it
> was much more painful than any of my wounds.

Campbell was forced to crawl across the hot sand to the shade of a field hospital. Eventually, he was taken out in a launch to a hospital ship where he had his first proper meal for six days. Shortly afterwards, he threw it all up and suffered from dysentery for the first part of his voyage home. His wounds grew infected and he saw nothing of the Mediterranean ports they passed through. At one point, it was thought his foot might have to be amputated.

They arrived in Southampton on 23 September and Campbell was transferred to Lady Caernarvon's hospital at Highclere Castle in

Hampshire. The greenness of the landscape and the care of the nurses made it feel like paradise to Campbell and his wounded comrades. Lady Caernarvon had promised personally to take care of the first Irishman they received and Campbell was that man. 'She, apparently had a penchant for the Irish', he remembered, 'and all the nurses and doctors were of that nationality.' The men were given homemade beer at lunchtime and wine and whisky with dinner, all served to them by Lady Caernarvon's butler and footmen.

The rest of the 10th (Irish) Division continued to suffer in Gallipoli. They took part in two more major assaults that achieved little. In total, the 10th Division lost 2,000 men killed or dying from wounds by the time the operation was acknowledged as a failure and the troops were evacuated from Suvla Bay in December. Campbell's Royal Irish Rifles had suffered 75 per cent losses and were too few in number to go back into action in Gallipoli. 'How futile seemed all our training, our field days, our reviews,' concluded Campbell. 'In a few days our grand battalion was shattered, wiped out without having achieved anything.'

Campbell returned to Ireland to a hero's welcome from his family and friends. His foot still bothered him and he had to spend a month in hospital in Dublin, but he eventually got back to his home in Crinstown and stood in the paddock he had dreamt of as he lay wounded at Gallipoli. A lot had happened since he kicked his Greek textbook in the air.

Campbell was declared fit in January 1916 and sent back to the 6th Royal Irish Rifles in the 10th (Irish) Division in Salonika in Greece, where he took part in a campaign against Bulgarian, Austrian and German forces. In April 1917, his company played host to Michael O'Leary VC. 'We were glad to have him but were at a loss how to employ him,' remembered Campbell. 'He had a habit of going on lone patrols and sometimes stayed away for days and filled us with alarm for his safety.' Campbell survived the war and was awarded the Military Cross. He returned to Trinity College to graduate with 1st Class Honours in Engineering.

The 10th (Irish) Division finished their war in Palestine as part of General Sir Edmund Allenby's army that defeated the Ottoman Turks, finally gaining vengeance for their humiliating losses at Gallipoli. They were the most widely travelled of all the Irish formations in the British Army in the First World War.

There were two other Irish divisions: the 16th (Irish) and the 36th (Ulster). Territorial and volunteer battalions raised in England included the Liverpool Irish, the London Irish Rifles and the Tyneside Irish Brigade. All served on the Western Front, but it was the soldiers of the 36th (Ulster) Division that took part in what has become one of the most infamous days of battle in the twentieth century – the first day of the Somme.

Chapter 11
Over the Top

In 1913, many Irishmen were preparing for war with the British Empire, but this time they were not Irish Catholic Republicans but Irish Protestant Unionists. Led by Sir Edward Carson, they feared the implications of the introduction of the Home Rule Bill, which proposed devolved government for Ireland within the United Kingdom of Great Britain and Ireland. To ready themselves for conflict with the British government, they raised militia units from Ulster Unionist clubs and the Orange Order – some 100,000 strong – and called them the Ulster Volunteer Force (UVF).

In July 1913, Carson arrived in Belfast for crisis talks with leading Unionists and to inspect the newly raised fighting men of the UVF. Arriving at Holywood in a carriage bedecked with Union Jacks, the fifty-nine-year-old barrister stepped down to shake the hands of the volunteers before making a rousing speech to them.

'You will find there is no comradeship more valuable than the comradeship born out of common danger', he told them, 'and it is when men are together prepared to meet a common danger that they find out the real qualities of those with whom they associate, and find out the men whom they can absolutely trust.' Little did any of the men know that night that this comradeship would be tested not in a contest with the British government, but in one of the bloodiest battles of the First World War.

When the Home Rule Bill was forced through Parliament in London in early 1914, it was feared that unrest in Ulster would turn into conflict. In April, a shipload of 24,000 rifles from Germany was imported to arm the UVF, but by August the bigger crisis in Europe had erupted into war, implementation of Home Rule was postponed, and loyal members of the Union rushed to join the British Army. Carson suspended his demands for a Protestant province of Ulster independent from the rest of Ireland and the threat of civil war within the island receded.

Thanks to its industry and trade throughout the Empire, Belfast had grown enormously and was the biggest city in Ireland. Its young men provided an entire division, designated the 36th (Ulster) Division, with the vast majority of them from the Ulster Volunteer Force. In fact, the original battalion designations included their origins within the UVF, as in the 8th Battalion, Royal Irish Rifles (East Belfast Volunteers). The divisional commander was Major General Sir Oliver S. W. Nugent, a highly experienced officer who had trained the Cavan UVF before they were incorporated into the 9th Royal Irish Fusiliers. Many of the soldiers benefited from their military training in the UVF.

It was not until October 1915 that the Ulster Division was shipped to France and, initially, it spent a quiet time on the Western Front in Picardy before being transferred to the Somme in the summer of 1916 to take part in the major Allied offensive of that year. The day chosen for the first day of this battle was 1 July – a day that resonated among the Protestant community of northern Ireland as the anniversary of the battle of the Boyne in 1690 when they defeated the Catholic army of James II. The Protestant fraternal organization known as the Orange Order got its very name from William III – William of Orange – their victorious commander at the Boyne.

In a letter written to the commander of the UVF back in Ireland, divisional commander General Nugent was very aware of the significance of the day:

> Before you get this we shall have put the value of the Ulster Division to the supreme test. I have no fear of the result. I am certain no General in the Army out here has a finer Division, fitter or keener. I am certain they will be magnificent in attack, and we could hardly have a date better calculated to inspire national traditions amongst our men of the North. It makes me very sad to think what the price may be, but I am quite sure the Officers and men reck [sic] nothing of that.

One of his soldiers, Lance Corporal John Kennedy Hope, 'A' Company, 14th Royal Irish Rifles (Young Citizens Volunteers of Belfast), had a more prosaic approach to the battle. 'I have no fear of death,' he wrote in his war diary on the night before. 'No fear at the moment. I do not yet know what, it is like to face death – not yet – it is only a matter of hours and then!'

In the forthcoming battle, the task of Lance Corporal Hope and his fellow Belfast riflemen was to take a position called the Schwaben Redoubt, near the German frontline and the village of Thiepval. A massive artillery bombardment preceded the assault on the morning of 1 July as thousands of Allied troops awaited the word to attack. Yet, rather than waiting for the bombardment to cease and then ordering his men forward, by which time the Germans would be dragging out machine guns from their dugouts, Nugent told his men to crawl out of their trenches and across no-man's-land during the bombardment, under the cover of smoke, until they were just a hundred yards from the enemy positions. It was a decision that would save hundreds of lives.

At Zero Hour at 7.30 a.m., the Irishmen bolted forward. They were still met by bullets but not the full fury the Germans directed at their British colleagues elsewhere along the line. Lance Corporal Hope clambered forward with a shovel and a large coil of wire over his shoulder. A shell exploded near him and his comrades and they ditched their heavy equipment, feeling speed was more vital to them. While 'bullets fall all round like a hail storm', they rapidly crossed the remaining yards of no-man's-land and plunged into the enemy trench.

'We get forward and into the Hun line and feel quite safe when we have clay walls to cover us, even in enemy territory,' noted Hope. 'There is little opposition at this point so what is left of our company operates up the line and we find many Huns who are afraid to come out of their deep dugouts.' The Germans fired random shots up the stairs from their bunkers and the Irish replied with grenades.

> We get well into the fray and I get curious. The excitement takes me on the prowl on my own. I seem to be alone somewhere, I take a look over the top and to my surprise I see a Hun officer standing on the parapet some distance away.

Ulstermen from other battalions joined them, including Rifles and Inniskillings. Excited by the relative ease of capturing their section of the enemy trenches, they were not sure what to do next. Aware that they were far more advanced than other British units along the line, they were told to prepare for a German counter-attack.

As they waited, casualties began to pile up from German artillery fire, their shells sending showers of shrapnel down on the Irishmen. One man was pushed to the top of the parapet to spot the enemy and rolled back down peppered with shell splinters. By midnight there was no support for them, for elsewhere along the line the British had suffered terrible casualties – up to 60,000 dead and wounded on this notorious first day of the battle.

There was nothing for Hope and his Ulstermen to do but give up their gains and go back to their lines. It was a task just as deadly as the early morning advance as Germans were now filtering back into their positions.

Hope sprinted across no-man's-land and ran smack into a barbed wire entanglement. As he extricated himself from it, he lost his sense of direction. A German flare shot up in the night sky and this helped Hope run in the right direction to join a group of Irishmen huddling in a shell crater. He was ordered to guard their withdrawal, but when he heard nothing more of the main unit, he joined the general retreat.

'We guess our position and run down the hill as fast as our legs will take us, over the Hun front line; over the famous sunken road and jump into our front line at the top of Elgin Av.' Hope was surprised to receive no challenge from the sentry on duty, but was glad to be back and gulped half a petrol tin of water. As German artillery continued to rain down on them, Hope concluded: 'The big day is a complete wash-out, a company wash-out or a Divisional wash-out if you like.'

Later the next day, after a breakfast of tinned pilchards, demoralized troops trickled back into his trench. One officer wanted to know where he could find some water to wash his feet. Hope pointed at the muddy lake behind them. 'He eyes the place and looks as if he would like to throw himself in. His company are all "sweating like pigs" and look as if they had been marching all night.'

Hope grabbed a few hours of sleep before waking for a roll call of his company. The soldiers cheered when they realized a companion had survived, but so many were missing. 'The company is but a shadow,' recorded Hope. 'Where are the officers? Gone to the place where there is no chin wagging, no kit inspections, no dirty rifles, no unshaven chins.'

Colonel J. A. Mulholland, in his War Diary of 14th Battalion Royal Irish Rifles, told a similar story to Hope, but was careful to state that the four battalions of the 109th Brigade, including the 14th Royal Irish Rifles and 9th, 10th and 11th Royal Inniskilling Fusiliers, all moved off at precisely 7.30 a.m. – Zero Hour – and not before as is generally understood. 'The Brigade moved off as if on parade,' reported Mulholland. 'Nothing finer in the way of an advance has ever been seen, but alas, no sooner were they clear of our own wire when the slow tat tat of the Hun machine guns from Thiepval Village and Beaumont-Hamel caught the advance.'

Several men fell under the deadly crossfire, but they pressed on. Mulholland stayed behind the main advance, gathering intelligence and noting the German prisoners being passed down the line and collecting their regimental shoulder badges.

A German counter-barrage shelled his HQ dugout and he asked for reinforcements to back up the achievements of his men in the German frontline, but none were sent.

By six o'clock, he finally got word of some Territorial troops moving up, but they were 'going the wrong way. The boy in command did not know in what direction he was to go so I put him right and gave him orders that he was to reinforce the remnants of the 109th Brigade.' But it had little effect as his troops began to make their own way back from the German positions during the night.

On 3 July, Mulholland received his copy of the Special Order issued by Major General Nugent, General Officer Commanding (GOC), in which he stated that

> in his opinion nothing finer has been done in the war than the attack by the Ulster Division on the 1st July. The leading of the Company Officers, the discipline and courage shown by all ranks of the Division will stand out in the future history of the war as an example of what good troops, well led, are capable of accomplishing … The GOC deeply regrets the heavy losses of Officers & Men. He is proud beyond description, as every

officer and man in the Division may well be, of the magnificent example of sublime courage and discipline which the Ulster Division has given to the Army. Ulster has every reason to be proud of the men she has given to the service of our country. Though many of the best men have gone, the spirit which animated them remains in the Division and will never die.

Subsequent accounts of the day began to elaborate on the heroic Ulster character of the advance. When Captain Arthur Samuels of 11th Royal Irish Rifles (South Antrim Volunteers) published his own account of the battle, he included a report that said that 'The men advanced as if on parade: one or two remembering the ancient watchwords, sang out " Dolly's Brae" and "No Surrender", but for the most part they kept the stiff upper lip and clenched teeth ...'

Lieutenant Colonel Ricardo, commander of the 9th Royal Inniskilling Fusiliers (Tyrone Volunteers), said:

Early on the 1st July (the boys were convinced the date had been chosen for their especial benefit) the battle began ... I shall never forget for one minute the extraordinary sight. The Derrys, on our left, were so eager they started a few minutes before the ordered time, and the Tyrones were not going to be left behind, and they got going without delay – no fuss, no shouting, no running; everything orderly, solid, and thorough, just like the men themselves. Here and there a boy would wave his hand to me as I shouted 'good-luck' to them through my megaphone, and all had a happy face.

Newspaper reports enhanced the legend of the Ulster Division at the Somme. 'I am not an Ulsterman', declared a correspondent in *The Times*, 'but yesterday as I followed the amazing attack of the Ulster Division on July 1 I felt I would rather be an Ulsterman than anything else in the world.'

'My position enabled me to watch the commencement of their attack from the wood in which they had formed up,' continued the reporter,

but which, long before the hour of assault, was being overwhelmed with shell fire, so that the trees were stripped and the top half of the wood ceased to be anything but a slope of bare stumps, with innumerable shell holes peppered in the chalk ... Then I saw them attack, beginning at a slow walk over no-man's-land, and then suddenly let loose as they charged over the two front lines of the enemy's trenches, shouting 'No Surrender, boys!'

Other accounts claim that some of the Ulstermen wore their Orange sashes and shouted 'Boyne!' All agreed, however, that the salient won by the Ulstermen could not be held and they had to retreat after their heroic gains. Even Ricardo had to admit that the situation was a 'cruel one for the Ulster Division. There they were, a wedge driven into the German line, only a few hundred yards wide, and for 14 hours they bore the brunt of the German machine-gun fire and shell fire from the sides; and even from behind they were not safe.'

The Ulster Division suffered 5,100 casualties on that first day and the scale of their sacrifice has seared itself into the collective memory of the Unionists and their movement, underpinning their connection to the United Kingdom. Four Victoria Crosses were won by the division. Today, in Northern Ireland, 1 July is still remembered as a day of tremendous significance for the Protestant community.

*

A later, almost equal sacrifice to that of the 36th (Ulster) Division has, however, been largely forgotten – that of the mainly Catholic 16th (Irish) Division, recruited from southern Ireland. They included battalions of the Connaught Rangers, Leinster and Munster Regiments, Royal Dublin and Inniskilling Fusiliers. Many moderate Irish nationalists fought in its ranks, believing their sacrifice might earn them the right to autonomy within the British Empire, like Australia and Canada. These nationalists had come together in 1913 as the Irish Volunteers, a military force intended to counter the influence of the northern Irish UVF and stand up against them in a civil war if necessary. But, again, war in Europe interrupted this process and John Redmond, leader of the Irish Volunteers, pledged their support to the British Empire.

Redmond, an MP in the British Parliament, supported the Home Rule Bill and believed it would be enacted once the war was over. He originally wanted the Irish Volunteers to form a separate Irish Brigade that would only be deployed in Ireland on defensive duties, but he was opposed by the British commander Lord Kitchener, and Redmond came under increasing pressure to see them serve abroad as a unit within the British Army. Redmond eventually accepted this mobilization of the Irish Volunteers and many of them were incorporated into the 16th (Irish) Division.

Redmond hoped that by sharing the dangers of the Ulster Division on the Western Front, the presence of so many Irish nationalists would encourage a mood of reconciliation and keep Ireland united. But the Irish Volunteers included a wide range of nationalists, from those, like Redmond, who wanted Home Rule under the British Crown to more hard-line Irish republicans who wanted a completely independent country. Redmond's decision to encourage the enlistment of the Irish Volunteers into the British Army split the movement. The majority were moderate followers of Redmond and became known as the National Volunteer Force. When they marched off to war in Europe, they left behind the hard-line republicans, who now turned the Irish Volunteers towards more militant action, exploiting the absence of so many moderate young nationalists.

In April 1916, radical members of the Irish Volunteers and other republicans led the most significant uprising in Ireland since 1798. Some 1,200 of them stormed key buildings in Dublin and fought a pitched battle with the British Army. After seven days of fighting, the Easter Rising was suppressed and its leaders captured. Redmond had been caught unawares by the rebellion, so out of touch was he with the republicans, but he pleaded with the British authorities to show leniency towards the rebel ringleaders. In no mood to show mercy, the British had the republican leaders executed. In the eyes of many Irish people, this punishment was too harsh and helped push them towards supporting the republican cause. The position of Irish moderates was not helped either by the fighting on the Western Front. Lasting for much longer than Redmond or any other politician had anticipated, the losses of so many young Irishmen called into question his judgement in sending them abroad in the first place.

The 16th (Irish) Division did not take part in the 1 July slaughter, but went into action on the Somme in September 1916. Advancing behind a creeping barrage, they had initial success capturing part of the German frontline near Delville Wood, but suffered in later assaults. Several of the Irish Volunteers distinguished themselves. County Monaghan-born Thomas Hughes was a private in the 6th Battalion, Connaught Rangers, when he was wounded on 3 September in the fighting at the village of Guillemont. Having had his wounds dressed, he went back into the front line and, single-handedly, charged a German machine-gun post, killing the gunner and capturing the position. Despite being wounded again, he brought back four prisoners. For his outstanding valour, he was awarded the Victoria Cross. On the same day in the same combat at Guillemont, a second VC was won by Lieutenant John Holland of the 3rd Battalion, Leinster Regiment, for leading his men under heavy fire and capturing fifty prisoners.

Irish courage came at great cost, however, and the casualties in the 16th (Irish) Division totalled over 4,300 men. In the following year, John Redmond suffered a personal loss when his brother Willie, a captain in the Royal Irish Regiment, part of the 16th (Irish) Division, was killed in fighting at the battle of Messines. His vacant seat in the Irish parliament was later taken by Eamon de Valera, the most senior surviving leader of the Easter Rising. Not only did the Great War take the lives of many Irishmen, but it also severely weakened the cause of moderate nationalism and encouraged the rise of more violent republicans.

*

Father Francis Patrick Duffy knew his men very well. As military chaplain to the 69th New York Infantry – the Fighting 69th – renumbered the 165th Infantry Regiment in 1917, he understood that many of the Irish immigrants fighting in the volunteer unit still harboured anti-British feelings.

This came to a head when their supply sergeant was shocked to see the combat uniforms supplied to them in France were not American but British Army issue, complete with brass buttons bearing the English crown. Some of the Irish soldiers wanted to burn the clothes there and then. The Easter Rebellion in Dublin in

1916 had brought Irish Republicanism to the fore once again and eighty-two Irish rebels had been killed by British soldiers in seven days of street fighting

Duffy took their concerns to the regimental colonel, John Barker, who at first did not take the complaints that seriously.

'At least they wouldn't object if they had to wear English shoes, would they?' said Barker.

'No,' quipped Duffy, 'they'd have the satisfaction of stamping on them.'

The forty-six-year-old military chaplain explained to the colonel the character of some of his men.

'We do not want you to feel that you have a regiment of divided loyalty or dubious reliability on your hands,' Duffy reassured him. 'If you put our fellows in line alongside a bunch of Tommies, they would only fight the harder to show the English who are the better men, though I would not guarantee that there would not be an occasional row in a rest camp if we were billeted with them. There are soldiers with us who left Ireland to avoid service in the British Army. But as soon as we got into the war, these men, though not yet citizens, volunteered to fight under the Stars and Stripes.'

Duffy asked the colonel if it would be acceptable for his men to wear – if there were a shortage of helmets – those of the Germans. Barker slammed the table with his fist, then laughed.

'You have a convincing way of putting things, Father. I'll see that they clothe my men hereafter in American uniforms.'

The 'mutiny of the buttons' was over and, fully equipped with clothing and weapons, the combination of Irish and Irish-Americans were sent to the front line. Part of the 42nd Rainbow Division, recruited from National Guard units across the USA, their first task was to help the British and French resist the massive last-ditch offensive of the German army in the spring of 1918.

Weathering that storm, they went on the attack later that year, as part of the Meuse-Argonne campaign in France aimed at penetrating the Hindenburg Line in September 1918. It was just one section in the Hundred Days Offensive that would finally break the German war machine and end the war.

Father Duffy was with the 165th throughout the fighting and his calm determination to bring spiritual and physical assistance to his men was much appreciated. An Irish-Canadian, born in Cobourg,

Ontario, he moved to New York as a young man where he was ordained. His father's family came from County Cavan and his mother's from County Roscommon in Ireland. Covered in mud and filth on the Western Front, exhausted by the strain of seeing so many deaths around him, the chaplain nevertheless kept a smile on his face for the soldiers.

'Never mind how Father Duffy looks,' said one soldier. 'All we remember is how he came running down ... during those last fateful minutes before zero hour, his hands and pockets full of cigarettes ... Some of the boys are gloomy, some are half-hysterical, some tense, some fidgety. If you could only jump over and get it out of your system! That's where the Father gets in his wallop. Along he comes, shoves you a cigarette, grips your hand, gives you a slap on the shoulder and an earnest "Go get 'em boys".'

It was the burying of the men after each attack that brought Father Duffy to the edge of nervous breakdown, but New York newspapers continued to report his positive contribution to the war, one journalist calling him a 'ministering angel truly affording the one human touch and supplying the last link between Christian civilization and the barbarism which is war'.

Although committed to supporting his men throughout the combat, Duffy was not above criticizing some of the decisions made by their commanders. He later wrote his own account of the war and described in detail the major assault in the Argonne Forest. Some 3,000 soldiers of the 165th advanced to their positions on 11 October 1918.

'It is interesting to watch the deliberate disintegration of a Division as it approaches the front line,' he noted. Marching along roads, it broke into brigades and regiments, and then battalions as it neared the frontline, one on the line and one in reserve. These separated into companies, which as they came close to shellfire broke down further into platoons, with some distance between them.

'In its last stages the warfare of these small groups is more like Indian fighting,' wrote Duffy. 'Often the resistance is overcome by a single sharp-shooter firing from the elbow of a tree, or by some daring fellow who works his way across hollows which are barely deep enough to protect him from fire, or up a gully or watercourse, until he is near enough to throw hand grenades. Then it is all over.'

Crossing a landscape of woods and ravines, the Irish-American soldiers were halted by a section of the German main line – the Kriemhilde Stellung – a fortified position of barbed wire, trenches and machine-gun nests. Duffy's heart sank as he realized there was no alternative but to attack this by direct assault across open ground; it was like going back to the murderous attritional warfare of 1916 on the Somme. The weather was appalling and heavy rain prevented observation balloons and aircraft seeing the enemy. The one piece of good news was that tanks were available to help the Americans cross the barbed wire fences. An artillery barrage opened the assault at 3.30 a.m. on the morning of 14 October.

Lieutenant Colonel William J. Donovan was in command of the Irish-American contingent. Born in Buffalo, New York, to first-generation Irish immigrants from County Cork, his grandfather had sheltered some of the Fenians that tried to invade Canada in 1866. Dubbed 'Wild Bill' Donovan after starring in his college football team, he was Catholic and proud of his Irish lineage. Duffy was very impressed by the thirty-four-year-old and considered him a natural leader. 'Donovan is one of the few men I know who really enjoys a battle,' observed the priest. 'He goes into it in exactly the frame of mind that he had as a college man when he marched out on the gridiron before a football game, and his one thought throughout is to push his way through. "Cool" is the word the men use of him and "Cool" is their highest epithet of praise for a man of daring, resolution and indifference to danger.'

As the 165th advanced, they came under withering machine-gun fire from a position to their right flank at the base of Cote de Chatillon. By midday, their 3rd Battalion had lost over half its men killed or wounded. Duffy praised the fighting spirit of his men but even he could see this advance across open ground undermined their morale.

> When a soldier gets where he can see the foe he develops a sort of hunter's exhilaration. His blood warms up and he actually forgets that the other fellow is shooting at him. Advancing in the open against trenches he has only the sensations of the hunted. Heavy fire begins to rain around them, men are hit, the line drops, each man in whatever shelter he can find.

Lieutenant Colonel Donovan ignored the usual advice of taking off all signs of rank – in order to avoid being targeted by enemy sharpshooters – and donned his Sam Browne belt with double shoulder straps so his men could see where he was. As the advance slowed down, Donovan made his way to the front. He stood in front of the soldiers sheltering in their shell-holes and read his map without any concern for the machine-gun bullets digging up mud around him. Smiling at their fearful faces, he shouted, 'Come on now, men, they can't hit me and they won't hit you.'

It was a bravura performance and ignited the courage of the Irish-Americans around him, but after six hours of non-stop firing, even Donovan had to accept defeat and helped carry the wounded back to his line. The 1st Battalion replaced them, but could make little headway against the barbed wire and trenches in front of them. The promised tanks failed to materialize.

The next morning, after an artillery barrage, Donovan returned to the fray to lead the 1st Battalion from the front, but this time a bullet broke his leg. Refusing to be evacuated, he continued to direct their struggle from a crater. All the time, the enemy artillery was closing in on their patch of mud.

'One of the creepiest feelings in war is that of being boxed in by artillery fire,' recalled Duffy. 'A shell lands to the right of a group of men; no harm in that – all safe. Then one lands to the left, to front, or rear, and the next is closer in between them. Then everyone knows what is happening. That square is in for a shelling until nothing living inside it will escape except by miracle.'

Fortunately for Donovan, tanks appeared in the late morning, but it was short-lived relief, for the precise German artillery targeted them, and they rumbled back to the rear, much to the disgust of the Irish-Americans around them. Eventually, another battalion replaced the 1st and Donovan agreed to be removed from the battle zone. The situation was a stalemate.

The 165th had advanced three kilometres but failed to take their final objective. Duffy criticized the corps commander for sending his troops against such a well-fortified position and compared the bloody struggle to Fredericksburg: 'the Kriemhilde Stellung was our Marye's Heights.'

Duffy visited Donovan at the regimental dressing station.

'Father, you're a disappointed man,' said the wounded Colonel from his stretcher. 'You expected to have the pleasure of burying me over here.'

'I certainly did, Bill,' replied Duffy, 'and you are a lucky dog to get off with nothing more than you've got.'

For his conduct during this offensive, Donovan was given the Medal of Honor. 'Colonel Donovan personally led the assaulting wave in an attack upon a very strongly organized position', said the citation, 'and when our troops were suffering heavy casualties he encouraged all near him by his example, moving among his men in exposed positions, reorganizing decimated platoons, and accompanying them forward in attacks.'

Corporal Martin J. Hogan was in Company 'K' of the 165th and he had his own story to tell of Argonne. He believed they were chosen for the tough mission because they were the 'Fighting Irish – that is, we felt all the élan of crack fighting corps'. He recalled the difficult advance through the forest and the numerous hidden machine-gun posts they had to deal with.

'Toward the end of this fight I had about made up my mind that the Germans hadn't cast any bullet yet which could find me' – it was the same kind of hubris possessed by Donovan – but then, advancing across a clearing, Hogan saw a German sniper and sheltered in a shell-hole. The Irish-American took careful aim at the sniper hidden in a tree and fired several shots. With a sickening realization, he knew he was more exposed than his target was. The German replied with a shot that struck his gun, sending splinters up in the air. Hogan fired more rapidly, but then a single rifle shot rang out from the German.

> Instantly I felt a sharp stab in my left hand, extended
> and holding my barrel. He had scored, hitting me on
> the knuckle of my left hand, tearing this knuckle
> away and ripping up the bones and flesh.

Hogan hid in his hole as the sniper moved on to another target. He lay there for hours, losing blood, his thoughts taking him back to when he first volunteered his service to the US Army. He was only seventeen, but his mother and father were dead and he felt he should do his growing-up in France.

'When I filled out my application, I chose the old 69th – because it and I were Irish.' Hogan made his way back to a dressing station and survived the war. His proud heritage was something he shared with Father Duffy, who said: 'I am a very Irish, very Catholic, very American person if anybody challenges my convictions.'

For his inspiration on the battlefield, Father Duffy became the most highly decorated military chaplain in the history of the US Army. He received the Distinguished Service Cross and Distinguished Service Medal, plus the Conspicuous Service Cross and two French awards, the *Légion d'honneur* and the *Croix de guerre*.

After the war, Duffy returned to New York to become a priest at the Holy Cross Church, near Times Square, where a statue to him was later erected after his death in 1932. In 1940, a feature film entitled *The Fighting 69th* recounted the exploits of Irish-American soldiers in the First World War and Pat O'Brien played the role of Father Duffy.

William Donovan also had a celebrated career after the war and later founded the Office of Strategic Services – precursors of the CIA – in the Second World War. In 1921, the 165th was consolidated within the 69th Infantry New York State Guard. There they stayed until another world war had need of their fighting spirit.

Chapter 12
Fascist Crusade

For Eoin O'Duffy, the Spanish Civil War was not a clash of political ideologies; it was a crusade. Throughout the summer of 1936, Irish newspapers had been running accounts of outrages committed by left-wing Republican forces against Catholic priests. 'Further heart-rending stories of the Communist atrocities in Spain are told by people who have escaped from that unhappy country,' blared the *Irish Independent*. They quoted an English businessman who had lived in the country for twenty-five years. 'In Badajoz I saw two priests who had been crucified by the Reds,' he said. 'Their bodies, hanging on the crosses, were exhibited in a public square. They had been knifed to death. Their eyes had been cut out.'

The forty-four-year old O'Duffy could not stand idly by and immediately appealed for volunteers to help the cause of the Spanish Nationalists led by General Francisco Franco. As he prepared to leave Dublin for Spain, he issued his own rallying call.

> We are leaving tonight for the Christian Front, and,
> to quote the words of a distinguished priest of the Limerick
> Diocese last Sunday, 'Irishmen had taken part in the
> Crusades of other days, and the Irish Legion of today
> will, please God, lead in the march on Barcelona', to the
> strains of the 'Faith of Our Fathers', and place the
> Cross of Christ the King high over that city, where
> every priest has been slain and where every church is
> a shambles.

Eoin O'Duffy was a man of strong convictions and had been a prominent figure in Irish politics for twenty years. Born in Lough Egish, near Castleblayney, County Monaghan, he trained as an engineer but became an auctioneer. In 1917, he made clear his political beliefs by joining the Irish Republican Army. Like many similar-minded Irishmen, he had been appalled by the harsh British response to the Easter Rising and rejected British attempts to introduce conscription in 1918. In the same year, Sinn Féin won a majority of Irish seats in the general election and set up their own parliament in Dublin called the Dáil.

In 1919, the IRA started a guerrilla campaign against British rule that evolved into the Irish War of Independence. At first, O'Duffy urged restraint. 'I know that he is opposed to assassination', noted the County Monaghan crown solicitor, 'and has so far prevented the shooting of policemen in this county though he may for all I know have taken part in the Ballytrain Barrack attack.' That was true.

In the early hours of 15 February 1920, O'Duffy led an IRA raid that captured the Royal Irish Constabulary barracks at Ballytrain in County Monaghan. The *Dundalk Democrat* reported the operation.

> All the men engaged in the early morning attack wore
> masks. They carried either revolvers or rifles and were
> led by a tall thin man [O'Duffy] who gave orders through
> a megaphone, addressing the leaders of the various gangs
> by numbers ... Several times they called loudly to the police
> to surrender, and the only reply received was a continuance
> of the rifle firing.

O'Duffy was imprisoned several times for his part in the insurgency, but avoided execution and became chief of staff of the IRA. A key Republican figure, he became a Sinn Féin member for Monaghan in the Dáil. Following the Anglo-Irish Treaty and the establishment of an Irish Free State in 1922, the Irish nationalists split – the IRA believing their republican cause had been betrayed by the creation of an independent Irish state within the British Empire. They wanted to stay true to their republican ideals and wanted to carry on fighting the British, but those who supported the treaty wanted an end to the conflict. The political clash descended into a bitter civil war. O'Duffy turned against the IRA and supported the

Anglo-Irish Treaty. He joined the Free State forces as a general of their army and led successful operations against his former IRA comrades, who were now regarded as rebels.

O'Duffy was rewarded for his loyalty to the new state by being appointed commissioner of its police force – *An Garda Síochána*, more familiarly known as the Gardaí. He stayed in this role for over decade, but in 1933 he was suspected of encouraging a coup, rather than accepting a newly elected Fianna Fáil government, and was dismissed as commissioner.

O'Duffy feared the rise of socialism in Ireland, and like many other politicians in Europe at the time he embraced fascism as a counter to it. He established his own Irish fascist movement with a blue uniform – called the National Guard – that became known as the Blueshirts in imitation of Benito Mussolini's Fascist Italian Blackshirts. Blueshirts and IRA members fought against each other on the city streets of Ireland.

In Dublin, it was feared the Blueshirts would launch their own rebellion, imitating Mussolini's March on Rome, and the movement was banned. O'Duffy simply changed the organization's name to the Young Ireland Association and linked up with other sympathetic groups to form the Fine Gael party, becoming its first leader. Unhappy with the more moderate views of his Fine Gael colleagues, O'Duffy resigned in 1934. He was convinced that Ireland faced a major threat from socialism and events elsewhere in Europe underlined this for him.

'It becomes increasingly evident that the Spanish War represents the first massed attack of International Communism against Christianity', declared O'Duffy in November 1936, 'and especially against the Catholic Church, which being international, stands as the obstacle to the world domination of Bolshevism. But yet I would not have urged any Irishman to go to the assistance of Christian Spain were I not persuaded that the war in that country is the opening action in the long expected clash of this new barbarism and the ancient Christian civilisation.'

*

Five thousand letters of support flooded into O'Duffy from Irishmen pledging to fight against the godless Communists, but when it came to appearing on the dockside, only around 700 men actually set sail for Spain. At first, it was agreed that the Irish volunteers would serve on the northern front with ultra-Catholic Carlist forces loyal to the king, but when it was discovered that meant fighting against equally passionate Catholic Basques, they were sent to central Spain to serve with the Spanish Foreign Legion.

There, they formed the 15th *Bandera*, comprising four companies. Many of them had military experience in either the Great War or as IRA recruits in the Irish Civil War and the Spanish were impressed by their professionalism. Short of uniforms, the Spanish clad them in Great War German combat dress, but armed them with modern guns supplied by Nazi Germany. Although wearing Spanish Foreign Legion insignia, O'Duffy designed their own unit flag, which featured an Irish wolfhound on the Irish tricolour.

The Irish volunteers first went into action on 19 February 1937, but it descended into a tragic farce. Advancing against the Republicans near Ciempozuelos, they came under enemy shell fire and dispersed behind their own lines to lessen the impact of the fire. Another Nationalist unit, from the Canary Islands, grew suspicious of these apparently alien soldiers near their own positions. A Spanish liaison officer attached to the Irish bandera tried to explain that they were members of the Spanish Foreign Legion but as they were not wearing the familiar Nationalist uniform, but old German kit, the Canary Islanders were not convinced and pointed their rifles at a Lieutenant Bove as he stepped forward to reassure them.

The captain of the Canary Islanders stepped back a pace, drew his revolver and fired point blank at the Irish Lieutenant. He missed Bove, but this provoked an outburst of machine-gun and rifle fire. In the hail of fire, Bove was hit and killed and so was the Spanish interpreter. Two more Irishmen died and one was wounded.

The only explanation for this was that the jumpy Canary Islanders had heard their foreign voices and presumed the Irish were volunteers from the Republican International Brigade, even though they had a Nationalist interpreter with them. The leader of the Canary Islanders was killed in the fire-fight and the rest of his officers court-martialled.

'The Irish bandera was held blameless', noted O'Duffy, 'and highly complimented for coolness, steadiness and determination.' When he shortly afterwards saw General Franco, the irrepressible

O'Duffy even managed to spin the incident into some kind of victory, as the generalissimo expressed his 'high appreciation of the courageous conduct of the Irish troops in their first engagement'.

It was a rude welcome to the realities of warfare in the Spanish Civil War. So was their entry into Ciempozuelos, as remembered by Sergeant Major Timlin of the Irish bandera.

> 'A' Company entered the town under cover of shell-racked buildings, finding desolation on all sides … Suddenly the air was rent with a terrific explosion, made greater by the previous quiet, and followed by another, and still another. Shells were coming screeching through the air, ploughing up the roads and knocking the sides and tops from already partly demolished buildings …
>
> I entered several houses on a tour of inspection. It required no great stretch of imagination to visualise the haste and terror in which some of these houses were vacated. Children's toys were trampled on, babies' shawls and bottles strewn about – one could almost hear the wailing of the mothers.

Timlin observed the menacing presence of Moorish troops fighting in the Nationalist army, 'arrayed in long multi-coloured robes and holding rifles cradled in their arms'. They became notorious for their brutal treatment of the enemy. In his book describing the campaign, *Crusade in Spain*, O'Duffy devoted several pages to justifying the deployment of Muslim warriors in a Catholic army. 'In my younger days I laboured under a very false impression that the Moors were savages, without culture or civilisation,' he wrote, 'and not until I went to Spain was the idea altogether dispelled … They are splendid soldiers, brave, loyal, reliable and well-disciplined.'

The first job given to the Irish in Ciempozuelos was to bury the Republican soldiers slaughtered by the Moors, although, in truth, many of the Irishmen found they got on better with the Moors than some of the more zealous Spanish fascists.

After their opening fiasco, the Irish were placed in trenches close to Ciempozuelos. 'The rain was torrential, and the trenches being on the crest of the hill, were exposed to the storm,' recalled O'Duffy. 'Often they were flooded. The boots supplied were not waterproof, the little forage cap was useless for keeping the head anyway warm, and there was no such thing as a waterproof ground-sheet.' A lack of good food, combined with this constant wetness, meant that many of the men went down with sickness.

On 13 March, the Irish bandera was ordered to attack the Republicans at Titulcia. They were given the unattractive task of drawing fire from the town, while two other banderas led the actual attack. But tired of weeks sitting in flooded trenches, the Irish were eager for action and marched off towards the Republican position. A squadron of Moorish cavalry trotted out before them. Once the Moors reached the open plain before the town, they came under heavy artillery fire and immediately dashed back to their camp, leaving the Irish to advance into the intense storm of shells. In two hours, some 250 rounds crashed among them.

'From my position I could observe our volunteers creep along,' reported O'Duffy, 'while a veritable rain of shells exploded in their midst. The shells fell four at a time, and the smoke had not subsided when the whistle of the next was heard.' Soldiers shuffled between clumps of hay only to be enveloped in smoke.

By midday, the Spanish officers with O'Duffy estimated that the Irish had lost between 200 and 300 men killed out of a total of 700 troops. With a heavy heart, he left his observation post to get closer to his soldiers, only to discover that there were no dead men among them, only a few wounded. The sodden ground had absorbed most of the impact of the shells.

'Rifles were split in two in their hands,' marvelled O'Duffy, 'packs were cut into pieces on their backs, they were time and again covered with showers of earth and stones as shell after shell exploded' – but after eleven hours of this only ten casualties were listed. O'Duffy considered it a miracle but wasn't taking any more chances and had the Spanish commanders call off the Irish attack the next day.

The Republicans were convinced they had annihilated the Irish bandera. The volunteers themselves were disappointed to endure all the misery of an assault without getting to grips with the enemy, but they were lucky to be alive. It turned out that they had received the full impact of the Republican artillery because the other main attackers had not even left their base.

At La Marañosa the rain gave way to intense summer heat and disease further reduced the morale of the Irish volunteers, who were fed up with being used as cannon fodder. Discipline broke down, with some getting drunk and even shooting each other. They needed fresh reinforcements to build up their numbers and, although there was no shortage of Irish Catholics willing to join their crusade, the Nationalists were committed to paying members of the Spanish Foreign Legion three times the pay of other units and they were reluctant to take on any more Irishmen.

When the Spanish Foreign Legion commander visited them, he felt their discipline had deteriorated to the point that they were more of a danger than a help to his other soldiers. O'Duffy agreed. He had been disappointed not to be leading a larger contingent in Spain, and with his men on the verge of mutiny he requested they be sent home.

There appears to have been a further source of friction in the character of O'Duffy himself. Rather than lead from the front, he preferred wining and dining with the Nationalist leadership, but his heavy drinking was not to the taste of General Franco. While Franco was the youngest man to be made a general in Europe, O'Duffy liked to boast that he was the second youngest, commanding a million men during a Papal visit to Ireland. However, he failed to properly look after his men in Spain and it was little wonder that the majority of them were keen to go home in June 1937. Only sixteen Irishmen stayed on with the Spanish Foreign Legion.

Back in Ireland, O'Duffy continued his dalliance with other fascist parties in Europe and made overtures to the Nazi German consulate in 1939. This culminated in him offering to raise an Irish Volunteer Legion – a Green Division – for service on the Eastern Front with the Germans against the Russian Army, all part of his continuing campaign to save Europe from Bolshevism. He was keen to fly to Berlin to explain further his plans but the Nazis failed to take his offer seriously. In 1944, he became ill and died at the age of fifty-two. He was given a state funeral by the Irish government.

*

For some Irishmen, the Spanish Civil War was not a crusade but just another source of employment. These were the restless youth who embraced the military life as an escape from home. Thomas 'Red' Cushing joined the IRA in his early teens during the Irish Civil War. When his father died, he left the country with his brother and sister to live with an aunt in Brooklyn, New York.

When he was sixteen in 1925, Cushing joined the US Army and served in China, Nicaragua, the Philippines and Panama. He loved a good scrap and stayed on his feet in a punishing boxing bout with the future Filipino middleweight champion of the world, Ceferino Garcia. After ten years, he left the US Army but was immediately at a loss to know what to do. He hung around with soldiers in Brooklyn and one morning, sitting in a bar with them, a former military man sat next to him.

'I'm recruiting for the Lincoln-Washington battalions serving in Spain,' said the man. 'Are you interested?'

Cushing pulled out his army papers detailing his specialist training. The recruiting officer was impressed. 'I can't guarantee it, but with qualifications like these you could swing a commission.'

'Never mind the commission,' said Cushing, adding bizarrely: 'My interests are tipple and bananas.'

The recruiter offered him $125 a month to lead a platoon, but warned him against making a snappy decision. He asked him when he thought he might be ready to go. Cushing slammed his whiskey glass on the counter and grinned.

'By eleven hundred hours, give or take five minutes. At what pier do I have to report?'

Two days later, after a medical, Cushing reported to a building on Eighth Avenue and Sixteenth Street. As soon as he stepped into the meeting he knew what he was in for. The men there were Communist Party members who viewed the Spanish Civil War as a golden opportunity to fight back against the fascists.

'Although I had no time for such crapology,' recalled Cushing, 'I decided to ride along with them and find out how they ticked.'

As a man of considerable military experience, Cushing was put in charge of forty young volunteers and escorted them onto a Greek ship flying the Panamanian flag. He had been warned before by the American Consul that if he took part in a war in which the USA was a non-belligerent, he would automatically forfeit his citizenship. He shrugged and took the job, but was not exactly impressed with the quality of his fellow recruits.

'There were intellectuals, homosexuals from the nearest freight yard, students from Columbia University and a generous sprinkling of Bowery bums and dead-beats, who had evidently espoused the Communist cause in order to be issued with meal tickets.'

The Communists tried to engage Cushing in their political beliefs, but the red-haired Irishman made it clear that was the only thing about him that was red. 'I'm a professional soldier, not a politician,' he told them. 'I've volunteered to go to Spain simply for the experience. As far as I'm concerned, you can stick your Communist racket up your jaxies!'

Over a farewell drink in an Irish bar on Second Avenue, Cushing ended up chatting to a couple of Irishmen who were about to sail for Spain, but fighting on the side of O'Duffy and his Catholic crusaders. He asked them what side the British were on. They said they hoped they were with the Republicans because then they could fight against them. It was at that point that Cushing wished he had spent more time studying international news reports than he had the sports pages, as he feared he was on the wrong side.

Far fewer Irishmen joined the Republicans than the Nationalists. Around 200 of them volunteered for the International Brigades. Most of them were socialists and sufficiently internationalist in their outlook to join the British battalion and fight alongside English left-wingers, but a few took exception to serving with at least one British officer who was identified as a former member of the Black and Tans, a paramilitary force pitted against the IRA in the early 1920s. Those Irishmen joined the American Abraham Lincoln or George Washington battalions.

Captain Frank Ryan was in charge of the Irish contingent in the Republican army. A newspaper journalist from Tipperary, he later edited a history of the XV International Brigade that included both the British and American battalions. In that, he made it very clear that part of the appeal for the left-wing Irish volunteers was fighting against O'Duffy and his fascists.

Some of the Irish volunteers were intellectuals who left comfortable academic posts to fight for their political ideals. Charles Donnelly was a twenty-six-year-old revolutionary poet who gave up his university career in Dublin to throw himself into what he considered a working-class struggle. He was jailed for leading strikers in Ireland and then travelled to Spain. He died on 27 February 1937 at the battle of Jarama, a few yards from the Nationalist trenches.

Kit Conway was one of Frank Ryan's key subordinates, commanding the First Irish Section as part of the British Battalion. He was also at Jarama, a bloody battleground in which Franco's Nationalist forces launched an offensive against Republican positions south of Madrid. A fellow socialist soldier, James Prendergast, described Conway in action on 12 February.

They came under heavy fire from the Nationalists who were supported by aircraft flown by the Condor Legion, German pilots sent by Adolf Hitler. 'Kit was everywhere at once, directing fire, encouraging us all,' recalled Prendergast. Many of the Irish and British volunteers of the XV Brigade were falling to the heavy fire and all the time fearing an advance by Moorish troops and the tanks of the Nationalist army.

> I reach the hill-crest where Kit is directing fire. He is
> using a rifle himself and pausing every while to give
> instructions. Suddenly, he shouts, his rifle spins out of
> his hands, and he falls back. He is placed on a blanket.
> No stretchers left now. His voice is broken with agony.
> 'Do your best boys, hold on!'

'Next morning they told me our great leader was dead,' wrote Prendergast. The Irish were savaged at Jarama, but the Republicans managed to rally and hold the Nationalists. Frank Ryan played his part by singing the socialist anthem, the *Internationale*, to the demoralized troops. In total, losses in the British battalion were 85 per cent and nearly every Irishmen was wounded.

'Red' Cushing arrived in Spain at the port of Cartagena and was transferred to a training camp north of Madrid. As a platoon leader of the American volunteers, he went into action against Italian fascist allies of the Nationalists south-east of Madrid in February 1937. Some of his fellow volunteers had argued that Cushing was insufficiently politically motivated to be a good socialist warrior, but his superiors were more practical, and, valuing his military skills, sent him back to America to raise more volunteers and imbue them with some tactical talent.

Cushing returned to Brooklyn where he tried to recruit ex-soldiers. 'I had to hang around the Army Base in Brooklyn, keep my weather-eye open for soldiers awaiting demobilisation, take them for a drink, paint an attractive picture of the pay and conditions in Spain.' But Cushing had little intention of deceiving soldiers into serving the socialist cause and spent the considerable sum of money he had been given for recruitment on drinking bouts. After six months, he was recalled to Spain.

Cushing arrived back in Barcelona and was dispatched to the Teruel front in the winter of 1937/38. There, he met Frank Ryan.

> Tall and scholarly-looking, Frank had a thin, hawk-like face, dark hair and a humorous mouth. He was serving as a machine-gun officer ... One of the men in his Company told me that thanks to Frank's intelligent siting of the guns in a defensive position farther south, practically the whole of an Italian Brigade had been cut to ribbons.

For the first time in Spain, Cushing experienced tough, intense fighting and felt the Nationalists were getting the best of it, forcing the Republicans back towards the coast. Along the Ebro River, he ventured out into enemy territory with a reconnaissance unit and, two or three miles into the patrol, they were ambushed. The Republicans scattered, running from the deadly crossfire, with Cushing heading into hilly scrubland accompanied by another volunteer called McClusky. Nervous, knowing that if they were picked up as members of the International Brigade they would be shot on sight, they trekked for several days and nights through the foothills of the Pyrenees until they reached the Mediterranean coast. From there, they persuaded a fisherman to take them to Marseilles where Cushing presented himself at the US Consulate, but because he had forfeited his citizenship by joining the International Brigade, there was nothing they could do for him. It was then that Cushing considered joining the French Foreign Legion.

The French recruiters were happy to see him, but bigger events were playing out across Europe and as Cushing read the newspapers, he could see that there would soon be a war with Britain and France against Nazi Germany. Like many left-wing volunteers who survived the Spanish Civil War, he decided to continue his military career in the service of the British. But while they did it for ideological reasons, carrying on their fight against fascism, Cushing was simply getting himself out of a tricky situation. He presented himself to the British Consul in Marseilles who gave him a rail and boat ticket and a letter of introduction to any recruiting office in England.

On a grey day in November 1938, 'Red' Cushing joined the Royal Inniskilling Fusiliers and took a train and a ferry to their depot in Omagh, County Tyrone. 'I should be on the wrong side of the border,' he recalled, 'but by all that was holy, it would be great to be back in Ireland again.'

The Spanish Civil War came to an end in March 1939 with victory for General Franco as Republican-held Madrid surrendered to his Nationalists. Hundreds of thousands of Spaniards had died in the savage conflict and many considered it a prequel to the Second World War, with Nazi Germany and Soviet Russia rehearsing their coming conflict in a foreign land.

Prisoners of war held by the Nationalists, including foreign volunteers, were released, but one Irish prisoner remained in Spanish hands. That was Frank Ryan, head of the Irish contingent on the Republican side, who had been captured as his troops retreated through Aragon in March 1938. He was considered highly useful by Franco's Nazi German associates and was spirited away to Germany where he was kept under house arrest. Nazi military intelligence officers believed that this highly competent Irish commander could be of use to them when war came against Britain.

Like Franco's Spain, Ireland declared itself neutral on the outbreak of war in Europe in September 1939. Having ceased to be the Irish Free State in 1937, following a referendum, Ireland – as known as Eire – was now an entirely sovereign state. The Irish government instituted an official state of emergency, which allowed them sweeping powers of internment and censorship, and the Emergency became the name they used for the war period. When America joined the world conflict in 1941, President Roosevelt was furious with Irish neutrality and blocked any aid to them.

*

Since 1922, Irish regiments in the British Army had been dramatically reduced. Five famous southern Irish infantry regiments disappeared completely: the Connaught Rangers, the Leinster

Regiment, the Royal Munster Fusiliers, the Royal Dublin Fusiliers and the Royal Irish Regiment (later reborn in 1992 as a result of amalgamations). As the British government seized the opportunity for ruthless military cost-cutting, further Irish regiments were poised for the axe, including the Royal Inniskilling Fusiliers, the Royal Ulster Rifles and the Royal Irish Fusiliers, but successful lobbying saved the three northern Irish regiments, although they were restricted in the number of battalions they could recruit.

Despite this, thousands of young men from the Irish Free State continued to enlist in the British Army. In the mid-1920s, almost a third of the Inniskillings came from south of the border. Although never recovering to nineteenth-century levels, the number of Irishmen serving rose to nearly 6 per cent of the total British Army's manpower just before the outbreak of war in 1939. Second battalions were added to the Inniskillings and Irish Fusiliers.

'Red' Cushing's Royal Inniskilling Fusiliers joined the 5th Division of the British Expeditionary Force in 1939. The following spring, the German blitzkrieg war machine was sweeping through northern France towards the Channel coast when Cushing and a handful of Inniskillings found themselves trapped behind enemy lines near Roubaix.

They burnt their army truck and kept to the fields and hedgerows in an attempt to find their way back to Allied lines. When they entered a ruined village, they headed for a bistro. Looking for somewhere safe to rest, they hauled up a trap door that led into a cellar. As they descended into it, an electric light illuminated shelves upon shelves of bottles of wine and spirits. Cushing couldn't believe his luck.

'We built an improvised bar out of a few empty crates,' recalled Cushing, 'helped ourselves to whatever we fancied and were soon embarked on what promised to be the greatest drinking bout of the century.'

The next morning, Cushing was roused out of a deep sleep by a comrade whispering to him that the Germans were camped directly outside the restaurant. Seeing no need to panic, they locked the trap door and survived for the next three days on wine and tins of bully beef, but the need for water eventually drove them to venture out. Fortunately, the Germans had moved on as they tightened the ring around the main British forces at Dunkirk.

The Irishmen gulped down pints of water from a well. Cushing wondered what to do next and accosted a local policeman. He explained to him their situation and the gendarme nodded, indicating he was happy to guide them. Armed with bottles of brandy, Cushing and the Inniskillings followed the smiling policeman as he led them to a nearby chateau. Once inside its walls, the Irishmen were surrounded by a dozen machine-gun wielding Germans.

'You are our prisoners,' barked a German officer. 'For you the war is over.'

For many other Irishmen, it was only just beginning.

Chapter 13
Churchill's Irish Brigade

It was a letter in *The Times* that caught the attention of British wartime Prime Minister Winston Churchill. 'It appears that very large numbers of Irishmen have joined HM Forces since the outbreak of war,' wrote retired General Sir Hubert Gough in September 1941.

> This is their own spontaneous and unsolicited act,
> since owing to Ireland's neutrality there have been
> no agencies where they could enlist at home and no
> recruiting campaign. It is a pity that the fact – well known
> as it appears to be in Ireland – is not more widely
> realized here, as it is valuable evidence that Irish
> neutrality is not a mask for a hostile spirit towards
> Britain and the Commonwealth at war.

Gough went on to suggest that the fighting spirit of the Irish was particularly strong when they served in units grouped together under an Irish banner. Just as American neutrality was not compromised by Americans volunteering to serve in the Eagle Squadron of the RAF, he recommended that Irish and Anglo-Irish serve together in an Irish brigade.

Churchill loved the idea and in an unguarded personal minute to the secretary of state for war wrote: 'I shall be glad to have an expression of opinion from the War Office on this suggestion. We have Free French and Vichy French, so why not Loyal Irish and

Dublin Irish?' Churchill's enthusiasm for an Irish Brigade was strengthened when he saw extracts from letters secretly intercepted in Northern Ireland for a Postal Censorship Report. 'Patrick is 19 years old,' wrote one correspondent from Waterford to a friend in Hampshire. 'He joined up entirely on his own bat and I must say that all his boy friends over here from three counties have done likewise, so Ireland shouldn't be damned so freely.'

Churchill underlined several similar passages in red and repeated his request for the War Office to look at this suggestion: 'I think now the time is ripe to form an Irish Brigade also an Irish Wing or Squadron of the RAF.' The prime minister recommended that the Dublin-born Battle of Britain RAF Spitfire ace Brendan Finucane would make an excellent figurehead for such a force. 'Pray let me have proposal,' insisted Churchill. Then, with an eye to post-war developments, he added: 'The movement might have important political reactions later on.'

It was the political ramifications of an Irish Brigade that concerned David Margesson, secretary of state for war, and Viscount Cranborne, secretary of state for the dominions, in their joint reply. They liked the idea of an official show of appreciation to all the volunteers coming from Eire, but they also did not wish to disrupt this flow.

> Up to now, men have gone from Ireland unobtrusively, and nothing has been said to underline their presence in our armed forces. It has therefore been possible for the Southern Irish Government to wink at it. But were we to blazon abroad the part which the citizens of neutral Eire are taking in the war, contrary to the policy of their own Government, the Irish Government might well feel bound to take action to prevent the departure of any further volunteers from their shores to join our forces. Were they to do so, we should have lost far more than we gained.

It would be estimated by the Dominions Office that some 43,000 Eire-born Irish men and women had joined the British forces by the end of the war.

In their letter to Churchill, Margesson and Cranborne made the case that southern Irish volunteers might not like it to be known that they had fought for the British as this might penalize them at home. 'Further, there is the possibility that completely Irish units, so far from being the symbol of the close connection between Britain and Ireland, might become a fertile breeding ground for subversive agitation by the IRA and other disloyal elements, who would join them for this very purpose.'

Consideration was given to establishing a Shamrock Squadron, formed from 'men of Irish blood from all parts of the world', but the view of the Air Ministry was that there was no demand for this within the service and that Irishmen would object to being removed from their current units. The only positive suggestion was to brigade together existing British Army Irish battalions, such as those from the Royal Inniskilling Fusiliers, Royal Irish Fusiliers and London Irish Rifles.

Somewhat deflated by the arguments coming from the War Office, Churchill scribbled his own reply on this joint memorandum: 'As proposed. It is a halfway house.' But, as if this wasn't disappointing enough, word of the suggested Irish Brigade got to John Andrews, then prime minister of Northern Ireland. In a forceful letter to Churchill, in which he apologized for burdening him with extra trouble, he appealed to the war leader's acute sense of military history. 'The name would inevitably be associated with the Irish who fought against England in the days of Marlborough, the Irish Brigade which fought against Britain in the Boer War ... and finally with a body of "Blue Shirts" organised in Eire a few years ago to fight in the Spanish Civil War.'

With Churchill abroad in the United States talking to President Roosevelt, Deputy Prime Minister Clement Attlee stepped into the growing controversy, saying that Andrews had got the wrong end of the stick. There was no intention to raise an Irish Brigade as originally suggested by General Gough, just to brigade together several Ulster regiments within the British Army. He reassured the Northern Irish prime minister that no particular publicity would be given to the proposed brigade 'until occasion arises to do so when it has distinguished itself in action'.

Andrews was unimpressed:

While, of course, I appreciate the desire of the British Government to give recognition in due course to those Eire citizens who are loyally supporting the Allied cause, we feel that the use of Ulster regiments for that purpose would arouse resentment here. In my view, any policy calculated to obliterate or blur the distinction between the belligerency of Northern Ireland and the neutrality of Eire would confuse and mislead public opinion and be detrimental to the highest interest of the Empire as a whole.

In the end, it was the will of Winston Churchill that prevailed, although in the moderated form suggested by the War Office. In January 1942, the 38th (Irish) Brigade came into being, consisting of the 1st Royal Irish Fusiliers, the 6th Royal Inniskilling Fusiliers and the 2nd London Irish Rifles. The London Irish were a Territorial unit associated with the Royal Ulster Rifles.

The Irish identity of the Brigade was strongly established from the outset, with a saffron-kilted pipe band for each battalion, a song-book full of Irish songs, and soldiers wearing the caubeen – a traditional Irish beret or tam o'shanter-style headdress worn with a feather hackle favoured by Irish warriors since at least the seventeenth century. Its first commander was Brigadier Morgan O'Donovan, who adopted the traditional clan title of 'The O'Donovan'. He was soon after succeeded by Brigadier Nelson Russell. The Irish 38th first went into action in November 1942 as part of the Anglo-American landings in French North Africa at Algiers in Operation Torch. It was the dramatic beginning to a very long and bloody series of campaigns for Churchill's cherished Irish Brigade.

*

Edmund 'Ted' O'Sullivan was a typical London Irishman. Born in Peckham in 1919, his father's side of the family had come from Limerick in the nineteenth century and his mother's side from Kerry. Raised a Catholic and winning a scholarship to the Brompton Oratory, he had just got his first job as a clerk at the uniform makers Hawkes of Savile Row when the war came.

Called up in September 1939 into the 2nd Battalion of the London Irish Rifles, he spent the first three years of the war in training, including shooting practice on centre court at Wimbledon. Promoted to colour sergeant, O'Sullivan was one of the Irish Brigade that landed in North Africa in 1942.

'We climbed out of Algiers in thick service dress,' he recalled, 'carrying everything in the hot midday sun. The pipers carried only their pipes. The first mile out of Algiers was a steady climb up a road that wound in a semi-circle. Gradually men collapsed from heat and exhaustion. At first, stretcher-bearers went to attend to them. Eventually, we left them where they fell.'

Their first night in North Africa, sunlight ended abruptly at six o' clock and the soldiers of the Irish Brigade had to huddle together under greatcoats and anti-gas capes against the intense cold of the night. The next morning, they had breakfast of biscuits spread with margarine and jam or potted meat, washed down with tea.

Part of the 6th Armoured Division, the London Irish and the rest of the 38th Brigade were transported by lorries to the battlefront in Tunisia along roads in the Atlas Mountains. The Italian and German forces were dug in along a north–south line thirty miles west of the capital of Tunis. The main Allied offensive came in January 1943. The weather was poor and heavy winter rain turned the ground to mud.

The London Irish were tasked with taking Point 286 on 20 January, a hill-top held by the Germans in the northern Bou Arada sector. They took it just after dawn, but were swept off it in a coun-ter-attack supported by tanks and armoured cars. As the London Irish went back to wrestle them off the hill, the Germans called in Stuka dive-bombers. 'It was practically impossible to dig in on the hard rocky slopes', reported Brigadier Russell, 'and all through the day they were subjected to heavy artillery and extremely accurate mortar fire. This fine battalion refused to be shelled off the position. What they had, they held. But at heavy cost.' As the Brigadier later noted, 'The Irish Brigade learnt at a hard school. From the very start we were opposed by the Koch Brigade of the Hermann Goering Division. They were paratroops – all unmarried volunteers and the average age was 22/23.'

Throughout the fighting, Colour Sergeant Ted O'Sullivan was back at the supply base getting hot food for his men. When he arrived at the captured position, he was shocked to see that several key officers had been killed or wounded. 'It was a shambles,' recalled O'Sullivan. 'There seemed to be no order or discipline.'

Some of the NCOs had dropped their weapons and fled. A total of 6 officers and 20 other ranks were killed, 8 officers and 78 other ranks wounded, and at least 136 other soldiers recorded as missing but later confirmed as either wounded or made prisoner.

Brigadier Russell considered it a tough but critical clash, whereas O'Sullivan believed it was poorly executed with men exhausted by previous night patrols. Along with the other colour sergeants, O'Sullivan was rebuked for not promoting NCOs from the survivors. 'The whole exercise was nonsense and the three colour sergeants had been used as scapegoats,' he commented bitterly.

In February, the Germans, led by General Erwin Rommel, assaulted the British and American lines. On the 26th, they came back to the Bou Arada position, west of Tunis, held by the London Irish. O'Sullivan was delivering rations to his men in the morning when his truck came under fire, tracer flashing past him. Armed with a couple of grenades and rifles, he and the driver jumped out of the vehicle.

> We did not a have a clear field of fire and could see little more than the bushes about 50 yards to our front. I was going to move forward when the undergrowth in front of us started to shake violently. I shouted a warning to Percy and we were preparing to open fire when a goat's head followed by about 20 others broke through the shrubs followed by a young lad.

Once they reached the rest of the Irish Brigade, they found them clinging on to their positions, and after twenty-four hours of hard fighting, the Germans had had enough and withdrew. A hill near Hadj was re-taken with an artillery barrage. 'For many weeks after the battle', remembered O'Sullivan, 'you could smell Hadj from almost a mile away. The stench of death was all pervading. Using an old towel, I cleaned the pieces of flesh which clung to the branches of trees. We buried our dead with honour but not the enemy who were interred without ceremony.'

The German breakthrough failed and the Allies pushed on towards Tunis. After a period of rest, the Irish Brigade, including the London Irish, were transferred to the 78th Infantry Division. On 22 April, a massive Allied barrage crashed down on the Germans and the Irish Brigade played their part in the assault on the German lines, which eventually cracked. As they closed in on the capital, Brigadier Russell drove past a mile-long column trudging along the dusty roadside. 'About 3,000 prisoners,' he noted, 'Bosche and Italian, soldiers, sailors and airmen – a mixed bag. It was a pleasant – though smelly sight.'

The Irish Brigade was given the honour of first entering Tunis, but they were not too sure what sort of reception they would get. Just in case, recorded Russell, 'The troops were all loaded up with bombs, Piats, mortars and petards – all set for a bellyful of street fighting – and the last lap.' They needn't have worried.

'I remained in my three-tonner,' remembered O'Sullivan, 'which soon became bedecked with flowers. The men were garlanded, kissed and cheered by the French colon[ial]s, who were relieved the war was over for them with little damage to their home.' Brigadier Russell was kissed twice by the delighted citizens. At a victory parade on 20 May, the Irish Brigade marched in their caubeens with saffron-kilted pipers before Generals Eisenhower, Alexander and Montgomery.

'I always felt I was very lucky to command the Irish Brigade,' wrote Brigadier Russell at the conclusion of the Tunisian campaign. 'It's the command an Irishman would court – and there a good many Irishmen in the Army. I wouldn't change my command for all the tea in China, or perhaps better, all the stout in Guinesses!'

The Irish Guards also fought in North Africa and it was in Tunisia in 1943 that Irish Guardsman John Kenneally won a Victoria Cross by charging German Panzer grenadiers firing a Bren gun from his hip. 'This outstanding act of gallantry', read his citation, 'and the dash with which it was executed completely unbalanced the enemy company, which broke up in disorder.' Kenneally then repeated this exploit two days later, inflicting so many casualties on the Germans that they cancelled their planned assault on the Allied lines. Although wounded in this attack, he refused to give up his Bren gun and carried on fighting throughout the day.

It was an extraordinary achievement, but Kenneally wasn't all that he seemed. In fact, he wasn't Irish at all, but half-Jewish – from Birmingham. His real name was Leslie Robinson. When war broke out he joined the Royal Artillery in an anti-aircraft battery, but found this boring and deserted. In Glasgow, he fell in with a gang

of Irish labourers who gave him a fake identity as John Patrick Kenneally and a fake past, which included a childhood in Tipperary.
Under this name he joined the Irish Guards.

Two years later, Churchill was delighted to hear of the VC, contrasting this 'Irish' hero with the Irish premier 'frolicking' with the
Germans. Such publicity was the last thing Kenneally needed. 'It
was the worst thing that could have happened to me,' he later said.
'I thought, "Now I'm bound to be rumbled", but I never was.'

*

In July 1943, the Irish Brigade joined the 78th Division in the Allied
invasion of Sicily. It was the stepping-stone towards attacking
Mussolini's Italy, considered the soft underbelly of the Axis forces.
The Americans had a relatively smooth advance across the island,
but the British and Canadians took the brunt of German resistance
as they tried to cover their retreat to the mainland.

The Irish Brigade was tasked with taking the hill-top town of
Centuripe. It was a hard but effective assault in which all three Irish
battalions played a part. Brigadier Russell concluded: 'The capture
of Centuripe had repercussions on both flanks – as it forced the
Bosche to re-adjust the whole line.' Many good men were lost in the
fighting, including Peter Fitzgerald of the London Irish. 'A great
character and a fearless leader,' noted Russell. 'He was, by trade, a
West of Ireland barrister – about 36 years old – and thus a volunteer
in the very highest sense.'

For Colour Sergeant Ted O'Sullivan it wasn't just the Germans
that posed a threat. Worn-out 25-pounders delivered their shells
short of the enemy, endangering their own side, while malaria and
dysentery invalided many men, including O'Sullivan. Even a
period of rest had its dangers, as the colour sergeant nearly drowned
in strong currents off the island as he tried to swim to a nearby
beach; two other adventurous soldiers were not so lucky and perished at sea.

On 24 September 1943, the Irish Brigade landed at Taranto on the
heel of the Italian mainland. Now part of the British 8th Army, their
mission was to advance along the Adriatic coast and break through
two German defensive lines between Termoli and Ortona. It was
merciless work. At one point, the London Irish discovered twenty

Germans in a deep dugout. When they refused to surrender, the London Irish dynamited the entrances and brought up a bulldozer to bury the Germans under tons of earth. Because of their relentless fighting spirit, the Germans developed a new respect for the Irish Brigade and dubbed them 'Die Irische SS'.

Following this, the Irish Brigade was shifted west to a posting in the Apennine Mountains. Fresh British soldiers joined them, many not from an Irish background but willing to adapt to their new military culture. Among the new influx of officers was Lieutenant Nicholas Mosley, the son of the imprisoned British fascist leader, Sir Oswald Mosley. He later wrote up his own account of fighting with the Irish Brigade, preferring it to the 'stuffiness' of the Rifle Brigade, saying, 'I had come to appreciate the anarchic style of the London Irish.'

For Christmas, they were billeted at Campobasso in a large Franciscan monastery. 'During Christmas Eve', recalled O'Sullivan, 'the monks carried around a harmonium and sang carols at each cell. The Catholics attended midnight Mass, formed a choir and sang the Credo. Our Christmas fare included pork chops.'

Brigadier Nelson Russell added his own observation of the feast: 'Each man was getting busy on a plate which held about 3lbs of turkey, pork and ham; happy in the thoughts that he would shortly follow it up with 2lbs of plum pudding – the whole thing diluted by a couple of pints of beers – steadied and solidified by great cans of steaming liquid – which smelt like an unauthorized rum issue (but who cares for local by-laws? certainly not the Irish Brigade on Christmas Day).'

In January, elite German mountain troops swooped on a patrol of the London Irish near Campobasso. Properly equipped with white smocks and skis, the Germans briefly captured the frozen-footed Irish until a counter-attack released them. In March, a new Brigadier, Pat Scott of the Royal Irish Fusiliers, took over from the ill Nelson Russell.

One of the departing brigadier's last acts was to turn over the body of a dead Irishman on a rocky crag in the Apennines. 'He was facing the right way,' wrote Russell, 'the last round of a clip in the breech and three dead Germans in front of him. His name was Duffy. After all is over – and the remainder of the Empire is quite understandably irritated with Ireland – I hope these countless

Duffys, from both the North and South, and in all three Services, will be remembered. We also supply quite a few Generals.'

In the same month, the Irish Brigade was moved westward again, to a position behind the Monte Cassino frontline, where the Germans had fortified a hill-top monastery and were defying all efforts to take it. From the nearby 2,300-foot peak of Monte Castellone, Brigadier Pat Scott witnessed a massive aerial bombardment of the German-held monastery. 'It seems questionable,' he wondered, 'if one wishes to attack a town or village, whether the right thing to do is to smash it all up first or not. If streets are an unrecognisable wreck of rubble two bad things happen, you cannot drive down the streets with tanks and it is quite impossible to tell which piece of rubble holds the enemy.'

Overlooking the battered monastery, the London Irish had to monitor the ongoing battle. Supplies could only reach them by mule up dangerous mountain tracks exposed to enemy shelling. 'We had to take particular care as the nervous muleteers were attempting to ditch their loads,' remembered O'Sullivan. 'I finally arrived at the top with about half a dozen mules. Loads were spread along the track behind us.' Brigadier Scott was impressed by the effort involved. 'The Battalion's administrative teams really came into their own during this period,' he noted – and that praise included O'Sullivan. 'The Irish Rifles bakery never failed to produce appetising cakes for the warriors on the mountain-top.'

The London Irish needed something to keep their spirits up as they were unable to dig slit trenches in the hard rock and had to clear up the rubbish and excrement left by the French troops before them. For the month of April, they carried out their sentry duty, sitting motionless during the day to avoid attracting the heavy mortar fire that pounded all the positions around Monte Cassino. At one point, Brigadier Scott was given a chilling task when General Harold Alexander asked him to work out a plan for capturing the monastery. Replied Scott: 'I said I thought the best plan was for someone else to capture it.'

Fortunately, Alexander agreed. 'We were very glad when some Poles started coming over to have a look around,' recalled Scott. 'They were being given the unenviable task of capturing the Monastery and breaking through the mountains behind it when the big battle came off.'

As the Poles finally took the summit of Monte Cassino in mid-May, the Irish Brigade was shifted to Monte Trocchio, east of the River Rapido, ready to advance along the Liri valley to link up with the Poles beyond Cassino. On 15 May, Colonel Ion Goff, London Irish commander, rode off in a jeep to carry out some reconnaissance, when his vehicle was hit by German shellfire. O'Sullivan was in the camp when a carrier came in acting as an ambulance.

> I went over and found the battalion's commander, Colonel Goff, seriously wounded and in agony. I helped unload him. With him was what looked like a midget who was obviously dead. It took me some time to recognise the body as Goff's driver who was more than 6ft tall. He had lost both legs.

Goff died shortly afterwards. 'His loss was a very sad one', wrote Scott, 'and it reflects the greatest credit on the London Irish that in spite of losing this trusted leader on the eve of one of the biggest battles they had ever fought, it in no way detracted from the magnificent performance they were to put in the next day.'

On the 16th, the battle began at nine in the morning with a tremendous artillery barrage by several hundred big guns. The London Irish surged along the road to Sinagoga, a fortified village that was part of the Gustav Line. A few were held up by Germans firing from the cellars of houses, but other riflemen poured into the enemy dugouts, using their bayonets to finish off the Germans before the barrage had barely passed over them.

When the London Irish were halted, supporting tanks from the 16/5 Lancers blasted the enemy positions with high explosive shells from their 75 mm guns. Many of the Germans were caught away from their anti-tank guns by the artillery barrage and those that managed to get to their guns were shot down by infantry fire. 'The show never really looked like stopping,' noted the battalion report.

The London Irish were most vulnerable on their open left flank across the Piopetto River when the Germans fired heavy machine guns and mortars at them. The Lancers helped by scoring several direct hits on German armoured vehicles and blowing up two ammunition dumps. 'H' Company of the London Irish eventually broke into the village of Sinagoga where they had to engage in fierce hand-to-hand fighting for over an hour as the Germans tenaciously defended the shattered buildings with grenades, MG 34 machine guns and 'Schmeisser' MP 40 submachine guns.

A self-propelled 75 mm gun proved the most deadly of the German weapons and Corporal Jimmy Barnes from County Monaghan went forward by himself, covered only by a Bren gunner, to deal with the vehicle. He killed one of the German crew with a grenade before being killed himself. Shortly after this, the Germans in the village surrendered. Barnes was unsuccessfully recommended for the Victoria Cross.

It took another hour of hard fighting for the rest of the London Irish to take their objectives. In total, their casualties numbered five officers and sixty other ranks. The Germans lost 100 killed and 120 captured, including Hermann Goering paratroopers – their old rivals from Tunisia. Two more days of hard fighting followed until the Germans realized their position was lost and they withdrew, the monastery at Monte Cassino falling on the 18th.

Another casualty of the fighting on the Gustav Line was Lieutenant Colonel Humphrey 'Bala' Bredin, battalion leader of the Royal Inniskilling Fusiliers. Shot through both legs, he remained in command throughout the battle, propped up in the front of a jeep. Commissioned into the Royal Ulster Rifles in 1936, he had been placed second-in-command of the Royal Irish Fusiliers during the earlier fighting at Cassino. He was then transferred to command the Inniskillings. Following his recovery from his wounds, he took over command of the London Irish Rifles. Thus, he held senior command of all three battalions in the Irish Brigade.

Already the recipient of the Military Cross in Palestine before the war, Bredin won a Distinguished Service Order for his leadership in Italy. 'Throughout this operation he commanded his battalion with the utmost skill and inspired his men by his examples of personal gallantry under fire,' ran the citation. Famously, he never wore a steel helmet, preferring to wear the Irish caubeen and carry a cane into battle.

Seven days after the fighting at Sinagoga, the German defensive Hitler Line was broken and the Allies could march on to Rome. At one point, a soldier in the Royal Irish Fusiliers remembered approaching a junction commanded by an officer of the Irish Regiment of Canada. 'Canadian Irish, this way,' he barked, enjoying the global span of Irish soldiers before him. 'English Irish that way.'

The Americans got to Rome first, but on 12 June the Irish Brigade accepted a special invitation to visit the Pope. Brigadier Pat Scott was an Irish Protestant but he most certainly was not going to miss such an honour for the brigade. He faced competition for the limited number of places for the papal audience. 'Many influential members of Orange Lodges were trying to get a seat in the party by virtue of their high rank or long service,' observed Scott. He intended that Catholic soldiers of long service should get first choice, and those born in Ireland, but there were not enough to fill the quota of officers from each battalion so Protestants took the spare places. 'The "heretic" element was almost entirely made up of out-and-out Orangemen. I would like to mention a few names, both of these officers and of some men of the other ranks who afterwards visited His Holiness, but it might be unkind to put their names in print and have them read out in their local Orange Hall at home.'

The Irish Brigade party arrived at the Vatican at 8.45 a.m. and were escorted by the elaborately clad Papal Guards to the audience. Pope Pius XII gave a short speech praising the Irish for spreading the Faith around the world to America, Australia, South Africa and other nations. Scott then asked the Pope if he would to like hear his pipers play. O'Sullivan was at the audience and noted the irony of what followed next.

> The massed brigade band in their saffron kilts and caubeens with the various coloured hackles and regimental badges played 'Killaloe' followed by 'The Sash My Father Wore'. This was probably the first and last time one of the signature tunes of the Orange Order was heard in the Vatican. His Holiness tapped his foot to the beat of the martial music and obviously enjoyed the alien sound.

The Pope then blessed the rosaries brought by the Catholic soldiers and they knelt to kiss his ring. The Orangemen remained in their seats.

Hard fighting for the Irish Brigade continued into late 1944 and 1945, as they advanced through Italy against stubborn German resistance. In a battle three miles south of Lake Trasimeno, the

London Irish lost more than seventy men killed, wounded and missing. For the final phase of the war, the London Irish were issued with armoured carriers called 'Kangaroos' and were dubbed the 'Kangaroo Army'.

The Irish Brigade ended the war in Austria, having fought their last major combat south of the River Po. From its fighting in Tunisia, all the way through Italy, the Irish Brigade has lost more than 900 men killed, of all ranks.

O'Sullivan survived the bitter last stages of the war. In Austria in May 1945, he was given twenty-eight days' leave in England. As he trekked back across Europe, he witnessed German cities in ruins and thousands of refugees wandering along roads back to their devastated homes. After three and a half years away from London, he arrived back in Brixton. 'My family did not know of my leave and my mother was overcome when she opened the door to me.'

O'Sullivan suffered a recurring bout of malaria he had picked up in Italy and his leave was extended. It was during this rest period that he met an ATS officer who later became his wife. His soldiering finally ended in August 1946. 'By that time', he recalled, 'I would have spent six years ten months in the army instead of the six months which I was originally called up to serve in October 1939.' After the war, he settled in Farnham Common with his wife to run a newsagent and tobacconist store.

Chapter 14
Secret War

'Ireland's No 1 soldier arrived here yesterday!' trumpeted the *Los Angeles Examiner* on 15 May 1939. Introducing the forty-nine-year-old Sean Russell to their West Coast readership, they described him as the blue-eyed chief of staff of the Irish Republican Army. He was looking for money and support for his war against Britain. Since the beginning of the year, Russell's comrades had set off a series of bombs in cities throughout England. No one had yet been killed, but several civilians had been seriously injured.

'You know these bombings in England you've been reading about,' Russell told the LA reporter, 'I ordered those and they'll keep on with systematic regularity until the British troops are taken out of Ireland and my men are released from jail.'

Shortly afterwards, the British Consul in Los Angeles dispatched a telegram to the British Embassy in Washington DC, warning that 'Russell had been in touch with local leader of the German American bund with a view to arranging an attempt on the King in New York, sabotage of British shipping etc'. The Bund was an American Nazi organization with ties to Adolf Hitler's Germany, and King George VI was due to visit the New York World's Fair in August of that year.

The Home Office in London took the whole affair very seriously and contacted the US government regarding Russell's progress through their country. The State Department reassured the British that their agents were keeping a close watch on Russell's activities, and in early June they informed the British Embassy in Washington that the FBI had swooped on Russell in Detroit and arrested him on a charge of illegal entry.

Disappointingly, however, for the British, Russell was soon after released, following a protest by Irish-American members of Congress, and continued his IRA fund-raising in New York and Philadelphia. This prompted the British ambassador, Sir Ronald Lindsay, to write a report in which he declared that a series of articles in the US press 'seemed to lend definite confirmation to the belief that Sean Russell and the Irish Republican Army were endeavouring to raise funds in this country to further the bombing campaign in England, and that certain members of the Irish organisations in this country were actively conspiring to assist the Irish Republican Army in this matter'.

The US State Department repeated their determination to hunt down Russell and for a moment he disappeared, prompting the British Consul in New York to declare that the IRA chief was running scared and hoped to be smuggled out of the country. In August, his passport was handed in to a lawyer, but then he popped up again to give an interview and two speeches in Chicago. Just days later, an IRA bomb exploded outside a busy store in Coventry, England, and killed five people, wounding fifty others. It was the bloodiest of the IRA's terrorist attacks and caused widespread revulsion. Russell was unrepentant and carried on promoting the campaign, but it was the IRA's last major assault on England that year.

On 3 September, Britain was at war with Nazi Germany and some felt that the IRA had scored an own goal with their terrorist activities. Lord Lothian, the new British ambassador to Washington, wrote a letter to the British foreign secretary, Lord Halifax, in which he declared he was convinced that 'the feeling of Irish-Americans is quite different from in 1914. Their sentiments are now pro-British and there is a great resentment among them at the outrages committed by the Irish Republican Army. Thousands were ready to volunteer to fight against Hitler.'

This didn't stop the British Consul in Los Angeles from feeling uneasy in the early years of the war. In March 1940, he sent a message of warning to the British Embassy in Washington. 'It may interest you to know', he wrote, 'that we have seen the first evidence of a renewal of that cooperation between Irish and German elements which was so noticeable during the last war.'

His point of concern was a paragraph in a Californian German-language newspaper inviting German sympathizers to join a ball celebrating American recognition of the Irish Republic. The ambassador in Washington dismissed the report as nothing serious, declaring that American support for Britain depended far more on events in Europe rather than a few Irish and Germans coming together for a dance.

*

'England's difficulty – Ireland's opportunity' maintained Sean Russell, and in early 1940 he sought to make the most of Britain being at war with Germany. He sent a friend, John McCarthy, to visit the German Consulate in Genoa, Italy, in February 1940. McCarthy was a steward on the transatlantic liner *George Washington* and told the German consul that he was an envoy for Russell who wished to come to Nazi Germany to discuss matters of common interest. The consul informed the Abwehr – German military intelligence – by telegram of the offer and they agreed to meet the Irishman.

Travelling as a stowaway on the *George Washington*, Russell arrived in Genoa in late April to be escorted immediately to Berlin, where he was put up in a hotel. He was then transferred to a small villa in Grunewald, where he was interviewed by an Abwehr agent, SS Colonel Dr Edmund Veesenmayer. He was also introduced to the head of the Abwehr, Admiral Wilhelm Canaris, and taken to watch a military exercise by the Brandenburg Regiment, an elite commando unit that was part of the Abwehr department II taking care of Russell.

In his discussions with Veesenmayer, Russell put forward his proposal for a joint IRA and German invasion of British-held Northern Ireland, beginning with an amphibious assault near Derry. He said the IRA could call upon 5,000–10,000 supporters and perhaps the support of members of the Irish Defence Force. Veesenmayer, however, was unimpressed, believing that Russell had been away too long from Ireland to have useful information on the organization of the IRA and its leadership. Russell proffered his links with left-wing Irish-American revolutionary groups, but the SS officer regarded this connection as too loose to be of any worth.

Dismissing Russell's plan for an assault on Northern Ireland, Veesenmayer was more interested in the limited idea of sending him back to Ireland to gather intelligence and conduct a campaign of sabotage. Russell was not keen on just becoming a German agent but in the end he agreed to take part in a secret mission to Ireland, called Operation Taube.

According to Kurt Haller, another German intelligence officer present, Russell showed an 'obstinacy and narrowmindedness, which made [him] unable to see the Abwehr preference for sabotage. No details of this could be discussed with him. He was even more vague when it came to facts, and had no clear picture of the future government of Ireland, except that it was to be in the hands of the IRA or their sympathisers.'

Veesenmayer and German Foreign Minister Joachim von Ribbentrop had their own doubts about Russell, and even wondered if he was an enemy agent planted on them by the English. The arrival of another Irishman changed their mind. Frank Ryan was the hero of the Irish Republicans during the Spanish Civil War. He had been captured by Franco's Nationalists, who handed him over to the Germans in July 1940. When he arrived in Berlin, Veesenmayer sprang Ryan upon Russell to see their reaction to each other. Their pleasure at seeing each other, even though they had originally belonged to different factions within the IRA, convinced the SS agent that Russell was genuine.

Frank Ryan was more pliant than Russell and was happy to accompany the IRA chief, so Veesenmayer decided to proceed with Operation Taube and include them both. The mission was to focus on Russell making contact with the German agent Hermann Goertz, who had been parachuted into Eire in May, to establish a Nazi link with the IRA.

Goertz had visited the Dublin house of Stephen Carroll Held, an Irishman of German origin who had earlier travelled to Germany to propose an invasion of Ulster by 50,000 Germans supported by 5,000 IRA members. He also made contact with the family of the Henry Francis Stuart, a novelist, and his brother-in-law Sean McBride, both IRA supporters who encouraged the idea of a link with German forces.

On 8 August, Russell and Ryan were placed in U-65 – a German submarine loaded with weapons and ammunition – and set sail for

Ireland. After six days at sea and a hundred miles short of Galway, Russell suddenly suffered from an acute intestinal ulcer and died. The mission was aborted and Russell's body was returned to the French port of Lorient (although some accounts have it that he was buried at sea). A stone statue was raised to the memory of Russell in Fairview Park, Dublin in 1951, but anti-fascists decapitated it in 2004. It was replaced with a bronze statue, which continues to be defaced with graffiti labelling Russell a Nazi.

The closeness of the link between Russell and Nazi Germany was the subject of an investigation by Colonel Dan Bryan of G2, the military intelligence section of the Irish Department of Defence. In a letter of 4 April 1946, titled 'Secret', Bryan flagged up his concern about documents in Germany that might reveal embarrassing contacts between the German spy Goertz and high-profile figures in the Irish government.

'While on the subject of German activities in Ireland', wrote Bryan, 'I should also state that information has now come to hand re the association of Sean Russell and the Germans during the period of the IRA bombing campaign in England. This information is to the effect that Russell obtained considerable financial aid from the Germans but that his line of contact with the Germans was known only to himself and a few other people and was handled entirely by Joe McGarrity in America.' This provides another reason for Russell's presence in the USA in spring 1939 and suggests that his relationship with Nazi Germany pre-dated the beginning of the war.

Frank Ryan returned to Berlin to advise German intelligence on Irish affairs. When Hitler invaded the Soviet Union in the summer of 1941, Ryan, as a fervent Communist, should have ceased his work for the Nazis, but he was treated well and continued his association with the Abwehr, even being presented to Hitler in August. Further operations were planned to send Ryan back to Ireland, especially when the Abwehr feared an invasion of Eire by US troops based in Northern Ireland in 1942. This failed to materialize and Ryan, now forty-one, suffered a stroke in 1943. He recovered, only to catch pneumonia the following year and he died in Dresden.

A memorandum prepared by the Department of Defence in Dublin in 1941 set out its ideas about the motives for Ryan's association with the Nazis: 'The Minister had no doubt that Frank Ryan went willingly to Germany and was apparently anxious to collaborate with the Germans on some basis.' But, said the minister for defence, 'he did not believe that Ryan would do anything underhand but would be inspired by his desire for the return of the Six Counties [of Northern Ireland] as part of the national territory. Any co-operation with the Germans was apparently to be with this object in view.'

*

John O'Reilly was a restless and disappointed young man. Born in County Clare, he was the son of Bernard O'Reilly, one of a party of Royal Irish Constabulary that had arrested Roger Casement during the Easter Rising of 1916. John was on course for a career in the civil service when he failed an oral examination in Irish. Fed up, he travelled to the East End of London where he met some priests and joined a monastic order. After three weeks of that, he moved on and took some odd jobs, until he ended up in Jersey working on a potato farm. He was twenty-four years old when the Germans occupied the Channel Islands in July 1940.

There were 200 Irishmen in Jersey and O'Reilly offered to take some of them to Germany to work there during the war, after which they would receive free passage home to Ireland. The German commandant of the island agreed and, with seventy-two of his fellow countrymen, O'Reilly set sail for Germany in July 1941. They ended up in Brunswick, working at the Hermann Goering steelworks.

Ever determined to try something else, O'Reilly put himself forward for a job in the Ministry of Propaganda in Berlin, making English-language broadcasts. In the summer of 1942, he was introduced to the Abwehr. At first, it was thought he could help them by talking to sailors and refugees in Spain with a view to getting information on shipping in Northern Ireland. But they then sent him to Bremen for espionage training and instruction in Morse code and radio operation, and planned to return him back to the west of Ireland by U-boat as an agent. There, he would gather information on Allied shipping convoys and troop movements.

In October 1943, O'Reilly returned to Jersey to recruit an accomplice and, on the recommendation of the local Gestapo, settled on Dublin-born John Kenny. At the time, Kenny was working as a driver for a German Marine officer, which kept him aloof from the remaining Irish on the island. The same age as O'Reilly, Kenny was less educated and had worked as a labourer, but had IRA connections in East London. He had also wanted to serve in the German armed forces but had been turned down because of language difficulties. O'Reilly now offered him a job in Germany. Kenny told him he didn't want to work in a factory, but O'Reilly explained it would be a post with the SS and he would be back in Ireland by Christmas.

Returning to Berlin, via occupied Paris, O'Reilly put Kenny in a room at the Hotel Roxy, a favourite with Waffen SS officers coming back from the front. He was paid 450 Reichmarks a month. During their time in Berlin, O'Reilly began to have doubts about the suitability of the under-educated Kenny for their mission, but two months later, on 13 December 1943, the two Irishmen left the capital for an airfield in Rennes, France. On the 15th, O'Reilly stepped by himself into a Junkers 88, thinking that his SS masters had decided to leave Kenny behind as he had recommended.

The flight took three hours and O'Reilly was dropped by parachute just south of his hometown of Kilkee in County Clare. It seems an odd choice, as O'Reilly would have been recognized by the local inhabitants who had been listening to his Berlin propaganda broadcasts. He landed at two o'clock in the morning with a radio transmitter set dropped by a second parachute. He dug a hole to hide his parachutes and then set off in the dark for Kilkee, but got lost. Knocking on the door of a house belonging to the Collins brothers, he explained he needed directions to Kilkee. Just setting off for a market fair, they offered to help him and one of the brothers carried a heavy case for him, which contained his radio set.

In the meantime, the local police had heard reports of a German aircraft flying overhead and sightings of a strange man carrying a heavy case. They followed this up by visiting O'Reilly's parents' house, where his mother explained that her son had arrived by air from Lisbon and that he had gone with her husband to be measured for some new clothes. O'Reilly was invited to the Garda barracks to explain himself, where he told a convoluted story in which German Luftwaffe friends had dropped him off by parachute while on a reconnaissance flight. His suitcase was heavy because it was especially weighted for the parachute drop, he maintained. On the 19th, however, John Kenny landed in Ireland.

Kenny landed badly, injuring his spine, and was taken to hospital. Under questioning, he immediately admitted details about his training and mission for the SS. Once news of this got back to O'Reilly, he too admitted his part in the German spying plot. He revealed that on top of his mission to note details of shipping and factories in Northern Ireland, he was to travel to England via Liverpool and gather information on the state of the political parties, especially those of the Left. The Germans believed these parties were at odds with Churchill and organizing a Glasgow-based underground movement against the UK government. O'Reilly was to infiltrate the Independent Labour Party and help them to call disruptive strikes as part of this covert movement. To this end, he was also instructed to talk to Scottish and Welsh nationalists. 'The importance of these organisations to the Germans at present', he told the Irish police, 'should not be underestimated.'

O'Reilly and Kenny were taken to Arbour Hill prison in Dublin. 'It can be said of Kenny that unlike O'Reilly', read a security report of the time, 'he has, since his detention, given such information as he could about his training and mission. Wherever it has been possible to check his story, it has been found to be correct, and the information as far as it goes has been of value.'

On the night of 5 July 1944, O'Reilly squeezed himself through his small cell window and climbed down a twenty-foot drainpipe. He clambered on top of a disused sentry box and loosened the barbed wire on top of the fourteen-foot-high outer wall to make his escape. Borrowing some money from relations in Dublin, he took a train to Limerick and then rode a bicycle to within fifteen miles of Kilkee. His one plan was to get back home.

After spending the night sleeping in a field, O'Reilly knocked on the door of his parents' home. After their reunion, his father informed the police and he was sent back to prison. Four months after the war ended in Europe, O'Reilly was released from jail. Shortly after that he bought the eighteen-bedroom Esplanade Hotel in Dublin near Phoenix Park.

*

As the war progressed, the Germans were determined to see the Irish prisoners of war in their captivity as a resource that could be turned against the British. To this end, they kept them isolated in their own camp at Stalag IIID in Berlin-Lichterfelde. William Royle of the Royal Irish Fusiliers came from Dromod in County Leitrim and was interrogated by a German officer in May 1941. He was asked if his parents still lived in Eire and what he would do if the country was invaded by the British. 'I told him as a British soldier that I could do absolutely nothing.'

Royle and his Irish comrades were treated well in their camp but supplied with a steady steam of propaganda pamphlets, some drawing attention to British atrocities committed in Ireland from 1916 onwards. Eventually, their camp leader, a Sergeant Murphy of the Irish Guards, told the Germans, as they all stood on parade, that they wished to be sent to a British camp and not kept separated. As a result of that protest, the Irish were banned from receiving Red Cross parcels of food and cigarettes. Murphy was later removed from the camp and declared insane, ending up in a Frankfurt asylum.

German reports of their own examination of Irish POWs revealed a similarly loyal attitude to their British military service. 'Only when a reference was made to the fact that Germany was not at war with the Free State did they venture to answer,' noted one German officer. 'From these questions it appears that many of them had joined the British Army before the war, following the slogan "Be a soldier and see the world." Others of them joined at the outbreak of war out of a patriotic feeling for the British Empire.' The officer concluded it was a waste of time putting spies among them.

Jupp Hoven, a former professor of archaeology at Leipzig who had spent some time in Eire, was given the task in 1941 of recruiting Irish POWs. His aim was to form separate units that might fight alongside German commando or landing forces. He found only a few dozen Irishmen willing to volunteer for this work and had them shifted to Damm camp near Friesack – also known as Stalag XXA/301 – the Irish camp. The designation of XXA indicated a camp in Poland, but it was in fact a secret camp near Berlin which was completely shrouded from the Allies and, as a result, received no Red Cross parcels.

In discussions with Hoven, Lieutenant Colonel John McGrath declared he would be interested in leading a group of his countrymen against the British. A forty-two-year-old reservist who had been wounded and captured at Rouen, McGrath had tried to escape and been at liberty for three days before the severe wound on his face gave him away and he was recaptured.

Manager of the Theatre Royal, Dublin, McGrath gave his private address as the Bank of Ireland, College Green, Dublin. He told Hoven he would lead the renegade Irishmen because 'he regarded himself as an Irishman first of all and that he was prepared to fight for Ireland if an opportunity should arise'. He later qualified this by saying, 'he meant an actual invasion of Ireland on the Irish ports by British troops'. There was then vague talk about forming an Irish Brigade.

McGrath, however, had no intention of leading Irishmen against Britain. He was merely playing along with the Germans in order to inveigle himself among the Irish in Stalag XXA. Arriving at Friesack on 10 April 1941, the 180 POWs were at first suspicious of him and did not regard him as an Irishman. He then explained to them in a series of secret talks that they were there to be exploited by the Germans. The majority of the Irishmen were surprised at this, claiming they were being given separate treatment because Eire was neutral. A handful among them reported McGrath's statements to the Germans.

McGrath was interviewed by an intelligence officer from Berlin and he managed to convince the German that he had to take this stance in order to persuade the prisoners of his genuine concern for their welfare. It was merely his way of getting to command them, but he was definitely on the side of the Germans. Allowed to carry on, McGrath organized entertainment for the prisoners and got Red Cross parcels sent to them.

Into this manageable situation came an Irish Roman Catholic priest from Rome called Thomas O'Shaughnessy. McGrath was sure he was planted by the Germans and questioned him in private. The priest admitted his surprise at the posting and agreed to pass on a secret message on the situation inside the camp to the British representative in Rome when he returned. He later reported to the British that McGrath was 'doing his best to prevent the men in Friesack from being used by the Germans'.

Not everyone was so easily controlled by McGrath and he identified a handful of Irishmen whom he felt were operating against him on behalf of the Germans. Among these was the celebrated soldier of fortune Sergeant Thomas 'Red' Cushing of the Royal Inniskilling Fusiliers, who had been captured in France in 1940. McGrath confronted the five Irishmen and they explained they were merely acting the role of impressing the Germans and would do nothing to endanger British interests. But shortly afterwards, the five left for another camp – an apartment attached to Dachau concentration camp – where they were treated well. When Cushing returned, he told McGrath that the Germans were interested in him because they planned to send Cushing to the Panama Canal, where he had formerly served in the US Army. McGrath considered this a tall tale, but typical of Cushing was the fact that he spent the little money given to him on booze and enjoyed the improved food without actually learning many of the espionage skills the Germans wanted him to. As a result of his laxity, he was returned to Friesack.

Father O'Shaughnessy later gave his own portrait of Cushing in the camp. He described him as a 'dare-devil' and 'addicted to drink'. 'He was too active a man to stand prison life', reported the priest, 'and although he would not do anything to help the Germans, he would do anything and say anything to get out of prison. If he had taken drink, he was unpredictable … [he] decided to fall in with the German plan in order to get away from Friesack.'

Cushing's own view of the shenanigans within the prison camp was that he and his comrades saw it as an opportunity to play along with the Germans in order to exploit the more relaxed regime and possibly escape. He did not fancy being part of a replay of Roger Casement's Irish Brigade of the Great War, in which the Irish nationalist sought to recruit Irish prisoners of war to fight with the Germans but faced indifference from mainly politically moderate soldiers.

As part of their initiation into working with the Germans, Cushing claimed that he and other Irishmen were addressed by a German agent pretending to be Frank Ryan. Cushing knew Ryan from his time in the Spanish Civil War and saw through the act as the agent explained that Churchill was intending to take over Irish ports and invade their country.

Contradicting McGrath's own scathing assessment of him, Cushing says that McGrath asked his advice on how to deal with the Germans and Cushing offered to act as a double-agent. Cushing recalls being sent to Brandenburg where a handful of Irishmen were trained in sabotage techniques, but throughout this Cushing says he sent McGrath coded messages describing the training. A German intelligence officer took particular interest in Cushing's American military service and suggested he might be useful to them in Panama blowing up the Gatun Dam, a crucial element of the Canal. Cushing would be smuggled across the Atlantic in a U-boat.

Cushing was delighted at the prospect of being sent away from the war to Central America, but made a major error by discussing his real intentions with other Irishmen in a Berlin apartment. Once in Panama, he told his comrades, he would give the Germans the slip and inform on them to the Americans. Shortly after this conversation, however, he was bundled off to Gestapo headquarters where a Nazi interrogator played him the tape recording of his planned deception. 'The German–Irish alliance had been dissolved,' recalled Cushing, who, after a beating, became an ordinary prisoner of war again.

By early 1942, the Germans suspected that McGrath was also playing a devious game and that his attempts to improve the living conditions of his fellow prisoners were delaying their willingness to serve them. In turn, the Irish became aggressive towards the Germans and burned their propaganda leaflets. That year, McGrath organized a tunnel-building scheme and twelve POWs escaped in February, but were recaptured five days later because of the poor weather. They were sentenced to twenty-one days' imprisonment.

Eventually, the game was up for McGrath and he was removed from his camp and interrogated by two Gestapo officers. Stripped of his uniform, every item was cut to pieces. He was sent to Sachsenhausen concentration camp, where he was kept in close confinement, and then to Dachau. For three years, he received no outside communication and no Red Cross parcels.

As for the rest of the Irish prisoners of war, a British wartime report concluded: 'It is difficult to estimate the number of prisoners who may have been subverted, for many of those who have come to our notice may have loyally tried to find out details of the German plan, or may merely have settled down to enjoy the conditions in preferential camp, without intending to assist the Germans in any material way.'

It was believed that 'the greater danger may lie in the individual agents who are recruited and removed from these camps to small Abteilung II training centres'. These could well have been intended as undercover saboteurs to be sent abroad to Britain or America. In the end, however, it all came to nothing.

Chapter 15
Cold War Irish

'Tokyo gives one the impression that it is rapidly becoming the Brussels of the last war,' recalled thirty-seven-year-old Major Gerald Rickcord, second-in-command of the 1st Battalion, Royal Ulster Rifles (83rd & 86th), as he arrived in the Japanese capital in January 1951, en route to Korea and the United Nations forces there. 'The Maranouchi Hotel provides very good service, good food and comfortable rooms for the equivalent of 8/- a night. Here a band plays, cocktails and drinks are in profusion. It is also patronised by Americans, Nursing sisters, Red Cross, War correspondents and many others whose knowledge of Korea seems unlikely to extend beyond reading the morning papers.'

Boarding an old Dakota, flown by an Australian courier service, Rickcord took two hours to reach Pusan in south-east Korea. A veteran of the Ulster Rifles during the Normandy landings and campaign, he had been called to Korea as the battalion's commanding officer was ill and the previous second-in-command had been killed. Another one and a half hours and he was in Taegu, a US airbase full of F-84E Thunderjet fighters and B26 bombers. From there, he proceeded north-west to the British base at Taejon. The main supply route north to Osan, where his battalion was located, was extremely rough and bumpy. Nearly all the bridges had been blown up by the Communist North Koreans and he had to drive over dry riverbeds. It was the middle of a bitter winter and the temperature dipped to minus 10°C at night.

'To see the Battalion for the first time again in these conditions reminded me of pictures of Christmas in the Crimea,' noted Rickcord. 'Groups of Riflemen standing round fires wearing caps fur lined with ear flaps, their peaks down, with the Harp and Crown above made a strange picture.'

Many of the men slept fully dressed and some wore pyjama trousers beneath their battle dress. Because most of the soldiers in the battalion were reservists, their average age was thirty years and although some thought they were too old to stand the conditions, Rickcord believed they were coping better than the younger men. Almost half the recruits came from south of the border in the Republic of Ireland.

Private Henry O'Kane from County Derry was also returning to the Ulster Rifles from Japan. He had followed his father and grandfather into the Royal Inniskilling Fusiliers but had been transferred to the Rifles for Cold War service in Austria and then Korea. He had first arrived at Pusan in November 1950 and been part of the general retreat during the Chinese intervention and attack on Seoul. He was caught up in savage close-quarter fighting on 3–4 January 1951 when the Rifles lost 208 men in the battle of Chaegunghyon or 'Happy Valley' as they called it. O'Kane was one of the wounded, peppered with shrapnel, and had been sent to Japan to recuperate.

When he was fit enough, O'Kane was escorted back to Korea with the rest of the wounded by the legendary Thomas 'Red' Cushing, who was continuing his eccentric military service with a spell of Cold War duty in the Ulster Rifles. 'After supper we spent a wild evening in the American PX,' remembered O'Kane, 'where Red Cushing entertained the audience as was his wont the world over with his blarney, rebel songs and Irish wit.' On that occasion USAF crew were paying the bar bill.

O'Kane arrived back in Korea to an icy wind blowing down from Manchuria. The land was hilly around the Royal Ulster Rifles' new position and they were experimenting with the best field service marching order for the country. 'Our problem was to devise a load which would not be too heavy, or too hot, for climbing', noted Major Rickcord, 'yet at the same time carry enough warm clothing or covering to withstand the climate on reaching the summit. The cold and terrain was also our enemy.' The solution was to carry a haversack loaded with one windproof suit, spare socks, spare insoles, a heavy woollen pullover and tin rations. Slung beneath the haversack was a blanket rolled in a waterproof ground sheet. They envied the Americans' lightweight sleeping bags.

On 10 February, the Royal Ulster Rifles marched north, singing 'Mule Train' and living off US combat rations, including cigarettes, chewing gum, biscuits, coffee, sugar and cocoa. Korean porters were employed to help carry their baggage up steep hills, but when they couldn't find enough rice to feed them they disappeared. Orphan boys were adopted by the battalion to help with tasks.

'These smiling little chaps are usually dressed as complete Riflemen,' recorded Rickcord, 'even with company colours. It is sad to think what will become of them eventually and at the best they would go to orphanages which have been set up in Pusan. The plight of refugees is very distressing and they present a sorry picture tramping along all shapes and ages.'

The weather continued cold and wet and the Irish soldiers were issued with American pattern rubber boots that reached up to below the calf and were fastened with metal clips. British supplies were far less efficient. 'Where one man may have an Irish Bonnet, the other has a khaki beret or if luckier a green beret. Under these circumstances uniformity of dress has been impossible.'

They frequently stayed in Korean villages, making the most of the cover provided by the little thatched buildings. The houses were heated by wood fires on the underside of the building and the smoke both warmed the floorboards and frequently choked the occupants. As they trudged along the roads north, the Irishmen were passed by US tanks with dragon faces painted on them in red, black and yellow, intended to scare their superstitious enemy.

On St Patrick's Day, the Royal Ulster Rifles celebrated with two eggs and bacon for every soldier at breakfast. After church services, they beat the 8th King's Royal Irish Hussars, an armoured unit, in a game of football. In the evening they had a dinner of turkey, ham, fruit and Guinness, and the Brigade Concert Party played for them.

On 30 March, the Rifles crossed American pontoon bridges over the Han River and passed by the capital Seoul on their way north. No longer reserve troops, they were directed to the front line. Their task was to push forward to the Imjin River against unknown enemy strength. News came in that their American allies were meeting stiff resistance on their right.

Their route was long and steep and some 200 Korean porters carried their supplies. Rickcord had a narrow escape when a Communist wooden box mine blew the track off an American tank just twenty yards behind his own jeep. The one piece of good news was that the weather was improving and the Irish soldiers set up their camp on a sunny slope overlooking the waters of the Imjin.

At nine o'clock on the morning of 7 April, Rickcord and a team of Royal Ulster officers, plus some American Rangers, set off on a patrol to find a crossing over the river. 'Everything was quiet,' observed Rickcord, until they reached the edge of the river 'when enemy automatic fire opened up from the opposite bank. It was an unpleasant experience returning for approximately 300 yards across open shingle through an old South Korean minefield.'

As a result of this contact with the enemy, they erected two footbridges further east of that point. Three days later, 'A' Company of the Ulster Rifles crossed over the river on the tanks of the 8th Hussars. A BBC reporter took photographs of them venturing into enemy territory. The rest of the battalion followed and secured their objectives. One of the footbridges broke during the operation and the river was too fast and deep for the soldiers to wade across, but Oxford Carriers – amphibious tracked vehicles – plunged into the water and helped them over.

Patrols pushed further north and Rickcord sensed that the enemy had withdrawn before them. Private O'Kane didn't like the landscape. 'The hills in this area were steep and covered in most parts with scrub timber,' he recalled. 'Devoid of the long fields of fire for proper defence it also meant our field of vision was limited and this made it possible for well trained troops to slip into [our] defended positions.'

Three days-worth of combat rations was delivered in case the soldiers found themselves cut off by a rise in the level of the river. It was a wise decision because at midnight on 14 April, the Communist Chinese attacked. It began when some seventy to eighty Chinese soldiers assaulted the isolated position of 'D' Company. The Irish used every one of their grenades as the fight lasted four and a half hours. They captured one of the enemy soldiers and identified him as belonging to the Chinese 19th Federal Army.

Over the next few days, the temperature rose and some of the Irish bathed in the river. News came through that a unit of Belgians would be taking over from the Ulster Rifles and they would revert to reserve battalion status. As a result, most of the Irish withdrew south of the river to act as brigade reserve behind the 1st Gloucestershire Regiment, 1st Royal Northumberland Fusiliers and the Belgian battalion. If they thought that meant they were out of harm's way they were mistaken, for on the bright moonlit night of 22 April, Chinese soldiers began to infiltrate the frontline positions. In response, a battle patrol of the Rifles moved forward to secure the bridges over the Imjin. By early the next morning, all the British and Belgian units were heavily engaged by the Chinese. 'The whole valley was filled with smoke, the smell of cordite and confusion,' recalled Rickcord. 'This was St George's Day…'

Soon, units of the Rifles moved forward to support the 1st Glosters. Rickcord was effectively the commanding officer and ordered his men to secure high ground over the river. For the next twenty-four hours, the Irish hung on to their positions. The 8th Hussars used their tanks to secure the main supply route, while an air strike was called for.

'It was noticeable that the Chinese were brave enough to engage the aircraft with machine gun fire just as they came out of the dive even though napalm, rockets and automatic fire was used.'

The Chinese were relentless, constantly trying to break through the perimeter held by the Irish and their comrades. O'Kane was part of 'C' Company and remembered the numerous attacks. 'During the night the Chinese mortars kept up their fusillade. Our positions were swept by rapid machine gun fire and red and green tracers raked through the sky. Determined attacks were driven off without loss. The bazookas were being used to wipe out parties of Chinese hiding behind rocks.'

Early on the morning of the 25th, 'D' Company deployed bazookas, machine guns, two- and three-inch mortars to fight off further Chinese assaults. A number of enemy dead and wounded could be seen strewn across the slopes up to their position. 'The feeling on top of the hill was one of the greatest confidence,' remembered Rickcord, hoping they had done enough to halt the enemy. 'Although everyone was becoming physically tired none ever spoke of withdrawing.'

Nevertheless, the Irish couldn't stay on the hill for ever, and they would need a large force to counter-attack the Chinese and drive them back across the river. Without these extra troops, the brigade commanders decided it was best to withdraw and sent orders to pull out to the Rifles, the Northumberland Fusiliers and the 8th Hussars. The Irish were told to evacuate the hill and join the main supply route but to watch out for snipers on the road.

It was late afternoon on the 25th when 1,000 Ulster Rifles, North-umberland Fusiliers and some Belgians and Americans were strug-gling along the route south away from the Imjin. Having withdrawn about a mile down the road at great speed, they ran into intense fire. Blazing tanks belonging to the 8th Hussars dotted the road-side. An American spotter plane flew over them and dropped a message warning them that a large body of 2,000 Chinese were fast approaching them from the west.

'The men of the platoon seemed fairly subdued,' recalled O'Kane; 'there was none of the usual banter and joking that went on; we all felt we were leaving safe defensive positions and going down into danger.'

Rickcord agreed. Although in his battlefield report of the combat he was uncritical of his commander, he later let it be known that he was very uncomfortable with taking his men off the hill and with-drawing along the valley road. He would have far preferred to march out of danger along the ridges of the high ground, keeping well away from the enemy below.

'Enemy fire was heavy', noted Rickcord, 'and every gap, opening or crossing place seemed to be covered.' The heat was getting to the Irish and their throats were parched. All they wanted to do was to withdraw in an orderly fashion. It was at that point that Major Henry Huth of the 8th Hussars swung into action and helped the Rifles when they needed it most.

Huth had only two Centurion tanks directly at his command. 'The attack developed rapidly, on a wide arc', reported Captain Winn, hunkered down behind Huth's turret, 'and was sustained with great ferocity.'

> With no protective infantry, the two tanks fought back in short bounds in constant danger of being enveloped on either flank. The enemy came forward at a remarkable pace, taking up fire-positions behind the banks, ignoring losses inflicted at every bound.

Huth coolly measured his firepower against the fire and speed of advance of the enemy, slowing them so as to allow the tired infantry to pass by safely behind him. He wasn't helped by the presence of injured soldiers clinging to his tank.

O'Kane was shot in the leg and was one of the wounded riding on another tank. 'It was a wild swaying, bouncing ride on the Centurion. It didn't last long – but I shall never forget it. The dust, the rattle of the tracks, the Besa machine gun, the screams of wounded men as we were repeatedly hit.'

The Chinese flung themselves at the Irish Hussar tanks, using charges on poles to break open the armoured vehicles or ram them into their tracks. Some climbed up on the turrets to batter open their hatches. One tank driver smashed through a Korean house to clear off the Chinese on his hull. Other tank gunners shot at each other's vehicles to sweep off the enemy. When machine guns ran out of bullets, high explosive shells were fired point blank at the road to bounce up at the Chinese. They suffered horrendous casualties in their hunger to decimate the UN column.

'Before the withdrawing infantry had reached safety', continued Winn, 'the powered traverse [turret mechanism] of Major Huth's tank failed, and it became impossible to bring fire to bear speedily where required, from the co-axial machine-gun.'

> Fire was continued by Brens and other automatic weapons from his tank, and the enemy was still kept at a distance without the speed of retirement being increased. In many instances it was necessary to engage at right-angles to the axis of withdrawal. Not until the last infantryman was seen to have reached the MSR [main supply route], where more powerful friendly gun power was available to them, did Major Huth give orders to draw out of the enemy's reach.

Rickcord was full of praise for Huth and the covering fire of the Irish tanks that allowed many of his men to escape a deadly situation. Huth was later awarded a DSO for his leadership. The Ulster Rifles gathered at an assembly area and the roll call was called. They numbered just 14 officers and 260 other ranks – at least 240 of them were missing. They marched another five miles until vehicles evacuated them from the combat zone. 'It was pathetic and cruel sight', recalled Rickcord, 'and not one easily forgotten.'

O'Kane was one of the missing. Chinese soldiers had surged along the road with Molotov cocktails and destroyed the tank he was riding on. He was thrown into a ditch, covered in blood, with his nose and ears bleeding from the concussion of an explosion. Another wounded soldier splashed some water over him and bandaged his head. The majority of the Chinese had rushed past, pursuing the retreating tanks.

For a moment there was silence on the battlefield, then three Chinese soldiers appeared in tatty cotton uniforms and gave them safe conduct passes, ordering them to the rear of their positions. With hands on his head, O'Kane marched off into Communist captivity. It was the beginning of over two miserable years as a Chinese prisoner of war.

Back at their barracks in Seoul, the rest of the Ulster Rifles who had escaped the battle of Imjin River bounced back the following day. After a breakfast of bacon and eggs, Rickcord was delighted to hear them singing an old Irish emigrant song along to a banjo: 'For we'll sell the pig and we'll sell the cow and we'll leave old Erin's Isle.'

The battle of Imjin River had cost the UN forces dearly, but the Chinese had lost many more men and the stiff resistance to their assault meant that they failed to press on to capture Seoul, their target. If the Ulster Rifles and 8th Hussars had had it bad, then their comrades, the Glosters – cut off and surrounded by the advancing Chinese – had had an even tougher time and they, quite rightly, featured in the media coverage of the battle. Only a few dozen men from the Glosters came off the battlefield, leaving over 600 killed or missing.

On 8 May, the Glorious Glosters, as they were henceforth known, paraded before the Eighth Army commander to receive the blue ribbon of the US Presidential Citation, the highest American decoration awarded to units. Pipers of the Royal Ulster Rifles played throughout the ceremony. A few days beforehand, *The Times* had published its own salute to the bravery of the soldiers at Imjin River.

The Northumberland Fusiliers, the Royal Ulster Rifles,
and other Commonwealth units, each with a past to live

up to, shared with the Gloucesters in this most testing of all hazards on the battlefield – attack by overwhelming numbers of enemy. The 'Fighting Fifth' wearing St George and the Dragon and the 'Irish Giants' with the 'Harp and Crown' have histories that they would exchange with no one.

The paper's editorial concluded by saying: 'The motto of the Royal Ulster Rifles may have the last word. Quis Separabit?' – Who Will Separate Us?

*

James Majury was a twenty-nine-year-old captain of a mortar platoon of the Royal Ulster Rifles when he was captured in earlier fighting with Communist forces in January 1951. He was defending Hill 195 in the battle of 'Happy Valley', some ten miles north of Seoul, when Chinese soldiers launched themselves at his position before dawn. At first, it was confusing because the Chinese were shouting, 'South Koreans – We Surrender.' Then, blowing bugles and whistles, they charged at the Irish, hurling grenades.

The firepower of the Ulster Rifles held them at bay for a period, but the sheer weight of numbers forced the Rifles from their position. Unfortunately, an American spotter aircraft, thinking it was being helpful, dropped a flare over the Irish, illuminating them for the Chinese. In the confusion, Majury's commanding officer was shot in the head. The battle continued and, as ammunition was running out, the rugby-playing Majury was forced to use his fists to punch out the enemy that closed in on him. In the end, however, Majury and his comrades had little choice but to become their prisoners.

Forced on a long march in sub-zero temperatures, the young Antrim-born captain took it upon himself to keep up the morale of his soldiers. When they reached the prison camp, the Communists took away all their Bibles and prayer books, but Majury had remembered enough prayers from his boyhood as the son of a reverend to write them down on rice paper and secretly passed them round. Majury took over the role of the chaplains who had been imprisoned separately, and in this way, he and his fellow Irishmen stoutly refused the attempts of the Chinese to convert them to Communism.

Private Henry O'Kane, captured at the battle of Imjin River, also had to fend off attempts to enforce Communism on him, most notably by English journalists. Michael Shapiro was a lecturer at University College London and one of twelve Communist councillors elected in Stepney after the war. In 1950, he travelled to China to work for the Communist News Agency and was more than happy to visit UN prisoners of war in north Korea. Standing before starving American and British soldiers, O'Kane remembered Shapiro calling them 'war-mongering dogs', saying they deserved to die like dogs. 'When he was verbally attacked by a sergeant of the Royal Ulster Rifles suffering from untreated wounds and beri beri which eventually killed him,' recalled O'Kane, Shapiro 'had the Chinese remove the brave man from his vicinity with the comment "I'll have you shot".'

When another Communist *Daily Worker* correspondent, Alan Winnington, and left-wing Australian reporter Wilfred Burchett, turned up at the same POW camp, the prisoners silently welcomed them by holding little string nooses in front of them.

Living conditions for the UN POWs in the north Korean town of Chongsong were poor. The camp was overcrowded and O'Kane was forced to sleep on the floor in a room with ten other men. With less than a square yard to each man, blankets were shared between two. There were no facilities for washing, and food was minimal, with a bowl of maize or sandy millet served twice a day. Rice was a luxury available once every two weeks. While the soldiers became malnourished and succumbed to disease, dysentery especially, the Chinese did not recognize the Geneva Convention and did not allow food parcels or Red Cross visits.

O'Kane suffered from a jaundice fever and had to be fed by Filipino prisoners he shared a hut with. While he was too ill to contemplate escape, others did, but all were recaptured. The Americans suffered particularly badly from the poor conditions, almost 400 dying in one summer alone at O'Kane's camp. But if the situation was dire in the Chinese camp, it was worse in those administered by the Korean Communists, who gained a reputation for being sadistic to their captors.

At one point, Irish prisoners from other UN units were brought in to join those from the Ulster Rifles. 'One I remember well', recalled O'Kane, 'was a large Tipperary man in the US Army who sported a Mohican haircut and was a camp cook in British 5 Company.' Occasionally, the prisoners were allowed to watch movies in the town cinema but they were mainly Russian Communist propaganda films about the achievements of Stalin. 'Many were concentrated on food production,' remembered O'Kane, 'not a subject for hungry men, but again and again in one form or another we were to witness row upon row of combines fighting the battle for production in an endless sea of grain.' The only news of Western events came via three-month-old copies of the *Daily Worker*.

The most popular diversion was when the POWs went on wood-collecting expeditions into the surrounding hills. There, they managed to gather a local weed, which when smoked had the same effect as marijuana. It made O'Kane feel quite light-headed, but a fellow Irishman under the influence usually pretended he was an aeroplane and ran around the camp with arms outstretched.

By 1953 the Korean War was over, but peace negotiations dragged on as most of the 60,000 Chinese and North Korean prisoners held by the UN refused to be returned home. This slowed the exchange of UN prisoners. News finally came through in July 1953 that the 2,000 captives at Chongsong were to be released. In order to show they had been well treated, the Chinese hurriedly introduced a new regime of feeding rice, bread and meat to the soldiers three times a day to fatten them up. Eventually, a train took them south to Kaesong, where they waited until a truck took them, group by group, to Panmunjom and Freedom Village.

> My first impression was that everybody seemed to look so big,
> strong, fit and healthy. Everyone seemed to be pink faced
> compared to the grey faces of my fellow ex-PoWs and I.

Captain James Majury also managed to survive the ordeal of over two years in a Chinese prison camp. Out of the 1,000 British soldiers captured, only fifty died in captivity, thanks in part to the commitment of soldiers like Majury and O'Kane to looking after their fellow prisoners. After his release, Majury was mentioned in dispatches for his particular efforts in taking care of his men.

After a long period of leave in Ireland, O'Kane was hospitalized on his return to the army for four months. After that, the army medical board told him he was fit only for service at home, so he took his discharge and returned to civilian life, taking up a career in catering. Majury returned to Staff College at Camberley and, despite the physical battering he received in Korea, he opted for service in the Parachute Regiment, commanding 'B' Company, 2 Para, which took him into another Cold War-period conflict.

The moderate pro-Western rule of King Hussein of Jordan was being threatened by left-wing Arab followers of Nasser of Egypt and Britain decided to send him some help. A unit of paratroopers was sent in, but was twice turned back over Turkey. On the third time, Majury was flying with the Paras in an RAF Hastings when his pilot again got the news to return home.

'You didn't get that message, did you?' Majury barked at the pilot.

'No,' said the pilot. 'Radio not too good.'

Majury and his Paras landed in Jordan, secured key positions in the king's capital, and were greeted enthusiastically by the Jordanians.

In 1961, Majury was appointed commander of 1st Battalion, Royal Irish Fusiliers, but had to give up the prestigious role because of a recurrence of tuberculosis caught in Korea. Overcoming that, he returned to soldiering, retiring from the army in 1974.

Major Gerald Rickcord also went on to further Cold War service after Korea. Handing over command of 1st Royal Ulster Rifles in Hong Kong in May 1952, he was appointed commandant of 1st Battalion, 2nd (KEO) Gurkha Rifles and was dispatched to engage Communist guerrillas in the jungle of Malaya during the Emergency for three years. On retirement from the army in 1961, Rickcord enjoyed a successful career working for Guinness.

In Korea, shortly after their first bloody clash at 'Happy Valley' in January 1951, a stone memorial was raised to the Irish dead near the battlefield on the outskirts of Seoul. The inscriptions were carved by a Korean mason. One of the faces was devoted to the Ulster Rifles while another commemorated the fallen of the 8th King's Royal Irish Hussars; the two others faces marked the sacrifice of the gunners of the 45 Field Regiment Royal Artillery and 170 Mortar Battery Royal Artillery.

In 1962, when the Korean capital was expanding, the memorial was brought back to Ireland on HMS *Belfast* and re-erected at the regimental depot in Ballymena, where it became the focus for many years for the annual Remembrance parade and service for the Korean Veterans Association of Ireland. When the barracks closed, the stone was moved to the grounds of Belfast City Hall, where it was re-dedicated in 2010. It is the only memorial in Ireland to the Korean War.

Chapter 16
Slaughter in the Congo

It was the wheelbarrow in the middle of the road near the bridge that caught the attention of twenty-year-old Private Danny Bradley as their vehicles rolled to a halt in the African village of Niemba at eight o'clock on the morning of 9 November 1960. He belonged to No. 2 Platoon, 'A' Company, 33rd Battalion of the Irish United Nations force sent to the Katanga region of the Congo. The wheelbarrow was used for repairs to the bridge and Bradley walked over to it. Inside, he saw rainwater mixed with blood. On the ground, he saw a poisoned arrow. Spent shell casings were scattered everywhere. One of his comrades pointed to where the elephant grass had been trampled flat to the side of the road. Bradley and two officers went to investigate.

As he entered the tall grass, Bradley felt the presence of evil all around him. It was then that he discovered the bodies of Lieutenant Kevin Gleeson and Sergeant Hugh Gaynor.

'I could see no obvious signs of recent bleeding,' recalled Bradley. 'It was as if they had been killed at another location, then the bodies had been brought to where I had found them to be displayed in some kind of ritual.'

The deliberate spreading out of the mutilated bodies, with no attempt to hide them, explained the purpose of the wheelbarrow – it had been used by the Baluba killers of the Irishmen to move their corpses.

Bradley's instinct was to turn and run from the awful place, but he kept his nerve and withdrew, facing the bush in case Baluba warriors were still out there. Secure among his comrades, Bradley just couldn't get the vision of the two dead Irish soldiers out of his head.

'I began to shake quite uncontrollably,' he remembered. 'I could not even trust myself to speak to the men beside me.'

*

In 1960, the former Belgian colony of Congo faced civil war as the mineral-rich province of Katanga sought to break away from the vast central African country. Belgian settlers supported the Katangans but were caught up in the violence and a United Nations army was sent to restore order. Among them were two battalions from the Irish Defence Forces. It was their first deployment abroad and thousands of Irish men, women and children had come out to line the streets of Dublin see them go overseas in September.

As they marched proudly along through the Dublin crowds, they were kitted out in First World War-style thick woollen tunics; and when they stepped off the aircraft at the other end of their long journey in the sweltering heat of equatorial Africa, they suffered. Told to keep their top buttons done up while on duty, they wore their pyjamas in barracks. It was five weeks before they were issued with proper tropical battledress.

Many of the Congolese were happy to see the peacekeeping Irish, selling them pineapples and bananas, but the Baluba tribesmen of northern Katanga were opposed to the breakaway Katangans and hated the intervention of the white soldiers. Lieutenant Stig von Bayer was a Swedish liaison officer and interpreter working with the UN at Niemba and understood the level of antagonism, but the Irish didn't pick it up. 'The general mood was quite optimistic,' recalled von Bayer. 'Very much nothing can happen as they all – the Balubas – know that we are there to help them. I advised Lt Gleeson to be extremely careful as the Balubas were very dangerous – he didn't listen.'

At one o'clock in the afternoon on 8 November 1960, eleven Irish soldiers of No. 2 Platoon, 'A' Company, set out in a Land Rover and a Volkswagen pick-up truck from the village of Niemba to repair a bridge over the River Luweyeye that had been destroyed by Baluba tribesmen. As the Irishmen got out of the vehicles, they saw a

Baluba warrior kneeling in the middle of the road wearing a leopard skin and holding a bow and arrow.

It was an ambush, and very quickly at least a hundred Baluba tribesmen surrounded the eleven-man group. Their vehicles were pointed in the wrong direction for a quick getaway and so Lieutenant Gleeson decided to talk with the tribesmen. They were there as policemen not soldiers, and the UN rules of engagement favoured negotiation over action. As Gleeson stepped forward to greet them with a raised hand, he got an arrow shot through his arm. He span round and told his men to withdraw into the bush. Followed by showers of arrows, they ran for cover among the elephant grass and trees. The Baluba followed them. 'They all appeared to be mad and I believe they were drugged,' recalled six-foot-two Private Joseph Fitzpatrick. 'Hearing them shouting would strike you dead!'

The Irishmen headed for a small hillock, where they made a brief stand with the wounded Gleeson, firing their .303 rifles at the warriors.

'A fellow came at me with a hatchet,' remembered Fitzpatrick. 'He was a young fellow of only about 21 and I shot him. One of the boys told me he was hit in the back with an arrow.' That was twenty-three-year-old Private Thomas Kenny.

> We grabbed whatever weapons we could lay our
> hands on. I was wounded with one arrow in the back.
> I saw one of the men get killed. We then went for
> deeper cover and I now had two arrows in me. I got
> weak and fell down but was not unconscious. I got
> a third arrow in the hip and I could not get up then.
> They then started hitting me in the back of the head
> with clubs. They did not seem satisfied with that and
> started beating me again.

Kenny was left for dead as the tribesmen rushed off to kill more of his comrades. Delirious with pain, he dragged himself away and disappeared into the bush. During the fight on the raised ground, someone shouted 'run for your lives' and Fitzpatrick sprinted down the slope through a swamp, throwing himself into a bush, where he watched the crowd of Baluba milling around, hunting down the other Irishmen.

Up to then I lay hidden with my face and arms blackened
with mud and did not fire any shots to reveal my position.
However, when I heard a pal's cry I opened up as I decided
I might as well die then as later that night.

The Balubas didn't find Fitzpatrick, but his pal crawled close to him
and said: 'I am dying, please pray for me.' He died shortly afterwards.

It was not until four o'clock that afternoon that officers in charge
at Niemba became concerned about the failure of the bridge-fixing
group to return. Even if their vehicles had broken down, they could
have marched back to camp. They radioed their anxiety to their
commanders, but as the sun set at six o'clock, they were told to stay
within their secure perimeter with a light machine gun placed on
top of their HQ. The machine-gun crew pointed their powerful
flashlights into the night sky in the hope that the patrol might signal
back.

The next morning a small convoy of armed Irish troops set off on
the hour's journey to the bridge. They found eight bodies and only
two survivors. Fitzpatrick had stayed hidden all night until the
patrol arrived. Kenny survived the night too, stumbling out of the
bush with two arrows still sticking out of his back. One soldier,
Trooper Anthony Browne, was missing. It was the worst casualty
level suffered by a United Nations peacekeeping force to that date
and remains the worst ever loss in a single incident in the Irish
army. The dead were flown back to Dublin and on 22 November
over 300,000 people paid their respects as the bodies were paraded
through the city streets.

For many Irish soldiers, the matter was made worse by the lack
of reprisals against Baluba tribesmen, but the UN had a peacekeeping profile to maintain and any sense of retaliatory justice had to be
suppressed. Or so it seemed – but a confidential letter from Cornelius Cremin, secretary to the Department of External Affairs in
Dublin, revealed a punitive expedition was taken against some of
the Baluba killers of Niemba.

Over lunch on 18 January 1961, Colonel Bunworth of the 33rd
Battalion told Cremin and his colleagues that he had got word of
five Baluba tribesmen recovering from wounds in a local hospital.
'He gave us to understand', recalled Cremin, 'that he had come to

learn that these Balubas had taken part in the Niemba ambush and had been directly responsible for killing our men.'

Bunworth subsequently commanded a mission in which his soldiers arrived at the hospital at dawn and dragged out the offending tribesmen. They were then transported to Albertville where they were handed over to the legal authorities to be put on trial. This, to some extent, satiated the hunger for punishment among the 33rd and even received the covert help of other UN contingents.

The private sense of dismay provoked by the massacre was expressed in Irish External Affairs correspondence between Brian Gallagher, Irish ambassador to The Hague, and Cornelius Cremin. Gallagher reported a candid conversation with a fellow ambassador in the Belgian Embassy in which he said: 'We had no interest to serve in the Congo. Our men had been sent there to help the Congo in its difficulties and to serve the cause of world order as represented by the United Nations Organisation. Now nine of our young men who had never done any harm to anybody had been savagely massacred. It was made worse by the fear that their sacrifice would be in vain.'

Ambassador Gallagher considered that the Congo crisis would only get worse and that any attempts by the UN to intervene were doomed to failure. 'The trouble', he concluded, 'was the rivalry of the great powers which was bringing the Cold War into the Congo situation.' It was true that among the mineral wealth of Katanga were mines rich in uranium – the raw material of nuclear weapons.

Questions were asked in the Dáil about the ambush and they revealed that the party were armed with two Bren guns, four Gustaf submachine guns and four rifles. No wireless equipment was carried by the patrol. Kevin Boland, minister for defence, replied that 'The patrol had been adequately armed' and 'would not normally carry radio and it was extremely doubtful if in the circumstances it would have been effective.'

On the anniversary of the Niemba ambush in November 1961, the Military Medal for Gallantry, Ireland's highest award, was given for the first time, posthumously, to the father of the missing Trooper Browne. The citation said that Browne had 'endeavoured to create an opportunity to allow an injured comrade to escape by firing his Gustaf, thereby drawing attention to his own position, which he must have been aware would endanger his own life'.

The story grew over the years that Browne had sacrificed himself to save the life of Thomas Kenny because he was married and had children. But after years of putting up with this version of events, Kenny felt he had to put the record straight.

'I am not trying to denigrate the bravery of Anthony Browne during that attack when it was every man for himself; I saw him firing and fighting with the best of them. But everyone believes he died to save me and that is not the truth,' Kenny told the *Irish Independent* forty years later. 'It is a terrible burden for everyone to think that the reason I am alive is because someone gave up his life to save me. It just isn't true and I want what really happened to become public knowledge rather than just among the Army, who have never come out and said what really happened.'

The remains of Browne's body were found two years after his death several miles away from Niemba. Local sources explained that what probably happened was that Browne did not die at the scene of the ambush but escaped into the bush, where he was later betrayed by local women to Baluba warriors. Kenny gave his original statement of what really happened to the army authorities as soon as he arrived back from the Congo, but this was lost, with the army preferring the legend of self-sacrifice that grew up around the award of the medal. While all the soldiers who died received posthumous medals, the survivors Kenny and Fitzpatrick did not, and felt somewhat victimized for surviving the ambush.

There was another horrific dimension to the ambush that was never mentioned at the time, but has ever since bothered those who witnessed the remains of the victims. Danny Bradley puts it bluntly: 'Acts of cannibalism perpetrated against captured Irish troopers – my knowledge and analysis of such matters has been continually disdained, hushed up and even whitewashed for whatever reasons.' Cannibalism was widely practised among the Baluba as part of their ritual of war.

After an earlier clash with Katangan troops, Stig von Bayer noted, 'the Balubas were roaming everywhere looking for bodies and parts of bodies to bring back to the camp to be smoked for eating later'. He came across a witchdoctor in a Baluba camp with half a bucket full of human testicles. 'He told me that if I took away his testicles he would simply collect new ones – UN General Policy was to never write about cannibal matters. You could circumvent it by using the term "Missing".' Bradley is convinced that this was the fate suffered by Trooper Browne.

*

Ten months after Niemba, trouble flared again for the Irish contingent of the UN forces in the Congo, but this time it wasn't from the Baluba tribesmen but the breakaway Katangans. In June 1961, a fresh Irish contingent had flown out to join the UN forces in the Congo. To keep them going on their thirteen-hour flight, each soldier of 'A' Company, 35th Battalion, was given a bag with an apple, orange, banana and two sandwiches.

Once on the ground in Katanga, their task was to assist the process of bringing an end to the rebel movement by rounding up white Belgian colonial mercenaries and their Katangan allies, but there was still plenty of fight left in the rebels and they were heavily armed. The 156 soldiers of 'A' Company were posted to the wealthy mining town of Jadotville, which had been previously controlled by the Belgian and Katangan troops. The Africans bitterly resented the outside intervention and gave the UN troops a frosty reception. A Swedish contingent had already got the message and rapidly moved out as the Irish soldiers moved in.

Far from appearing neutral, the UN Irish troops were perceived by the locals to be supporting the other side in the brewing civil war. With little transport, they were forced to leave some of their supplies and ammunition behind as they drove into the hostile town.

Fortunately, their commanding officer, forty-two-year-old Kerry-born Commandant Patrick Quinlan, ordered them to dig five-foot-deep trenches at night around their encampment on the outskirts of the town as soon as they arrived. While they did so, the far from cowed mercenary troops drove around the camp in their jeeps pointing their mounted machine guns at the Irish.

An official report later revealed how unprepared the Irish peace-keepers were for their presence among battle-hardened mercenaries.

> Our men were not adequately security conscious. They were not suspicious enough as sentries, on patrol or off

duty. This fault prevailed right through. They are very
much inclined to be 'cushy' and easy going. They trust
too much in the other fellow's good intentions.

Early on Wednesday, 13 September 1961, the Katangans blocked
the bridge that linked the regional capital of Elizabethville and the
Irish camp at Jadotville. A Belgian mercenary tipped off African
comrades that the Irish soldiers were at Mass and the Katangan
rebels advanced on the camp. Luckily, one of 'A' company's soldiers was less religious than the rest. Sergeant John Monaghan was
coming out of his tent after shaving, with his towel around his neck,
when he saw a group of about thirty Katangans fast approaching in
jeeps and on foot. He jumped into a trench and started firing a
Vickers machine gun.

Unknown to Quinlan, a major UN operation against the Katangans had been initiated that morning. Throughout Katanga, UN
units were instructed to take over the region in order to reunite it
with the rest of the Congo. 'I received a message just as the Katangans started shooting at us,' reported Quinlan. 'I was upstairs
shaving when the message arrived. I rushed down to the rest of the
men and by that time we were already under fire.'

Unsurprisingly, the operation had provoked the Katangans into
outright warfare to protect their independence. Quinlan quickly
understood the seriousness of the situation and instructed that
every container within the camp – every bath, bucket and bottle –
be filled with water. 'We were fortunate to have taken this precaution', he later recalled, 'because that day the water was cut off.'

Some 2,000 to 4,000 Belgian-led enemy troops quickly surrounded 'A' Company. Aside from the mercenaries and black gen-
darmerie, many white townspeople picked up guns and joined in
the attack. Heavy firing broke out from 11.30 a.m. onwards with
the Katangans deploying machine guns and mortars. The Irish
returned fire with their own mortars, Bren and Vickers guns and
knocked out an enemy artillery piece as well as their ammunition
dump, leaving it burning all day and night. Despite these successes,
the enemy presence was overwhelming and Quinlan had to make
quick decisions.

'Our position was untenable if the enemy attacked in strength or
infiltrated at night,' noted Quinlan. 'I decided to withdraw our

forward platoon at last light into a new defensive position. We got every man who could be spared to dig trenches in the new position. At last light we thinned out the forward positions and one hour after last light our new position was fully organised.'

Quinlan's plan was to break up the enemy attacks at long range before they reached the thick bush surrounding their trenches. For most of the young Irish soldiers, this was their first time under live fire and it was terrifying. Not wanting to let down their comrades was the main motive that kept many of them from showing their fear, but as the fire poured into their positions, some fell wounded. Private John Manning, nineteen years old, was one of the casualties. 'It was about 10.30 at night on September 14,' he recalled. 'I was behind a fence, half-kneeling at the time. There was a burst of fire and I happened to catch an FN rifle bullet on the right shoulder.'

Private John Gorman, at just seventeen years old, was one of the very youngest soldiers there. From County Wicklow, he had been a restless youth, running away from home at fifteen before he joined the army for a sense of adventure. But as he crouched in a trench at Jadotville, this was not exactly what he was expecting. 'The only thing we knew about Africa was when we were going to school – we would have to bring a penny in for the black babies to feed them. I didn't know the black babies would be trying to kill me afterwards.'

For Gorman, the role of their senior NCOs was vital in helping to keep their nerve. 'I was never under fire before, but we had great leadership. If you are a young lad, you say, "Well he's not afraid, I'm not going to be afraid either." Company Sergeant Jack Prendergast was a powerful man, about 6′4″.'

Worse was to come as the Katangans had a Fouga Magister jet fighter that strafed the Irish trenches and dropped bombs. 'Each time the jet plane came over it came in out of the sun', recalled Quinlan, 'and we prepared a barrage of small arms fire should it come again. On Friday morning the jet came in low and into our barrage of SA and MMG fire from armoured cars. It dropped two bombs but failed to come in on a strafing run. We felt that we had hit it. This was confirmed later as it returned to Kolwezi with bullet holes. After this attempt it bombed and strafed from very high altitude and was inaccurate.'

Having survived the first assault, the Irish held out for four more days, fighting through the nights with no opportunity for sleep. They had little food and ammunition, and conditions in their trenches quickly deteriorated.

'Jack Prendergast broke up our "dog biscuits" – very hard,' remembered Gorman, 'put them in a bucket, poured water over them, stirred them up and he'd go round the trenches at night and give us a spoonful. That's all you'd get. But he never took his own spoonful until the very last. That's the kind of man he was.'

The sun hammered down on the soldiers in their open dugouts. With water running low, they could only wet their lips. Cans of pineapple juice were handed round with penknives used to stab them open so they wouldn't attract swarms of flies. Fighting continued throughout the night and into the next day with little prospect of rescue for 'A' Company.

Commandant Pat Quinlan radioed the UN HQ for help, but two columns sent out to reinforce them from the regional capital of Elizabethville couldn't get across the bridge. The second attempt consisted of Irish and UN Gurkha troops, but they were heavily outnumbered and outgunned. Fearing they would themselves be surrounded, they had to fight their way back to Elizabethville, suffering five Gurkhas killed along the way. Only one helicopter with water supplies made it over the enemy lines but the water was tainted by the unwashed jerry cans it was carried in.

News reports in Ireland fed upon Katangan propaganda that claimed up to fifty-seven Irish soldiers had been killed, much to the distress of 'A' Company families. In fact, amazingly, after five days, despite their desperate position, the Irish had inflicted up to 400 casualties on the attacking Katangans and not suffered one death, with only five wounded. Eventually, knowing they would soon be out of food, water and bullets, Quinlan agreed to a cease-fire with the Belgian mercenaries.

The Irish soldiers were ordered out of their trenches, but rather than being allowed to march away from the action, the UN troops were disarmed and taken hostage. It was a humiliating moment and full of anxiety for the Irishmen, who were now completely at the mercy of the angry Katangans. The locals were delighted to see them made prisoners and made it clear they would rather see them dead.

Even some fellow countrymen – long-term settlers in Africa, who styled themselves the Mashonaland Irish Association – railed against them. In a letter written to the Irish Taoiseach on 17 September 1961, the Association declared: 'We cannot overstress the deep sense of shock felt by Irish men and women, who have made their homes in the Federation of Rhodesia and Nyasaland, at the action taken by the United Nations against the Government and people of Katanga and at the part taken in this brutal exercise by the Irish contingent and the Irish civil administrator.'

When this failed to garner any desired reaction, the Irish-Africans argued that the UN mission 'unleashed an attack which, we have reason to believe, can justly be compared with the suppression of the Hungarian people by Russia in 1956'.

As the outside world argued over the Cold War politics of the situation, Quinlan and his men faced indefinite imprisonment among a hostile population. When 'A' Company was joined by other UN soldiers captured in Elizabethville, including Irish members of 'C' Company, this confinement took a sinister turn as anonymous interrogators accused the Irish of atrocities. One man, identified only as a German doctor, shouted at 'C' Company's Commandant Cahalane: 'You do not understand what has happened – the Irish shot and raped white women in the town.' Cahalane vigorously denied the accusation, asked for proof, which the doctor declined to provide, and concluded 'an Irish soldier never did such a thing'.

To keep his men occupied during the deteriorating situation, Quinlan organized activities for them, including physical training, lectures, discussions and indoor games. They were not allowed to drill or train outside, their post was censored and their radios taken away from them. Quinlan presumed a rescue mission was being organized for them and prepared accordingly.

'We had plans to take over the guard in the event of any attempt to relieve us,' he recorded. 'We had plans to defend ourselves to the last in the event of any attempt on our lives. Most of the men still had jack-knives or daggers and we prepared fuel for Molotov cocktails from petrol provided for our cooker, candle grease from some candles that we had and oil from the sump of a car.'

Prisoner John Gorman had an additional concern: he hadn't told his mother he had come out to the Congo – she assumed he was still based in Ireland. 'She would get down on her knees at night and say the rosary for the lads fighting in Jadotville, but she didn't know I was one of them.'

Quinlan was interviewed by an Irish journalist during his imprisonment and expressed his concern at the fact that his unit had not been given prior warning of the UN operation. 'Had his force been warned that the Sept 13 operation was to start', wrote *Irish Independent* reporter Colin Frost, 'he could have controlled the bridge on the main Jadotville–Elizabethville road where the UN effort to relieve his garrison was time and again pushed back.'

At one point, it was mentioned that local tribesmen were going to be sent into the attack and had threatened to eat the Irishmen. To this, Quinlan reputedly declared: 'If they do, we will give them indigestion.' The commandant later qualified this, saying: 'As to being eaten, I don't think it worried any of us unduly what happened to us after we were killed. In any case, the propaganda did not get down to the men. Three or four men … knew of it all right and they seemed to enjoy the joke.'

As the weeks dragged by, the prisoners were moved around, exposed to threats and jeers from locals, subject to beatings, and given little food and drink. The only hope for the Irish was that the UN would swap captured Katangans for them. For the Katangans, it was an opportunity to embarrass the UN and they took full advantage of it, allowing photographs of the prisoners to appear in the world media.

Back home in Ireland, rumours spread that the cease-fire had, in actual fact, been a surrender. This was countered by a quote from Quinlan, who during the height of the siege had declared: 'We will fight to the last man – could do with some whiskey.' The latter request was Irish myth-making; in truth, he asked for more water.

After over a month of captivity, the UN prisoners were finally freed on 26 October. 'A' Company came back to Ireland to a mixed reception, with some saying they should have fought on. Even though Quinlan recommended several of his men to be awarded the Military Medal for Gallantry, no such awards were made and the Irish Defence Forces buried the memory of Jadotville.

'We were ignored when we came home – completely,' recalls Gorman. 'Everything that happened in the Congo was spoken about – like Niemba – but Jadotville was never spoken about. If Pat

Quinlan had come back with two-dozen body bags, he would be a hero. But we had just five wounded.' Other Irish servicemen taunted them with accusations of cowardice and fights frequently broke out in barracks as Jadotville veterans defended their record.

This attitude was in stark contrast to the praise of Quinlan expressed in a letter of appreciation written just three months after the events at Jadotville and included in the official report of the mission. It came from Brigadier KAS Raja, officer in command of the UN forces in Katanga.

> I should like to make particular mention of Comdt Quinlan, who was in command of the company that had the misfortune to suffer so much at Jadotville. This officer needs little commendation as his performance in maintaining the discipline and high morale of his men during a particularly difficult stage of Katanga Operations speaks for itself. I have great personal admiration for the initiative, courage, drive and restraint of this officer and I believe that he could be held as an example for all soldiers.

Quinlan eventually retired with the rank of colonel but was never again posted abroad. The soldiers under his command felt his role in saving the lives of every man at Jadotville was never fully appreciated in Ireland. 'Later, when I met veterans in the street, like Pat Quinlan, I could see the pain in that man's face,' said Gorman. 'At least ten or twelve of 'A' Company committed suicide – some drinking themselves to death.'

John Gorman doggedly led a campaign to hold an official review of the battle, and, in 2004 as a result of this, Quinlan was cleared of any charges of soldierly misconduct. Forty-four years after the combat, the veterans of Jadotville received honorary scrolls and a memorial stone was erected at Custume Barracks in Athlone. A portrait of Commandant Quinlan now hangs in the Congo Room of the Irish Defence Forces' UN School.

Chapter 17
War on Terror

On the afternoon of 14 September 2001, US President George W. Bush visited the remains of the World Trade Center in New York City. He was shocked at the scale of the gnarled and twisted remains of the giant twin skyscrapers that had dominated the Manhattan skyline until Islamic hijackers crashed two passenger jets into them. He clambered up onto a charred fire truck, put his arm around an exhausted fire-fighter and spoke to the crowd of rescue workers around him.

'We can't hear you,' shouted one of them.

'I can hear you,' Bush bellowed back into a bullhorn. 'The rest of the world hears you, and the people who knocked these buildings down will hear all of us soon.'

'USA! USA! USA!' chanted the hard-hat wearing workers.

Among those sifting through the debris and remains of the nearly 3,000 people who died there three days earlier were members of New York's National Guard. That included soldiers of the 1st Battalion of the 69th Infantry Regiment – the Fighting 69th – the most famous Irish-American military unit in the country. On the day of the assault, these part-time soldiers had rushed from their Armory headquarters on Lexington Avenue, less than fifty blocks away from the devastated site of the World Trade Center, to help evacuate the wounded, remove the rubble and provide instant security.

The scenes they saw were like those of a battle zone: shattered buildings, trees wrenched in the direction of the blast, bodies and bits of bodies strewn across the streets. A fine layer of grey ash covered everything, constricting their throats, making it hard to breathe. As the day progressed, news came through that a soldier of the 69th – Gerard Baptiste, a fire-fighter – had died in the south tower trying to evacuate terrified office workers. A second member of the 69th, police officer Thomas Jurgens at the city courthouse, had leapt into a van with his comrades to help but had died with three of them as the twin towers collapsed. Another soldier told his commander, Lieutenant Colonel Geoffrey Slack, that his brother was missing.

'I asked him, "Why didn't you tell anyone?"' said Slack. 'He told me, "Sir, because I think maybe I can find him."'

A total of 5,000 National Guardsman were mobilized in the New York area, including soldiers from the 101st Cavalry from Staten Island and the 258th Field Artillery Regiment from Queens, alongside the Fighting 69th. Their duties evolved from helping the injured and gathering bodies to providing perimeter security, transporting fuel and construction equipment, traffic control, and distributing 1,000 tetanus shots to the doctors at the scene.

The cavernous drill hall of the 69th's Armory HQ was turned into a processing centre for information on the thousands of missing people. Long lines of distraught civilians shuffled inside the building to give DNA samples and fill out questionnaires so that victims could be identified. For Lieutenant Michael Rodriguez this was particularly difficult as his sister was last heard of on the 82nd floor of the south tower.

'She was crying hysterically, and then the phone line went dead,' said Rodriguez. At one point, an identification was made in a hospital, but it proved to be a false hope. 'We've experienced every emotion you could ever feel. I feel like I've been to the moon and back 15 times.'

Three days after the attack, Colonel Slack gave his soldiers a break. They gathered in the hall of the Armory. 'I told them I was proud of what they had done and that I hoped that we would get a call to war,' he said. 'I know we have a score to settle.' Four hundred men of the Fighting 69th roared their approval.

*

In response to the 9/11 terrorist atrocities – a death toll that surpassed that of Pearl Harbor in 1941 and included mainly civilians

– President Bush launched a global 'War on Terror'. The first phase of this was an invasion of Afghanistan in October 2001 to remove the Taliban regime that had harboured the Al-Qaeda terrorists responsible for the suicide attacks. The second, more controversial phase was an assault on Iraq.

At the time of the attack on the World Trade Center, Iraqi President Saddam Hussein had made it clear where his sympathies lay. An official Iraqi statement declared: 'The American cowboys are reaping the fruit of their crimes against humanity.' Although Saddam had no direct links with Al-Qaeda, he was promoting himself as a leader of Islamic opposition to American foreign policy and supported many terrorist organizations. The American and British governments feared that Saddam's posturing, allied to his past use of weapons of mass destruction, made him an increased risk to their own security and they authorized the invasion of his country in 2003. Many American-Irish and British-Irish soldiers would join in the military consequences of 9/11.

On the morning of 19 March 2003, the 1st Battalion, Royal Irish Regiment grabbed the attention of the world. Poised to go into battle, their colonel, forty-two-year-old Belfast-born Tim Collins, addressed his men at Fort Blair Mayne camp in the desert of Kuwait, just twenty miles from the border with Iraq. Little did he know it at the time, but those words, reported by Sarah Oliver of the UK's *Mail on Sunday*, would go round the world, be quoted in TV news reports, and end up framed on the wall of President Bush's Oval Office in the White House.

Collins spoke through a microphone without notes to the young Irishmen before him.

> We go to liberate, not to conquer. We will not fly our flags in their country. We are entering Iraq to free a people and the only flag which will be flown in that ancient land is their own. Show respect for them.
>
> There are some who are alive at this moment who will not be alive shortly. Those who do not wish to go on that journey, we will not send. As for the others, I expect you to rock their world. Wipe them out if that is what they choose. But if you are ferocious in battle remember to be magnanimous in victory.

He told them that Iraq was steeped in history. It was the land of the Garden of Eden and other biblical sites: 'Tread lightly there.' It was this combination of respect for his enemy's land plus a professional determination to demonstrate their fighting spirit that struck a chord with many who supported a war to punish Saddam Hussein but also wished to help liberate the Iraqi people.

The Royal Irish Regiment is the last remaining Irish infantry regiment of the line in the British Army. Its former incarnation as the 18th (Royal Irish) Regiment of Foot could trace its history back to 1684, but was disbanded in 1922. The title of the regiment was resurrected in 1992 with the amalgamation of the Royal Irish Rangers and the Ulster Defence Force. It forms part of the 16th Air Assault Brigade, fighting alongside Apache attack helicopters and the Parachute Regiment. It is proud of its Irish identity and a good 70 per cent of the regiment are from southern or northern Ireland, with others descended from Irish families living in Britain. Catholics serve alongside Protestants. Serving previously in Bosnia, Kosovo and Sierra Leone, the Royal Irish was deployed in February 2003 as part of Operation Telic 1 – the Coalition invasion of Iraq.

Thirty-one-year-old Royal Irish Platoon Sergeant Dominic 'Brummie' Hagans came from a Belfast family that had moved to Birmingham. 'I joined up because my granddad said it would do me good,' recalled Hagans. 'We lived on a rough estate in Birmingham and most of my mates were living on the wrong side of the law. I wanted something different. I kept myself fit with boxing. The army appealed to me. I only meant to serve three years but I've loved every minute of it.' Hagans was standing on parade in the desert when Colonel Collins gave his famous speech. 'It hit us hard,' he remembered. 'When he said that soldiers would die and that we would put them in sleeping bags and just carry on, that was quite daunting. That was the first time I heard that.'

Hagans had already been on tour in Northern Ireland and Bosnia, but this was the first large-scale conventional battle for the Royal Irish. 'He was right to talk about treading lightly, because once you've taken a position, you've got to switch your mentality from a fierce fighter, calm yourself down, there's civilians in the area, let's sort them out. By doing that, you can bring a good or bad name to the Royal Irish.'

Captain Doug Beattie of the Royal Irish was more critical of Tim Collins's speech. He later wrote that it made the soldiers fearful and apprehensive and he had to snap them out of it by 'bollocking them'. Unlike the quasi-Shakespearian words of Collins, Beattie was more straightforward – 'like most Ulstermen my language is straight out of the gutter'.

As it turned out, there was no great set-piece battle with the Iraqi forces. Crossing the border on 22 March in a variety of vehicles, including four-ton Bedford trucks, the Royal Irish battalion helped secure the strategically important Rumaylah oilfields. Once they arrived there, they found the air was black with burning oil and it smelled terrible, but there was little resistance. 'The Iraqis kept bugging back,' said Hagans. 'There was no way they were going to fight us.' From there, they advanced north to secure the towns of Al Medina and Al Qurnah in the region, thought to be the location of the biblical Garden of Eden. 'You wouldn't think it was the Garden of Eden,' said Hagans, 'a few trees and houses.'

With the rapid advance of the entire Coalition force, the Royal Irish operated alongside their Brigade's elite Pathfinder Platoon paratroopers on the River Euphrates to conduct a lightning raid over 150 kilometres to take the city of Al Amarah. 'This was the toughest part of the operation,' said Hagans, 'patrolling and securing Amarah. Once the fighting was over, the attitude of the locals changed – they just wanted us out. That was when on patrol we'd get bricked, the odd shots fired at us. It was like going back to Northern Ireland days. Much more dangerous – you never know where the trouble's coming from. But we had the solid patrol skills experience of Northern Ireland behind us and that helped.'

*

The Irish Guards were the other major Irish unit in the British Army fighting in Iraq in 2003. Deployed as part of the 7th Armoured Brigade, the battalion was split up and attached to various units of the Desert Rats. As they crossed the border in March they saw the burnt-out hulls of Iraqi tanks and armoured personnel carriers destroyed by the Americans before them. Assigned the job of processing prisoners of war and guarding key locations, the Irish Guards came under fire at night as Iraqis in civilian clothing – the first insurgents – shot at them. They also came under attack from looters keen to get their hands on anything valuable. In the distance, across the desert at night, the Guards could see the flashes and hear the explosions of artillery shelling around Basra. As they approached the major southern city, organizing road blocks along the way, searching for weapons, they came under heavier fire from insurgents armed with Rocket Propelled Grenades (RPGs) and mortars.

Whereas much of the military activity seemed like an exercise, Irish Guardsman Sergeant Bryn Taylor thought the strangest aspect of the campaign was the large number of journalists accompanying them. 'There were occasions when their zeal for a story perhaps overrode their responsibility to act sensibly,' he recalled. 'This could make life very difficult for us.' Sometimes the media presence could exacerbate a situation. As the Irish Guardsmen organized a vehicle checkpoint outside Basra, the local population were, on the whole, quite willing to be patient and wait for roads to re-open, but as soon as reporters appeared with cameras, this encouraged some members of the crowd to play up and make the situation seem worse than it was.

Moving into Basra was the most challenging aspect of the operation and, for forty-eight hours, the Irish Guardsmen came under intense fire from paramilitary soldiers loyal to the old regime. Early on the morning of 6 April, Challenger tanks and Warrior armoured vehicles from the Black Watch and the Royal Scots Dragoon Guards, 7th Armoured Brigade, supported by the Irish Guards in an armoured infantry section, advanced into the south and west of the city. Further armoured battle groups moved into other parts of the city. 'The people of Basrah are getting their first real glimpse of the courage, tenacity and professionalism of our armed force,' declared Air Marshal Brian Burridge, UK National Contingent Commander.

One of the Irish Guardsmen attached to the Royal Scots Dragoon Guards was twenty-eight-year-old Dublin-born Lance Corporal Ian Keith Malone. He came from a Catholic working-class family of five and served in the 20th Infantry Battalion of the FCA – the Reserve Irish Defence Forces – the Irish equivalent of the British Territorial Army. At the age of twenty-two, he wanted to carry on and join the Irish Army, but he was considered too old, as they were only recruiting teenagers. Desperate for a military career, Malone considered joining the French Foreign Legion, but, like so many young Dubliners, he chose instead to enlist in the Irish Guards – a still controversial decision in the eyes of many Irish Republicans.

In 2002, Malone was interviewed on Irish radio about joining the British Army. 'At the end of the day,' he said, 'I am just abroad doing a job. People go on about Irishmen dying for freedom and all that. That's a fair one. They did. But they died to give men like me the freedom to choose what to do.'

While getting ready for action in Iraq, Malone met, by extraordinary coincidence, a US Marine Lance Corporal, also called Ian Malone, attached to the British 3rd Commando Group during Operation Telic. Sharing the same name and rank, they immediately struck up a conversation.

'My family originally came over from Dublin, Ireland in the 1840s', recalled the American Malone, 'and I was surprised when he said he was from Dublin, Ireland. We got to talking about the fact of my ancestry and his and both of our families had lived in Dublin, Ireland around the same time. I figured it was a small world, here a Marine from America and an Irish Guard from Ireland take part in a military Operation in Iraq and are probably blood relatives.'

On 6 April in the streets of Basra, Irish Guardsman Malone was shot in the head by a sniper. He was the first Irishman to die in the war. He was a valued member of the Irish Guards Pipe Band and the other Irish Guardsman to die on that day was a fellow piper, Zimbabwe-born Christopher Muzvuru. 'It really brought home to us that we were truly at war and not on exercise,' recalled Bryn Taylor. 'It knocked everyone sideways, but in true "Mick" style we raised our game and got on with the job in hand.' 'He loved the Army and lived for the excitement and challenges that being a soldier brought,' said the Malone family. 'He was proud to be an Irishman and proud to serve in the Irish Guards.'

Malone's body was taken to the Church of the Holy Assumption on the Ballyfermot Road, close to where his family lived. Two pipers – one from the Irish Guards, the other from the Irish Defence Forces – played at his funeral, which was attended by hundreds of local people.

Malone became the first serving British soldier to be buried with a military honour guard in the Republic of Ireland – thanks in part to the Good Friday peace process – although neither a national nor a regimental flag draped his coffin, nor was there a firing party. It was the first time that British soldiers were seen in uniform in Dublin since independence in 1922. Representatives from the British and American embassies attended the funeral.

It marked a new acknowledgement of those Irishmen who had fought for Britain over the previous century, many of them proudly wearing their regimental blazers for the first time in Dublin. A year later, the Irish Defence Minister attended a ceremony in Westport, County Mayo, honouring the memory of an Irish Victoria Cross winner in the British Army during the Indian Mutiny. In total, 188 Victoria Crosses have been won by Irishmen. In 2005, the 1st Battalion, Irish Guards became the first British Army unit to be awarded battle honours for service in Iraq.

*

The Fighting 69th finally got their opportunity to participate in the War on Terror in 2004. On 15 May, the 1st Battalion of the 69th Infantry Regiment, New York Army National Guard, was federalized for combat duty in Iraq. Although beginning its proud history as an Irish-American regiment and maintaining a strong Irish identity into the twenty-first century, many of its recent recruits are drawn from the ethnically diverse population of New York and that includes a large portion of Puerto Ricans.

Being national guardsmen, these soldiers also have other jobs in the civilian world. Their commander was Lieutenant Colonel Geoffrey Slack, the forty-seven-year-old owner of a tree-cutting company in Seaford. He had overseen the grim tasks at Ground Zero and was ready for payback time. 'I've made my peace with God,' he told his soldiers and, unusually for a commander of his rank, he would lead his troops on daily patrols in Iraq. 'I like nothing more than to be in a tussle.'

Originally destined for a tour of duty in the Balkans, nearly 800 men of the 69th were redirected at the last moment to Iraq. Given desert training at Fort Hood in Texas then Fort Irwin in California, they were detached from their familiar service with the 42nd New York Rainbow Division to become part of the 256th 'Tiger Brigade' of Louisiana. 'Although antagonists in the American Civil War,' recalled Slack, 'these two gallant old units bonded together to achieve a common purpose.' Given extra strength with a company of Bradley Fighting Vehicles, the 69th were dubbed 'Task Force Wolfhound' in acknowledgement of their Irish ancestry.

In October 2004, the fully trained and equipped 69th were flown to Kuwait. They then hit the road for the long drive north, arriving at Camp Liberty in Baghdad on 6 November. Their mission was to provide security in occupied territory thirty miles north of the capital at Al Taji. At first it looked like a peaceful farming community dotted with a few small villages. That view changed within days of arrival.

Tasked with keeping Iraqi insurgents armed with rockets and mortars away from Camp Cooke, Slack led patrols day and night along the dusty roads, seeking out enemy groups. The enemy frequently found them in bitter, fast-moving ambushes. 'Taji?' remembered Sergeant Javish J. Rosa. 'It's one of those things when you get in the vehicle and you say, "Is today my day?" Anywhere you ride, you feel like you're going to die.'

On 29 November, that fear became reality. Insurgents triggered a massive roadside bomb that ripped into a Humvee, killing New York fire-fighter Staff Sergeant Christian P. Engeldrum and Long Island volunteer fire-fighter Private Wilfredo F. Urbina. Engeldrum had been at 9/11 and served in the First Gulf War, but had had a bad feeling throughout this tour of duty that he would not make it back. They were the first combat deaths of the Fighting 69th since the Second World War. 'It made it all a lot more scary,' said a twenty-one-year-old college student from Manhattan serving with Task Force Wolfhound. 'It was a moment of clarity – but terrifying clarity.' Remote-controlled bombs continued to take a toll on the unit. Staff Sergeant Henry Irizarry was blown out of his Humvee and killed on 3 December. Born in Puerto Rico, he was appreciated in the 69th for his 'great disposition and warm smile'. He left behind a wife and four children.

On 6 January 2005, 200 pounds of explosives devastated an armoured Bradley Fighting Vehicle, killing all seven men inside, including twenty-year-old Private Kenneth von Ronn, alongside his Louisiana comrades. 'He was a good kid,' said his mother, 'and he died doing what he wanted to do. He wanted to serve his country, and he went with honours.'

When fellow national guardsmen arrived at the site to deal with the casualties they found the blast had torn away their friends' limbs and heads, leaving their torsos untouched inside their bullet-proof vests. For Slack it was the World Trade Center all over again, bodies mangled beyond recognition. Determined to give the victims back their dignity, he would insist on personally scouring the area for all body parts, even scooping up blood-soaked sand to put into body bags. Diesel fuel was then poured onto the surrounding ground and the landscape set on fire.

A total of ten soldiers from the Fighting 69th died in Taji and seven were seriously wounded. 'The men of the Task Force grieved at their losses', noted Slack, 'but proved their mettle by working all the more intensely to find and destroy the enemy.' They raided enemy safe houses, destroyed arms stores, disrupted their net-works and captured their leaders. Some of the soldiers were New York policemen and made the most of their specialized skills to purse the terrorists. 'Day after day, Task Force Wolfhound forced the enemy to fight on an ever smaller battlefield', concluded Slack, 'and lose its effectiveness as a fighting force.'

Later in January, the combat-experienced 69th were reassigned to duties inside Baghdad as part of an operation to secure the city for upcoming elections. Making their base in a ruined department store, they did their best to protect the democratic process. Follow-ing the successful completion of that, an exhausted unit was given the task of guarding the five-mile stretch of road linking Baghdad airport to the Green Zone compound that housed American and Iraqi government buildings – it was called Route Irish.

Slack was disappointed by the task, feeling they were being reduced to the role of state troopers again. 'I'm agitating to get off this mission,' he complained. 'It's been deathly quiet.' For others it was a welcome relief and they grumbled that their commander took too many risks, but none could criticize him for not leading from the front. Investigating a building used by Iraqi snipers along the highway, Slack ignored the fear that it might be booby-trapped. 'Nothing around here comes without risk,' he said, as he climbed to the top of the building.

For seven months, the 69th patrolled Route Irish, checking every piece of suspicious-looking garbage for the sign of roadside explosives. It was not just the presence of IEDs (Improvised

Explosive Devices) that inspired fear, but also car-borne explosives driven by suicide bombers. These caused enormous casualties among soldiers and civilians and grabbed international headlines – serving the purposes of the insurgents to portray Iraq as a land of anarchy.

This frustrated Slack and his soldiers, but they kept on with the patient job of patrolling the highway. Their task was helped by the presence of two battalions of Iraqi Special Police attached to their unit and together they created secure checkpoints to intercept terrorist assaults. Unable to directly clash with the insurgents, the extent of their success could only really be measured by the explosions that didn't happen: the people that weren't slaughtered by the terrorists because of their presence.

A year after they arrived in Iraqi, the Fighting 69th were sent home. Nineteen of them would not make the journey back to America, many of them the victims of roadside bombs. For some of them, the contrast of life as a civilian returning to New York – rather than to a military base like a regular soldier – was too much.

'What I was doing over there was exciting,' said Private Carlo Giordano, 'like an adventure. So I'm not sure what I'm planning to do now. Maybe I'll be a cop.' Captain Sean Flynn was a public relations executive in upstate New York but he too was unsettled by the experience in Iraq. 'I was just talking to my wife and I said, "Now what?" I got the feeling this is going to be period of metamorphosis for me.'

In the end, Flynn would write a critically praised book about the Fighting 69th on duty in Iraq. In the meantime, he had the satisfaction of a job well done. 'I will never forget that January election. There was something huge going on, and I thought, holy cow, we're part of this.'

For Slack, it was a time to remember the missing. 'For those 19 wonderful guys who made the ultimate sacrifice,' he wrote, 'for a free Iraq, a secure America, their brothers in arms and their families now bear the painful burden of continuing life's journey without the love and support of their gallant soldier – they have joined the legion of the fallen of the Fighting 69th, their memory must be kept forever green.' A framed Honor Roll inside the entrance hall of the Lexington Avenue Armory – the scene of so much heartbreak during 9/11 – records their passing.

In August 2006, the Mayor of New York, Michael Bloomberg, flew to Ireland to attend the unveiling of a monument to the Fighting 69th in Ballymote, County Sligo, the birthplace of Michael Corcoran, colonel of the 69th at the first battle of Bull Run. The base of the bronze column contained a fragment of steel from the destroyed World Trade Center. Fine Gael TD John Perry said: 'The monument represents the unbreakable link between all those who emigrated from Ireland to the United States over the past 200 years. It is a link of dedication. It is a link of service to others. It is a link of sacrifice to others.'

Bloomberg added his own speech to the ceremony in which he revealed how the Fighting 69th now embraced many other nationalities within its ranks.

> When the Fighting 69th was re-activated for World War
> One, about 95% of the men who joined the regiment were
> Irish. Their chaplain, Father Francis Duffy, said the rest of
> the men were 'Irish by adoption, Irish by association, or Irish
> by conviction'. Today, the 69th is as diverse as New York
> City itself – but Father Duffy's words still hold true.

Chapter 18
Blown up in Afghanistan

The Fighting 69th in the twenty-first century might draw its troops from New York's broader ethnic mix, but when they came back from deployment in Afghanistan they enjoyed a purely Irish welcome. Selected to head Manhattan's St Patrick's Day Parade along Fifth Avenue in March 2009, they dined first on a traditional Irish breakfast at the Lexington Avenue Armory of black pudding and soda bread. They then attended Mass at St Patrick's Cathedral, where New York's Catholic cardinal stood on a rug decorated with green shamrocks.

Putting out its largest ever contingent for the parade, the Fighting 69th was led by a piper and a unit of mounted New York policemen. More than 1,000 of them marched along the Manhattan streets in four formations wearing army desert camouflage fatigues and black berets adorned with green boxwood in memory of the shamrock substitute worn by their predecessors in the American Civil War.

Among the 300 soldiers from the US 1/69th who were deployed to Afghanistan in 2008 as part of Task Force Phoenix was thirty-two-year-old Staff Sergeant Brandon Luchsinger from Bayside, Queens. The day before he went, he made headlines by marrying his long-time girlfriend. Having already served two terms in Iraq, he volunteered to go to Afghanistan where the task of the 69th was to train the local Afghan police force.

'It's a very humbling experience,' said Luchsinger of his time out there. 'In New York, we get angry if we can't get theatre tickets.

Over there, it's about survival, finding a school for your children that's not been destroyed by the Taliban. As National Guard, we are more used to dealing with civilians and 98 per cent of the population are really friendly.'

*

In the same year that the Fighting 69th helped train Afghan policemen, more than 500 soldiers of the Royal Irish Regiment also served in Afghanistan. Part of Operation Herrick 8, they were deployed, as in Iraq, with the 16th Air Assault Brigade. This usually meant they went into action by helicopter, but in Afghanistan the lack of availability of helicopters was to be a controversial point. On that occasion, the task of the Royal Irish was to mentor and support the Afghan National Army (ANA) so that, in due course, the Afghans could take over the security of their own country.

Several of the Royal Irish soldiers who had served in Iraq were back in Afghanistan and this time they saw a lot more action. 'After Iraq I was a bit disappointed, after all that training and no major action,' said Dominic 'Brummie' Hagans, promoted to company sergeant major and acting warrant officer class 2. 'But in Afghanistan, it got a lot more intense.'

Charged with knocking into shape the Afghan soldiers, the role of the Royal Irish was to join them on patrols through land contested with the Taliban. This meant driving in convoys of Land Rovers across a countryside rigged with the most effective weapon possessed by the Taliban – the roadside bomb or IED.

On the morning of 3 July 2008, forty-two-year-old Ulsterman Captain Doug Beattie was in command of a re-supply mission to a base in Marjah, in central Helmand Province, in the south of the country. He had already been on one tough tour of duty in 2006 when he had won the Military Cross for his part in recapturing an Afghan town. Beattie's disdain for the poor performance of the ANA was a matter of record – 'more chance of killing birds than the enemy' – and he wondered at the value of fighting so hard for territory that would then be promptly given up. 'Is it a country worth saving?' But his Royal Irish professionalism triumphed over his doubts and he saw it as a job that had to be finished properly.

On that summer morning, Beattie knew they'd already had problems with attacks on their road patrols and he had a bad feeling about going back to Marjah.

'You know we should be doing this by helicopter,' he told a comrade, but there were none available. They had no choice but to get into their WMIKs – Land Rovers fitted with a Weapons Mounted Installation Kit that meant it could become a platform for a machine gun or any other large calibre weapon.

Three British vehicles set off from the British base at Lashkar Gah at 4.30 a.m. Dominic Hagans was in the lead WMIK, with a British-crewed Snatch Land Rover behind him, then twenty Afghan soldiers packed into a Humvee and two pick-up trucks, and lastly Beattie at the back in the other WMIK.

Beattie was disappointed to see the WMIKs were armed only with a pair of 7.62 mm General Purpose Machine Guns; he would have preferred something with a bigger punch. He also wanted the British vehicles to travel together, but they had to sandwich the Afghans, otherwise they could very well fall behind and disappear as they had done on previous occasions. The discipline and fighting spirit of the ANA was no match for that of the Royal Irish.

It was tough going with roads running out into dirt tracks in the middle of fields cut up by irrigation channels. The sky was clear blue with the sun hammering down on the Royal Irish clad in body armour and equipment. At one point, Beattie's Land Rover slid off a narrow bridge into the stinking water of an irrigation ditch. The palaver of negotiating the treacherous farmland was attracting crowds of locals amused at the efforts of the Royal Irish.

After six hours' driving, they were approaching the outskirts of Marjah at an intersection called Green 1, when Hagans noted an ominous sight. He saw a family running from a house with the man carrying an old woman on his back. At that moment, an RPG whooshed over his vehicle and a burst of automatic fire dug up the ground in front of him. All at once, he was in the middle of an ambush with fire coming from three sides.

Hagans' orders were to push on and he drove through the storm of AK47 bullets towards Green 1. At the same time, Beattie was being engaged from the rear. The Snatch Land Rover followed Hagan's WMIK into cover behind compound walls. They could see the Taliban rushing forward from woods and scattered buildings.

Hagans radioed back to base but got the bad news they were on their own for 45 minutes until air support could get to them.

Behind him, the ANA had tumbled out of their vehicles and were spread out over 500 metres along the road, hiding in the roadside canal, with Beattie stuck at the rear. 'They just froze,' said Hagans, who wanted to get the Afghans moving towards Green 1. 'I had to act quickly. I ordered my gunner, Ranger Stewart, to give me covering fire and then fire manoeuvred down the track for about 200 metres. It felt a life time – the rounds were landing around me.'

Hagans shouted to the ANA soldiers to stop hiding and start fighting. He grabbed them out of the canal and pushed them back up to the road. Without their imput, the Irish were outnumbered five or six to one. Most importantly, the ANA had to move their vehicles so that Beattie could join Hagans with his WMIK.

When Hagans got back up to the road, he saw an Afghan 15 metres away in a compound doorway and shot him dead with his pistol. Barking instructions to the ANA, Hagans was clearly the leader, the prime target for the Taliban, and the fire became heaviest around him. Suddenly, he was swept off his feet as a bullet smacked into the heel of his left boot and knocked him over. Shaken but undeterred, Hagans got up and ran back to his WMIK team.

'We were in a 360 degree ambush, pinpointed down,' said Hagans. 'The Taliban had the advantage. We could see four or five in one firing position in the wood to my northwest. We continued to engage with GPMG and 40 mm HE grenades. I saw two enemy dead in the wood, but they were moving rapidly around us, giving each other covering fire as they moved. This was well planned.'

Hagans shouted at his driver, Corporal Brown, to get his satellite communications antenna in the air, but as he did so it was shot out of his hands. Shocked, Brown said, 'I need a fag.' 'What a time to ask for one!'

With RPG airbursts above them and their own ammunition running low, Hagans was relieved to hear the approaching drum of an Apache helicopter gunship. Unfortunately, someone had given the Royal Irish the co-ordinating codeword of 'Boulevards', which in the midst of a battle was proving difficult for them to spell out precisely to the Apache pilot.

Hagans could see the enemy moving around on motorbikes to buildings at Green 2, an intersection nearer to Marjah, but valuable

minutes were lost trying to convince the pilot of their identity
because they were misspelling the code word. Finally, the Apache
opened fire with its 30 mm cannon. 'I saw one man split in half –
just disappear.'

As the Taliban fled from the helicopter fire, Beattie told Hagans
it was their opportunity to get moving and they sped towards
Green 2. One RPG passed by Hagans' WMIK, but a second hit it.

'It ripped my door off – it flew in the air. There was a big cloud of
desert around me and my team. I shouted we are ok. The vehicle
had stopped. We got our belt buckle [7.62 mm GPMG] firing at the
enemy.'

They fired their SA80 assault rifles, but to Beattie it felt like
engaging the enemy with a peashooter. Radio instructions to the
Apache brought down more fire on the Taliban at Green 2 and they
moved on to Green 3, a small village with several shops. Completely clear of villagers, the Taliban were using the buildings as
cover to shoot at the Royal Irish. Hagans' driver kept his foot down
and they hurtled on to the patrol base in Marjah, where the garrison
brought their own fire down on the Taliban.

With the fire-fight finally over, Hagans studied the bullet hole in
his boot. He considered it a miracle that none of the Royal Irish had
been hit. A local elder later told him that eighteen Taliban fighters
had been killed. Truly, the luck of the Irish had been with Hagans,
Beattie and his comrades, but their good fortune couldn't last
forever. On 27 July, Sergeant Jon Mathews of OMLT 4 (their Opera-
tional Mentoring and Liaison Team) was killed.

*

In August 2008, OMLT 4 moved out of Marjah and headed south to
the notorious Garmsir area, where they took over from the American soldiers based there. The Royal Irish carried out daily patrols.
On 11 September – the seventh anniversary of the 9/11 New York
attacks – Hagans took out two vehicles to visit his men at a patrol
base. It was about 12.15 p.m. when a roadside bomb exploded
under his Land Rover.

I felt an initial surge of pain in my legs, then, just like
the war movies show, time stood still. I moved very slowly

and was floating in the air. It seemed as though I was there
for ages, then I was on the floor. I sat up, looked to my
right and saw the radio had landed by me.

Remarkably, Hagans sent an initial contact report, but couldn't
hear the reply.

My legs were badly damaged. The left leg below my knee
was hanging off and my right leg shattered, I couldn't even
administer morphine because my body armour and helmet
had been blown off me by the blast – my morphine was in my
body armour. It was mad because I should have been in pain
but I wasn't.

Hagans saw his comrades move towards him and told them to get
metal detectors to look for more bombs. He couldn't believe that
the Taliban had managed to lay a bomb on that stretch of the road.
It had been checked just days before, and it was only 200 metres
from an ANA-manned patrol base. But that was the weak point.
Sometimes the ANA guards just wandered off.
    Hagans shouted out to his crew. He wanted to know they were
okay and they shouted back to him, describing their injuries.
Hagans was then placed on a stretcher and given first aid. He was
losing a lot of blood.

I felt my heart racing even faster and I was struggling for air.
I must have been in shock. I started to close my eyes, but before
I did I told Corporal Imrie to tell my kids I love them. My eyes
closed and I thought that this was it for me. But then a smack
around the face and a scream of 'Brummie' woke me up.

Hagans felt a sudden pain in his left leg as the tourniquet was tightened. The injured were evacuated by Chinook helicopter to the
main British base at Camp Bastion. Just two days later, Hagans was
flown back to Selly Oak hospital in Birmingham, his home town.
    When his friend Captain Beattie saw the twisted wreckage that
was all that was left of Hagans' vehicle, he knew that he was very
lucky to be alive. Not many soldiers in Afghanistan survive an IED
blast directly under them. 'If I had been wearing my seat belt,' said

Hagans, 'I would have been cut in half.' Fortunately, the blast threw him and his comrades clear of the wreckage.

Since arriving in Selly Oak, Hagans has had numerous operations to rebuild his shattered legs, which are held together by wire. After seven weeks, he was moved to Headley Court where he began his rehabilitation. At first, he was told he would be in a wheelchair for the rest of his life, but he got out on two crutches, then graduated to a walking stick and now he walks unaided.

Hagans would like to re-join the Royal Irish in Afghanistan. 'To be honest, if they said to me tomorrow you're going back, my Bergen would be packed and I'd be on the first plane out, because that's what we are trained to do and that's what we want to do. You don't join the army to drink loads of beer. You join to go to war.'

In total, the Royal Irish won three Conspicuous Gallantry Awards, more than any other unit over a six-month tour in Afghanistan.

But Hagans' injuries are serious and it is unlikely he will ever be able to run again. 'When I got took out, there was somebody straight there to take over my job. The machine doesn't break because Brummie Hagans got blown up. You need someone to plug that gap to make the sure the momentum of the battle group carries on.'

Hagans would like to be commissioned as an officer, but if it is not to be he is determined to help other injured soldiers rebuild their lives at Headley Court. 'Some of the casualties are really bad and bringing them back into the public eye is a challenge. I know what they are going through.' He has no regrets.

> The Royal Irish have got over 300 years of
> history and it can only continue with the likes of Iraq
> and the likes of Afghanistan.

Together, American-Irish, British-Irish and Irish from the Republic of Ireland continue to fight for freedom around the world.

Appendix 1
Irish-Born Winners of the Victoria Cross

The Victoria Cross is the highest British military decoration.

Crimean War

John Alexander
Edward Bell
Joseph Bradshaw
Hugh Burgoyne
John Byrne
Daniel Cambridge
William Coffey
John Connolly
John Connors
Thomas Esmonde
John Farrell
George Gardiner
Thomas Grady
Henry Jones
William Lendrim
Charles Lucan
John Lyons
Ambrose Madden
Frederick Maude
Charles McCorrie
William McWheeney

Andrew Moynihan
Luke O'Connor
James Owens
John Park
Joseph Prosser
Philip Smith
John Sullivan
Mark Walker
Alexander Wright

Indian Mutiny

Charles Anderson
Abraham Boulger
William Bradshaw
Francis Brown
James Byrne
Patrick Carlin
Cornelius Coughlan
Denis Dempsey
Bernard Diamond
John Divane
Patrick Donohue
William Dowling
Thomas Duffy
John Dunlay
Denis Dynon
Richard Fitzgerald
Thomas Flinn
George Forrest
Stephen Garvin
Peter Gill
Henry Gore-Browne
Patrick Graham
Peter Grant
Patrick Green
Thomas Hackett
John Harrison
Henry Hartigan
Robert Hawthorne
Samuel Hill
Charles Irwin
Edward Jennings

Thomas Kavanagh
Richard Keatinge
George Lambert
Thomas Laughnan
Samuel Lawrence
Harry Lyster
Patrick Mahoney
John McGovern
James McGuire
Patrick McHale
Peter McManus
Bernard McQuirt
Michael Murphy
Patrick Mylott
William Nash
William Olpherts
James Pearson
Dighton Probyn
John Purcell
George Richardson
Patrick Roddy
John Ryan
Miles Ryan
John Sinnott
Michael Sleavon
James Travers
Joseph Ward

Anglo-Persian War

Arthur Moore

Second Opium War

Nathaniel Burslem
Andrew Fitzgibbon
Thomas Lane
Robert Rogers

New Zealand Wars

John Lucas
William Manley
John Murray
John Ryan

Frederick Smith
Dudley Stagpoole
William Temple

Canada
Timothy O'Hea

Andaman Islands Expedition
David Bell
William Griffiths
Thomas Murphy

Abyssinian Campaign
James Bergin
Michael Magner

Cape Frontier Wars
Hans Moore

Zulu War
William Beresford
Neville Coghill
Edmund Fowler
William Leet
Edmund O'Toole
James Reynolds

Basuto War
Francis Fitzpatrick
Richard Ridgeway

Second Afghan War
James Adams
Garrett Creagh
Walter Hamilton
Reginald Hart
Edward Leach
Patrick Mullane
George White

First Boer War
John Dannaher

John Doogan
James Murray

Burma Campaigns
John Crimmin
Owen Lloyd

Sudan Campaign
Thomas Byrne

Siege of Malakand
Edmund Costello

Second Boer War
John Barry
Edward Brown
Thomas Crean
William English
Charles FitzClarence
Robert Johnston
James Masterson
George Nurse
Hamilton Reed
Robert Scott
Alexander Young

Somaliland Campaign
Alexander Cobbe

The Great War
Eric Bell
Edward Bingham
George Boyd-Rochfort
John Caffrey
Geoffrey Cather
Hugh Colvin
William Cosgrove
James Crichton
John Cunningham
Maurice Dease
Edmund De Wind
Martin Doyle

James Duffy
Frederick Edwards
James Emerson
Frederick Hall
Robert Hanna
Frederick Harvey
John Holland
Thomas Hughes
Henry Kelly
William Keneally
Edward Mannock
William McFadzean
Martin Moffat
Robert Morrow
John Moyney
David Nelson
Claude Nunney
Michael O'Leary
Martin O'Meara
Michael O'Rourke
Gerald O'Sullivan
Robert Quigg
Clement Robertson
George Roupell
James Somers

Baltic Campaign

Augustus Agar

Waziristan Campaign

William Kenny

Second World War

Harold Ervine-Andrews
Eugene Esmonde
Edward Fegen
Donald Garland
James Jackman
Richard Kelliher
David Lord
James Magennis

Appendix 2
Irish-Born Winners of the Medal of Honor

The Congressional Medal of Honor is the highest US military decoration. The 202 Irish recipients are the largest body of soldiers born outside America to win the medal.

American Civil War

David L. Bass
Terrence Begley
Felix Brannigan
Christopher Brennan
John Brosnan
Michael Burk
Thomas Burke
William Campbell
Hugh Carey
David Casey
Thomas Connor
James Connors
John Cooper
Thomas Cosgrove
John Creed
Thomas Cullen
Timothy Donoghue
Patrick Doody
William Downey

Thomas T. Fallon
Thomas Flood
Christopher Flynn
George Ford
William Gardner
Richard Gasson
Patrick Ginley
James H. Gribben
John H. Havron
Patrick Highland
Michael Hudson
John Hyland
Patrick Irwin
Andrew Jones
William Jones
John Kane
Joseph Keele
Thomas Kelly
John Kennedy
Hugh Logan
John Lonergan
Richard C. Mangam
Edward S. Martin
James Martin
Peter McAdams
Charles McAnally
Bernard McCarren
Michael McCormick
Patrick H. McEnroe
Owen McGough
John McGowan
Thomas McGraw
Patrick McGuire
Alexander U. McHale
George McKee
Michael McKeever
Patrick Monaghan
Robert Montgomery
Charles Moore
Charles W. Morton
Dennis J. F. Murphy
John P. Murphy

Thomas C. Murphy
John J. Nolan
Peter O'Brien
Timothy O'Connor
George C. Platt
Thomas Plunkett
John Preston
Peter Rafferty
John Rannahan
George Reynolds
Thomas Riley
John Robinson
Thomas Robinson
Peter J. Ryan
Patrick Scanlon
Bernard Shields
William Smith
Timothy Spillane
Joseph Stewart
Timothy Sullivan
William Toomer
George William Tynell
M. Emmett Urell
John Walsh
Richard Welch
Thomas Wells
Edward Welsh
Christopher W. Wilson

Indian Frontier Campaigns

Richard Barrett
James Bell
Edward Branagan
James Brogan
Patrick Burke
Richard Burke
Edmond Butler
Denis Byrne
Thomas J. Callen
Thomas Carroll
George Carter
John Connor

Charles Daily
Charles H. Dickens
Cornelius Donavan
John S. Donelly
James Dowling
William Evans
Daniel Farren
James Fegan
John H. Foley
Nicholas Foran
Michael Glynn
Patrick Golden
Frank Hamilton
Richard Heartery
Thomas P. Higgins
Henry Hogan
Bernard J. D. Irwin
Daniel Keating
John Keenan
Charles Kelley
Philip Kennedy
Thomas Kerrigan
David Larkin
James Lenihan
Patrick J. Leonard
Patrick T. Leonard
George Loyd
Patrick Martin
William McCabe
Bernard McCann
Michael A. McGann
Michael McLoughlin
James McNally
William McNamara
Robert McPhelan
John Mitchell
John J. Mitchell
John Moran
James L. Morris
Myles Moylan
Edward Murphy
Jeremiah Murphy

Phillip Murphy
Thomas Murphy
Thomas Murray
John Nihill
Richard J. Nolan
Moses Orr
John O'Sullivan
William R. Parnell
Frederick Platten
James C. Reed
Joseph Robinson
David Roche
Patrick Rogan
David Ryan
Dennis Ryan
Thomas Sullivan
John Tracy
William Wallace

1866–70

Thomas Burke
James Carey

Korean Campaign 1871

John Coleman
James Dougherty
Patrick H. Grace
Michael McNamara

1871–98

Thomas Cramen
John Dempsey
John Flannagan
Hugh King
Patrick J. Kyle
John Laverty
John O'Neal
Patrick Regan
Thomas Smith
James Thayer
Michael Thornton

Spanish–American War

George F. Brady
Thomas Cavanaugh
Thomas M. Doherty
John Fitzgerald
Philip Gaughan
Michael Gibbons
Michael Kearney
John Maxwell
David Montague
John E. Murphy
Edward Sullivan

Philippine Insurrection

Cornelius J. Leahy
Thomas F. Prendergast
Patrick Shanahan

China Expedition

James Cooney
Martin Hunt
Joseph Killackey
Samuel McAllister

1901–11

Thomas Cahey
Edward Floyd
John King
Patrick Reid
Thomas Stanton

The Great War

Joseph H. Thompson

Notes

Chapters 1 and 2

Gerald O'Connor quotes are from Morris, W. O. (ed.), *Memoirs of Gerald O'Connor*, London: Digby, Long & Co, 1903. Other Sarsfield-related quotes are from Wauchope, P., *Patrick Sarsfield and the Williamite War*, Dublin: Irish Academic Press, 1992; Todhunter, J., *Life of Patrick Sarsfield*, London: T. Fisher Unwin, 1895; Hand, J., *The Life of Sarsfield*, Liverpool: J. Denvir, 1875. See also Hennessy, M., *The Wild Geese*, Old Greenwich: Devlin-Adair Company, 1973 and Murtagh, H., 'Irish Soldiers abroad, 1600–1800' in Bartlett, T. and Jeffrey, K. (eds), *A Military History of Ireland*, Cambridge: Cambridge University Press, 1996. Historian's comment on Ulstermen at Boyne from Boulger, D. M., *The Battle of the Boyne*, London: Martin Secker, 1911. See also McNally, M., *Battle of the Boyne 1690*, Oxford: Osprey, 2005 and Doherty, R., *The Williamite War in Ireland*, Dublin: Five Courts Press, 1998.

Captain Robert Parker quotes are from *Memoirs of the Most Remarkable Military Transactions from 1683 to 1718*, Dublin: G & A Ewing, 1746; see also Chandler, D. (ed.), *Military Memoirs of Marlborough's Campaigns 1702–1712*, London: Greenhill Books, 1998. Career of Alexander O'Reilly told in Beerman, E., 'Alexander O'Reilly: an Irish soldier in the service of Spain', *The Irish Sword*, Vol. XV, No. 59, Winter 1982, and in Ireland, J. de C., 'General Alexander O'Reilly and the Spanish attack on Algiers', *The Irish Sword*, Vol. XII, No. 47, Winter 1975.

Chapter 3

Wellington quote about Ireland from Hibbert, C., *Wellington: A Personal History*, London: HarperCollins, 1997. For Daniel O'Connell quote regarding Wellington, see his speech of 16 October 1843 in *Reports of State Trials: New Series*, Vol. V, 1843–1844, London: HM Stationery Office, 1893.

For soldiers' first-hand accounts see: Grattan, W., *Adventures of the Connaught Rangers from 1808 to 1814*, 2 vols, London: Henry Colburn, 1847 (reprinted 2003); O'Neil, C., *The Military Adventures of Charles O'Neil*, Worcester, Mass.: Edward Livermore, 1851 (reprinted 1997); McGrigor, Sir J., *The Scalpel and the Sword: The Autobiography of the Father of Army Medicine*, Dalkeith: Scottish Cultural Press, 2000; Harris, J., *Recollections of Rifleman Harris (Old 95th) with Anecdotes of his Officers and Comrades*, London, 1848 (reprinted 1996).

For a detailed description of the battle of Badajoz, see Fletcher, I., *In Hell Before Daylight*, Staplehurst: Spellmount, 1994. For a concise profile of Irish Regiments in the Peninsular War, see Chappell, M., *Wellington's Peninsula Regiments (1) – The Irish*, Oxford: Osprey, 2003.

Chapter 4

Quotes from letters by Emmet are from Emmet, T. A., *Memoir of Thomas Addis and Robert Emmet*, Vol. 1, New York: The Emmet Press, 1915. O'Connor's account of the relationship between the Society of United Irishmen and the French government is recorded in 'The Examination of Arthur O'Connor, before the Secret Committee of the House of Commons, 16 August, 1798', part of a pamphlet bound in the British Library (8145.ee.20.1-2). The conflict between Sweeny and Corbet is thoroughly described by John G. Gallaher in his article, 'Conflict and tragedy in Napoleon's Irish Legion: The Corbet/Sweeny affair', *The Irish Sword*, Vol. XVI, No. 64, Summer 1986. His principal sources for his account are letters contained in the Archives de Guerre in the Chateau de Vincennes, near Paris. A further description of the affair appears in Kennedy, B. A., 'Light on a revolting duel fought in 1804', *Irish Sword*, Vol. IV, No. 15, Winter 1959.

The best account of the Irish Legion is Gallaher, J. G., *Napoleon's Irish Legions*, Carbondale and Edwardsville: Southern Illinois University Press, 1993, but see also Dempsey, G. C., *Napoleon's Mercenaries: Foreign Units in the French Army*, London: Greenhill Books, 2002. Byrne quotes come from *Memoirs of Miles Byrne, Chef de Bataillon in the Service of France*, Vol. II, Paris: Gustave Bossange, 1863 (reprinted 1972).

Chapter 5

Robertson's quotes about Don Pedro Campbell come from Robertson, J.P. and W. P., *Letters on South America*, London: John Murray, 1843. See also Pyne, P., *The Invasions of Buenos Aires 1806–1807: The Irish Dimension*, Liverpool: University of Liverpool, Institute of Latin American Studies, Research Paper 20, 1996 and Cutolo, V. O., *Nuevo Diccionario Biografico Argentino*, Buenos Aires: Editorial Elche, 1969. John Devereux's 1824 letter is in O'Connell, M. R., *The Correspondence of Daniel O'Connell, Vol. III, 1824–28*, Dublin: Irish University Press, 1974; Bolívar's proclamation is in *The Times*, 2 March 1820. Description of Irish mutiny in Brazil appears in *The Times*, 28 August 1828.

John Riley correspondence and related quotes are from: Miller, R. R., *Shamrock & Sword*, Norman: University of Oklahoma Press, 1989; Stevens, P. F., *The Rogue's March*, Washington DC: Brassey's, 1999; Hogan, M., *The Irish Soldiers of Mexico*, Guadalajara: Fondo Editorial Universitario, 1997. Original correspondence of Riley held in US National Archives RG153, EE531, Case 27, John Reilly [Riley]; interesting material on Riley in British National Archives, FO203, 93:367. For a reconstruction of San Patricio uniform, see Field, R., *Mexican-American War 1846– 48*, London: Brassey's History of Uniforms, 1997.

Chapter 6

Irishness of 28th Foot comes from 'The Twenty-Eight and Forty-Second', *The Nation*, 13 May 1843; see also Daniell, D. S., *Cap of Honour – The Story of the Gloucester Regiment*, London: George G. Harrap & Co, 1951 and 'Fenianism in the 61st Regiment', *The Back Badge – Journal of the Gloucestershire Regiment*, Vol. IV, No. 14, June 1953. Bace quotes from transcript of *Journal of Captain George Alexander Bace, Her Majesty's 61st Regiment of Foot, 1844–55*, in the archive of the Soldiers of Gloucestershire Museum, Gloucester. Additional Chillianwallah description in Ford, Sgt J., as told to Walter Wood, 'Survivors' Tales of Great Events', No. XX, *The Royal Magazine*, 1906. Career of Redmond told in McConnel, Dr J., 'An Irish Colonel of the 61st', *Newsletter of the Friends of the Soldiers of Gloucestershire Museum*, Spring 2010.

Rogers and McWheeney VC citations from Creagh, Sir O'M., *The VC and DSO*, Vol. I, London: Standard Art Book Co., 1924. See also Burrows, J. W., *The Essex Regiment – 1st Battalion (44th) 1741–1919*, Southend-on-Sea: Burrows and Sons, 1923.

For Fenian British soldier trials, see reports from Ireland correspondent
    in *The Times*, from 23 February 1866 onwards, plus editorial of 5 June
    1866. Devoy quotes from his *Recollections of an Irish Rebel*, Shannon:
    Irish University Press, 1969.

Chapter 7

William McCarter quotes come from O'Brien, K. E. (ed.), *My Life in the
    Irish Brigade – the Civil War Memoirs of Private William McCarter, 116th
    Pennsylvania Infantry*, Campbell: Savas Publishing, 1996. Irish
    immigrant to Wisconsin letter published in *The Times*, 'From our
    own correspondent – Dublin', 14 May 1850. Meagher quotes from
    'Cead Mille Failthe', *New York Times*, 26 July 1862 and 'The Irish
    Brigade – resignation of Gen Meagher etc.', *New York Times*, 14 May
    1863. See also Wylie, P. R., *The Irish General: Thomas Francis Meagher*,
    Norman: University of Oklahoma Press, 2007. Joseph Stuart quote
    from 'The Irish Brigade – to the public', *New York Times*, 1 November
    1861. For early months of Irish Brigade, see also 'Irish Brigade off to
    the war', *New York Times*, 14 November 1861 and 'A riot among the
    soldiers of the Third Regiment Irish Brigade', *New York Times*, 30
    November 1861.
Description of Irish Brigade uniforms in Smith, R., *American Civil War:
    Union Army*, London: Brassey's History of Uniforms, 1996; for a
    reconstruction of their uniform at Fredericksburg, see Smith, R., 'The
    Fighting Irish', *Military Illustrated*, No. 101, October 1996.
    Confederate Irish quotes from O'Grady, K. J., *Clear the Confederate
    Way! – The Irish in the Army of Northern Virginia*, Mason City: Savas
    Publishing, 2000. Full list of Irish-American Civil War medal winners
    in 'Irish-born Recipients of the US Congressional Medal of Honor',
    Irish Sword, Vol. XII, No. 47, Winter 1975.

Chapter 8

John O'Neill and Daniel Murphy quotes from *Official Report of General
    John O'Neill on the attempt to invade Canada*, New York: John J. Foster,
    1870. Canadian quotes from Macdonald, J. A., *Troublous Times in
    Canada*, Toronto: W. S. Johnston & Co, 1910. Letter from owner of
    Fort Erie in *The Times*, 15 June 1866; see also 'The Fenian Invasion of
    Canada', *The Times*, 18 June 1866, for a round-up of contemporary
    Canadian and American news coverage. A thorough recent study of
    the Fenian campaign is given by Senior, H., *The Last Invasion of
    Canada*, Toronto: Dundrun Press, 1991.

Details of Keogh's military career in a lecture given at University
College, Galway, 19 October 1965, and later published as Hayes-
McCoy, G. A., *Captain Myles Walter Keogh*, Dublin: National
University of Ireland, 1966. See also www.myleskeogh.org. Gibbon
quote from Gaff, A. and M. (eds), *Adventures on the Western Frontier*,
Bloomington: Indiana University Press, 1994. Trapper Ridgely quote
from interview published in Minneapolis *Pioneer Press and Tribune*, 8
September 1876. Thanks to Robert Doyle for his suggestion that
Wooden Leg may be referring to Keogh, and quote from *St Paul
Pioneer Press* in the *Army & Navy Journal*, 4 May 1878.

Chapter 9

Tynan stories in 'Tynan "No1" Arrested', *New York Times*, 14 September
1896, and '"Number One" Reveals Himself', *New York Times*, 24 May
1883. Tynan letter to Boers and Transvaal Irish Volunteers notice in
the anonymous *The Great Transvaal Irish Conspiracy*, Cape Town: Ross
& Lewis, 1899 (*Tracts relating to the Transvaal War*, British Library:
8154.B.18). For the suggestion that this booklet was written by
Tynan, see Brown, M., *The Politics of Irish Literature*, London: Allen &
Unwin, 1972. MacBride quotes from MacBride, Major, 'The Irish
Brigade in South Africa', *Freeman's Journal*, 13, 20, 27 October and 17
November 1906, plus 'City Water Bailiff – Major MacBride's
Candidature', *Freeman's Journal*, 31 December 1910. See also Jordan,
A. J., *Major John MacBride*, Westport: Westport Historical Society,
1991 and McCracken, D., *MacBride's Brigade*, Dublin: Four Courts,
1999.

Numbers of Irish settlers and soldiers in South Africa from Akenson, D.
H., *Occasional Papers on the Irish in South Africa*, Grahamstown:
Institute of Social and Economic Research, 1991. Quotes from the
diaries of Auchinleck and Bryant in Cassidy, M., *The Inniskilling
Diaries 1899–1903*, Barnsley: Pen & Sword, 2001. Davidson quote at
Tugela River in Regimental Historical Records Committee, *The Royal
Inniskilling Fusiliers*, London: Constable, 1928. Glyn account of
Driscoll quoted in Monick, S., *Shamrock and Springbok*, Johannesburg:
South African Irish Regimental Association, 1989; see also Hales, A.
G., *Driscoll – King of Scouts*, Bristol: J. W. Arrowsmith, 1901. Kruger
thanks to MacBride in 'The Transvaal Irish Brigade', *The Times*, 30
November 1900; Dublin Irish Transvaal Committee statement in
'Ireland', *The Times*, 30 October 1900. Irish Yeomanry Trooper Earl
account in Gilbert, S. H., *Rhodesia and After*, London: Simpkin,
Marshall, Hamilton and Kent, 1901.

Chapter 10

O'Leary-related quotes from 'O'Leary's Ovation', *The Times*, 12 July 1915, 'Sergeant O'Leary – A Personal Sketch', *The Times*, 10 July 1915, 'Michael O'Leary, VC, is killed in battle', *New York Times*, 28 May 1915, 'The Cuinchy Hero', *Irish Independent*, 5 July 1915; see also 'Michael O'Leary, of the Irish Guards, winning his VC', *Illustrated War News*, 3 March 1915 and Batchelor, P. F. and Matson, C., *VCs of the First World War: The Western Front 1915*, Stroud: Sutton Publishing, 1997. Macdona letter, 'Why not Irish Guards', *The Times*, 1 March 1900. Irish Guards Regimental Diary quoted in Kipling, R., *The Irish Guards in the Great War: The First Battalion*, Staplehurst: Spellmount, 1997. Irish Guards trench newspaper quotes from *The Morning Rire*, 3rd edition, January 1916, 5th & 6th editions (British Library: European War Magazines, Miscellaneous PP.4039.W). Lowry quote from 'Story of the Feat', *Cork Examiner*, February 1915. Captain David Campbell's recollections of service in the 6th Royal Irish Rifles come from his war diary and later narrative privately published in 1962, which is now in the possession of the Royal Ulster Rifles Museum in Belfast; thanks to Terence Nelson of the RUR Museum for drawing my attention to this.

Chapter 11

Carson quote from 'Sir Edward Carson at Belfast', *The Times*, 18 July 1913. Nugent letter and Ricardo quotes in Samuels, A. P. I. and D. G. S., *With the Ulster Division in France – A Story of the 11th Battalion Royal Irish Rifles (South Antrim Volunteers) from Bordon to Thiepval*, Belfast: William Mullan & Son, 1921. Hope quotes from transcript of his war diary in Royal Ulster Rifles Museum, Belfast. Other Somme quotes from transcript of War Diary of 14th Battalion Royal Irish Rifles by Colonel J. A. Mulholland, also in RUR Museum. Newspaper report, 'Ulstermen in the Great Battle', *The Times*, 7 July 1916. See also Orr, P., *The Road to the Somme*, Belfast: Blackstaff Press, 1987. For a good account of the 16th (Irish) Division, see Denman, T., *Ireland's Unknown Soldiers*, Dublin: Irish Academic Press, 2008.

Duffy quotes come from his own wartime memoirs: Duffy, F. P., *Father Duffy's Story*, New York: George H. Doran Co., 1919. Newspaper reports on Duffy from *New York Tribune Sunday Magazine*, 20 April 1919, and *The Advocate*, 18 January 1919, both quoted in Harris, S. L., *Duffy's War*, Washington DC: Potomac Books, 2006. Donovan's medal citation quoted in Reilly, H. J., *Americans All: The Rainbow at War*, Columbus: F. J. Heer, 1936; see also Cave Brown, A., *The Last*

Hero – Wild Bill Donovan, New York: Times Books, 1982. Hogan
quotes from Hogan, M. J., *Shamrock Battalion of the Rainbow*, New
York: D. Appleton & Co., 1919.

Chapter 12

Republican atrocities quoted in 'The Red Reign in Spain', *Irish
Independent*, 29 August 1936. O'Duffy's views on Spanish Civil War
in 'General O'Duffy's Message', *Irish Independent*, 21 November 1936.
Quotes from County Monaghan crown solicitor and the *Dundalk
Democrat* from McGarry, F., *Eoin O'Duffy: A Self-Made Hero*, Oxford:
Oxford University Press, 2005. Quotes from Sergeant Major Timlin
and O'Duffy in Spain are from his own recollections of the Spanish
Civil War in O'Duffy, E., *Crusade in Spain*, Clonskeagh: Browne &
Nolan Ltd, 1938. For a reconstruction of the uniform worn by Irish
soldiers fighting with the Spanish Foreign Legion, see Hall, C. and
Sumner, G., 'Ireland's Fascist Volunteers', *Military Illustrated*, No.148,
September 2000.

For profiles of Irishmen fighting on Republican side, see *The Book of the
XV Brigade: Records of British, American, Canadian and Irish Volunteers
in the XV Brigade in Spain 1936–1938*, Madrid: Commissariat of War
XV Brigade, 1938. Cushing quotes from Cushing, R., *Soldier for Hire*,
London: Four Square Books, 1967. The veracity of Cushing's
memoirs has been questioned by several people, including Peter
Lunt, who served with him in the 1st Battalion Royal Irish Fusiliers
in Berlin and Korea after 1945. 'If the rest of the incidents in the book
are as inaccurately described as those with which I am familiar',
stated Lunt, 'then the title should probably be changed to "Soldier
For Hire – a work of fiction, written by Charles Connell [ghost writer
of the book], loosely based on the experiences of an Irish soldier by
the name of 'Red' Cushing."' However, Lunt later qualified this by
saying, 'most military biographies tend to glorify the individual
being portrayed – Let's just say that "Red" is in good company!'
Source: www.irelandscw.com. For figures of Irish in the British
Army after 1922, see Bartlett, T. and Jeffrey, K. (eds), *A Military
History of Ireland*, Cambridge: Cambridge University Press, 1996.

Chapter 13

Gough letter proposing Irish Brigade appears in *The Times*, 26 September
1941. All subsequent government correspondence contained in
British National Archives file, PREM 3/129/5: Prime Minister's
Personal Minutes dated 6 & 8 October 1941, extract from Postal
Censorship Report, 1 October 1941, 'Proposed Formation of an Irish

Brigade' – Joint Memorandum by the Secretary of State for War and
The Secretary of State for the Dominions, 25 October 1941, letters
from John M. Andrews to Churchill and Attlee, 12 December 1941 &
23 January 1942, letter from Attlee to Andrews, 2 January 1942.
O'Sullivan quotes from his privately published memoirs, *All My Brothers*,
King's Lynn: O'Sullivan, 2007; thanks also to his son, Richard
O'Sullivan, for his recollections and assistance. Brigadier Russell
quotes from his official campaign accounts, 'The Irish Brigade in
Tunisia 1942–43', 'The Irish Brigade in Sicily July and August 1943',
'The Irish Brigade in Italy January and February 1944' and Brigadier
Scott quotes from 'The Irish Brigade in Italy March–July 1944', all
kindly provided by Captain Nigel Wilkinson, London Irish Rifles
Regimental Association. Kenneally quotes from obituary in the *Daily
Telegraph*, 20 September 2000. Mosley quotes from Mosley, N., *Time
at War*, London: Weidenfeld & Nicolson, 2008. See also *The London
Irish at War*, London: London Irish Rifles Old Comrades' Association,
1949.

Chapter 14

Russell interview in *Los Angeles Examiner*, 15 May 1939. Subsequent
Consulate and Embassy correspondence contained in British National
Archives file, FO 371/22831: LA British Consul warning telegram to
British Embassy, 20 May 1939, Russell arrested British Embassy
telegram, 5 June 1939, Sir Ronald Lindsay's report to Halifax, 13 July
1939, New York British Consul telegram, 24 July 1939, Lindsay
telegram, 11 August 1939, Lord Lothian letter to Halifax, 21 September
1939. LA Consul letter to British Embassy, 14 March 1940, in FO
371/24256.
Account of Russell in Germany based on British interrogation of German
Abwehr officer Kurt Haller, 7 August 1946, in Security Service file
KV 2/1292. For discussion of continuing desecration of Russell
statue, see 'Seán Russell and Frank Ryan', *Irish Times*, 16 July 2009.
Dan Bryan's G2 secret information on Russell's financial support
from Germany in letter, 4 April 1946, in Irish National Archives in
Dublin: A20/4 Part 1; file also contains report on Sean Russell's
death; Department of Defence memorandum on Frank Ryan's
motives for working with the Germans, 20 October 1941, in A20/4
Part 3.
Account of O'Reilly and Kenny based on Security Service documents in
British National Archives file, KV 2/119, including 'Note on the Case
of John Francis O'Reilly', two wartime reports dated 30 December
1943 and 6 January 1944, Northern Irish interrogation report of 15

January 1944, Royal Ulster Constabulary report on O'Reilly's escape of 15 July 1944, 'Parachute man buys Eire hotel', *Daily Express*, 5 October 1945, and 'Security Note on the Application by John Kenny for Release on Medical Grounds', 22 December 1944 (turned down).

Reports on Irish prisoners of war in German camps contained in Security Service file in British National Archives, KV 3/345, including Royle's statement, 12 November 1945, translation of German reports on POWs, 10 September 1945, Jupp Hoven's statement, 13 June 1945, British interrogation report of Lt Col. McGrath, 22 May 1945, 'German plan for recruiting Irish Prisoners of War to act in conjunction with the IRA', 6 August 1942, and report on Father O'Shaughnessy, 29 April 1943, both by I. G. Philip. Cushing's story from his *Soldier for Hire*, London: Four Square Books, 1967. See also Carter, C. J., *The Shamrock and the Swastika*, Palo Alto: Pacific, 1977, and O'Reilly, T., *Hitler's Irishmen*, Cork: Mercier Press, 2008.

Chapter 15

Major Gerald Rickcord quotes come from his official report of 1st Battalion, Royal Ulster Rifles in Korea, 26 January to 26 April 1951, in British National Archives, WO 308/46. For obituary of Rickcord, see *Daily Telegraph*, 5 September 1990. For Rickcord criticism of orders to leave high ground at Imjin River, see Hastings, M., *The Korean War*, London: Pan Books, 2000, p.263. Captain Winn's report of Major Huth's action with 8th King's Royal Irish Hussars tanks, May 1951, is in British National Archives, WO 281/1142. *The Times* salute to RUR in 'Fore and Aft', 3 May 1951; see also 'Heroism of the Glosters', *The Times*, 9 May 1951. Account of James Majury comes from his obituary in the *Daily Telegraph*, 18 September 1996. O'Kane's story and quotes come from his self-published memoir of the war, *O'Kane's Korea*, Kenilworth: Mokan Publishing, 1988 and 2008, and correspondence with him.

Chapter 16

Quotes from Bradley and Stig von Bayer come from author's correspondence with them. Fitzpatrick quotes come from 'Graphic Story of Niemba Ambush', *Irish Independent*, 18 January 1961. Kenny quotes come from 'Stumbled From Jungle Beaten and Wounded', *Irish Independent*, 19 January 1961. Cremin description of Bunworth expedition in letter, 20 January 1961, and Gallagher comments on Irish mission to Congo in letter, 17 November 1960, both contained in government file in Irish National Archives in Dublin: DFA/305/384/15; Dáil question and answer in file S16959A. Browne

citation from 'First Army Medal for Gallantry', *Irish Independent*, 9
November 1961. Later Kenny quotes from 'Congo massacre survivor:
Army must tell real story', *Irish Independent*, 5 November 2000. See
also veteran interviews in 'War Stories – The Congo: Niemba', RTE
documentary, directed by David Whelan, 2008, and O'Donoghue, D.
(ed.), *The Irish in the Congo*, Dublin: Irish Academic Press, 2006.
John Gorman quotes from author interview, 19 May 2010. Main source of
Quinlan quotes is from his official report written on 2 December
1961, appearing as an appendix in 'History 35 CN COIS in the
Republic of the Congo, June–December 1961', a copy of which is held
in Irish National Archives: DFA/305384/51. This also contains a
report by Commandant Cahalane on being interrogated by white
Katangans. Other Quinlan quotes at Jadotville from 'With the Irish
Prisoners at Jadotville', *Irish Independent*, 26 September 1961; 'Green
Badge of Courage', *Irish Independent*, 10 October 1961 and Doyle, R.
and Quinlan, L., *Heroes of Jadotville – The Soldiers' Story*, Dublin: New
Island, 2006. Manning quote from 'Graphic Story of the Battle', *Irish
Independent*, 1 December 1961. Quote from Mashonaland Irish letter
comes from government file in Irish National Archives: S/16137
J/61. See also 'War Stories – The Congo: Jadotville', directed by Trish
O'Connor, RTE documentary, 2008 and Power, D., *Siege at Jadotville*,
Dublin: Maverick House Publishers, 2004.

Chapter 17

Bush 9/11 quote from 'After the Attacks: the President', *New York Times*,
15 September 2001; Lt Col. Slack quote from 'A Nation Challenged:
the National Guard', *New York Times*, 18 September 2001; Lt
Rodriguez quote from 'After the Attacks: the President', *New York
Times*, 14 September 2001; Iraqi statement on 9/11 from 'Attacks
draw mixed response in Mideast', CNN.com, 12 September 2001.
Dominic Hagans quotes from author interview, 26 April 2010. Bryn
Taylor quotes from his website www.irishguards.org.uk. Burridge
quote from his official statement in Kuwait on 7 April 2003. Ian
Malone quote from RTE documentary, 'True Lives', November 2002.
US Marine Malone quote from recollection posted on Irish American
Story Project website on 12 January 2008. Malone family quote from
MoD statement. For the full story of Colonel Collins's military
career, see Collins, T., *Rules of Engagement*, London: Headline Books,
2005; see also Beattie, D., *An Ordinary Soldier*, London: Simon &
Schuster, 2008.
Story and quotes about Fighting 69th in Iraq come from Lt Col. Slack's
own account of deployment on www.thewildgeese.com; 'New York

Nerve, Tested on Mean Streets' by Kirk Semple, *New York Times*, 4 March 2005; 'After Duty in Iraq' by Jeffrey Gettleman, *New York Times*, 10 September 2005; see also Flynn, S. M., *The Fighting 69th*, London: Penguin Books, 2008.

Chapter 18

Beattie quote from Beattie, D., *Task Force Helmand*, London: Simon & Schuster, 2010; see also review of his previous book, *An Ordinary Soldier*, by Christina Lamb, *Sunday Times*, 26 October 2008. Hagans quotes from his own unpublished accounts of the ambush and explosion, plus author interview with him in April 2010. Luchsinger quote from author interview with him in Lexington Avenue Armory, March 2010; see also 'Fighting 69th member marries girlfriend before leaving for Afghanistan'¯ by Stephanie Gaskell, *New York Daily News*, 28 March 2008.

Bibliography

For precise archival references to unpublished sources, newspaper and journal articles, see Notes.

Akenson, D. H., *Occasional Papers on the Irish in South Africa*, Grahamstown: Institute of Social and Economic Research, 1991.

Bartlett, T. and K. Jeffrey (eds), *A Military History of Ireland*, Cambridge: Cambridge University Press, 1996.

Beattie, D., *An Ordinary Soldier*, London: Simon & Schuster, 2008.

Beattie, D., *Task Force Helmand*, London: Simon & Schuster, 2010.

Book of the XV Brigade: Records of British, American, Canadian and Irish Volunteers in the XV Brigade in Spain 1936–1938, Madrid: Commissariat of War XV Brigade, 1938.

Boulger, D. M., *The Battle of the Boyne*, London: Martin Secker, 1911.

Bredin, A. E. C. Brig., *A History of the Irish Soldier*, Belfast: Century Books, 1987.

Bruce, S. U., *The Harp and the Eagle*, New York: New York University Press, 2006.

Burrows, J. W., *The Essex Regiment – 1st Battalion (44th) 1741–1919*, Southend-on-Sea: Burrows and Sons, 1923.

Bury, P., *Callsign Hades*, London: Simon & Schuster, 2010.

Carter, C. J., *The Shamrock and the Swastika*, Palo Alto: Pacific, 1977.

Cassidy, M., *The Inniskilling Diaries 1899–1903*, Barnsley: Pen & Sword, 2001.

Cave Brown, A., *The Last Hero: Wild Bill Donovan*, New York: Times Books, 1982.

Chandler, D. (ed.), *Military Memoirs of Marlborough's Campaigns 1702–1712*, London: Greenhill Books, 1998.

Chappell, M., *Wellington's Peninsula Regiments (1) – The Irish*, Oxford: Osprey, 2003.

Clark, G. B., *Irish Soldiers in Europe*, Cork: Mercier Press, 2010.

Coogan, T. P., *1916: The Easter Rising*, London: Cassell & Co, 2001.

Cushing, R., *Soldier for Hire*, London: Four Square Books, 1967.

Daniell, D. S., *Cap of Honour – The Story of the Gloucester Regiment*, London: George G. Harrap & Co., 1951.

Dempsey, G. C., *Napoleon's Mercenaries: Foreign Units in the French Army*, London: Greenhill Books, 2002.

Denman, T., *Ireland's Unknown Soldiers*, Dublin: Irish Academic Press, 2008.

Desmond, J. and D. Desmond, *Heroic Option: The Irish in the British Army*, Barnsley: Pen & Sword, 2005.

Devoy, J., *Recollections of an Irish Rebel*, Shannon: Irish University Press, 1969.

Doherty, R., *The Williamite War in Ireland*, Dublin: Five Courts Press, 1998.

Doherty, R., *Helmand Mission – with the 1st Royal Irish Battlegroup in Afghanistan in 2008*, Barnsley: Pen & Sword, 2010.

Doyle, R. and L. Quinlan, *Heroes of Jadotville – The Soldiers' Story*, Dublin: New Island, 2006.

Duffy, F. P., *Father Duffy's Story*, New York: George H. Doran Co., 1919.

Dungan, M., *Distant Drums*, Belfast: Appletree Press, 1993.

Emmet, T. A., *Memoir of Thomas Addis and Robert Emmet*, Vol. 1, New York: The Emmet Press, 1915.

Falls, C., *The History of the 36th (Ulster) Division*, Belfast: M'Caw, Stevenson & Orr, 1922.

Falls, C., *Elizabeth's Irish Wars*, London: Constable, 1996.

Fletcher, I., *In Hell Before Daylight*, Staplehurst: Spellmount, 1994.

Flynn, S. M., *The Fighting 69th*, London: Penguin Books, 2008.

Gallaher, J. G., *Napoleon's Irish Legions*, Carbondale and Edwardsville: Southern Illinois University Press, 1993.

Gilbert, S. H., *Rhodesia and After*, London: Simpkin, Marshall, Hamilton and Kent, 1901.

Grattan, W., *Adventures of the Connaught Rangers from 1808 to 1814*, 2 vols, London: Henry Colburn, 1847.

Hales, A. G., *Driscoll – King of Scouts*, Bristol: J. W. Arrowsmith, 1901.

Hand, J., *The Life of Sarsfield*, Liverpool: J. Denvir, 1875.

Harris, J., *Recollections of Rifleman Harris (Old 95th) with Anecdotes of his Officers and Comrades*, London, 1848.

Harris, R. G., *The Irish Regiments*, Tunbridge Wells: Nutshell Publishing, 1989.

Harris, S. L., *Duffy's War: Fr Francis Duffy, Wild Bill Donovan, and the Irish Fighting 69th in World War I*, Washington DC: Potomac Books, 2006.

Hayes-McCoy, G. A., *Captain Myles Walter Keogh*, Dublin: National University of Ireland, 1966.

Hennessy, M., *The Wild Geese*, Old Greenwich: Devlin-Adair Company, 1973.

Hibbert, C., *Wellington: A Personal History*, London: HarperCollins, 1997.

Hogan, M., *The Irish Soldiers of Mexico*, Guadalajara: Fondo Editorial Universitario, 1997.

Hogan, M. J., *The Shamrock Battalion of the Rainbow: A Story of the Fighting Sixty-Ninth*, New York: D. Appleton & Co., 1919.

Jordan, A. J., *Major John MacBride*, Westport: Westport Historical Society, 1991.

Journal of the Battle of Fontenoy, As it was drawn up and published by Order of his Most Christian Majesty, London: M. Cooper, 1745.

Kenneally, I., *Courage and Conflict: Forgotten Stories of the Irish at War*, Cork: Collins Press, 2009.

Kipling, R., *The Irish Guards in the Great War: The First Battalion*, Staplehurst: Spellmount, 1997.

Macdonald, J. A., *Troublous Times in Canada*, Toronto: W. S. Johnston & Co., 1910.

Malcolm, J. L., *Caesar's Due – Loyalty and King Charles 1642–1646*, London: Royal Historical Society, 1983.

McCracken, D., *MacBride's Brigade*, Dublin: Four Courts, 1999.

McGarry, F., *Eoin O'Duffy: A Self-Made Hero*, Oxford: Oxford University Press, 2005.

McGrigor, Sir J., *The Scalpel and the Sword: The Autobiography of the Father of Army Medicine*, Dalkeith: Scottish Cultural Press, 2000.

McLaughlin, M., *The Wild Geese*, London: Osprey, 1980.

McNally, M., *Battle of the Boyne 1690*, Oxford: Osprey, 2005.

Memoirs of Miles Byrne, Chef de Bataillon in the Service of France, Vol. II, Paris: Gustave Bossange, 1863.

Memoirs of the Most Remarkable Military Transactions from 1683 to 1718, Dublin: G. & A. Ewing, 1746.

Miller, R. R., *Shamrock & Sword*, Norman: University of Oklahoma Press, 1989.

Monick, S., *Shamrock and Springbok*, Johannesburg: South African Irish Regimental Association, 1989.

Morris, W. O. (ed.), *Memoirs of Gerald O'Connor*, London: Digby, Long & Co., 1903.

Mosley, N., *Time at War*, London: Weidenfeld & Nicolson, 2008.

Murphy, D., *Irish Regiments in the World Wars*, Oxford: Osprey, 2007.

Newark, T., *Celtic Warriors*, Poole: Blandford Press, 1986.

O'Brien, K. E. (ed.), *My Life in the Irish Brigade – the Civil War Memoirs of Private William McCarter, 116th Pennsylvania Infantry*, Campbell: Savas Publishing, 1996.

O'Callaghan, J., *History of the Irish Brigades in the Service of France*, Glasgow, 1870.

O'Connell, M. R., *The Correspondence of Daniel O'Connell, Vol. III, 1824–28*, Dublin: Irish University Press, 1974.

O'Donoghue, D. (ed.), *The Irish in the Congo*, Dublin: Irish Academic Press, 2006.

O'Duffy, E., *Crusade in Spain*, Clonskeagh: Browne & Nolan Ltd, 1938.

Official Report of General John O'Neill on the attempt to invade Canada, New York: John J. Foster, 1870.

O'Grady, K. J., *Clear the Confederate Way! – The Irish in the Army of Northern Virginia*, Mason City: Savas Publishing, 2000.

O'Kane, H., *O'Kane's Korea*, Kenilworth: Mokan Publishing, 1988.

O'Neil, C., *The Military Adventures of Charles O'Neil*, Worcester, Mass.: Edward Livermore, 1851.

O'Reilly, T., *Hitler's Irishmen*, Cork: Mercier Press, 2008.

Orr, P., *The Road to the Somme*, Belfast: Blackstaff Press, 1987.

Power, D., *Siege at Jadotville*, Dublin: Maverick House Publishers, 2004.

Pyne, P., *The Invasions of Buenos Aires 1806–1807: The Irish Dimension*, Liverpool: University of Liverpool: Institute of Latin American Studies, Research Paper 20, 1996.

Regimental Historical Records Committee, *The Royal Inniskilling Fusiliers*, London: Constable, 1928.

Reilly, H. J., *Americans All: The Rainbow at War. Official History of the 42nd Rainbow Division in the World War*, Columbus: F. J. Heer, 1936.

Robertson, J. P. and W. P. Robertson, *Letters on South America*, London: John Murray, 1843.

Samato, C. G. (ed.), *Commanding Boston's Irish Ninth – the Civil War Letters of Colonel Patrick R. Guiney*, New York: Fordham University Press, 1998.

Samuels, A. P. I. and D. G. S. Samuels, *With the Ulster Division in France – A Story of the 11th Battalion Royal Irish Rifles (South Antrim Volunteers) from Bordon to Thiepval*, Belfast: William Mullan & Son, 1921.

Senior, H., *The Last Invasion of Canada*, Toronto: Dundrun Press, 1991.

Stevens, P. F., *The Rogue's March*, Washington DC: Brassey's, 1999.

Stevenson, D., *Scottish Covenanters and Irish Confederates*, Belfast: Ulster Historical Foundation, 1981.

Stradling, R. A., *The Spanish Monarchy and Irish Mercenaries*, Dublin: Irish Academic Press, 1994.

The Great Transvaal Irish Conspiracy, Cape Town: Ross & Lewis, 1899.

The London Irish at War, London: London Irish Rifles Old Comrades' Association, 1949.

Todhunter, J., *Life of Patrick Sarsfield*, London: T. Fisher Unwin, 1895.

Two Remarkable Letters Concerning the King's Correspondence with the Irish Rebels, London: F. Neile, 1645.

Verney, P., *The Micks – The Story of the Irish Guards*, London: Peter Davies, 1970.

Walsh, M., *G2: In Defence of Ireland*, Cork: Collins Press, 2010.

Wauchope, P., *Patrick Sarsfield and the Williamite War*, Dublin: Irish Academic Press, 1992.

Whelan, M., *The Battle of Jadotville*, Dublin: South Dublin Libraries, 2006.

White, G. and B. O'Shea, *Irish Volunteer Soldier 1913–23*, Oxford: Osprey, 2003.

Wylie, P. R., *The Irish General: Thomas Francis Meagher*, Norman: University of Oklahoma Press, 2007.

Index

1st Battalion (French Army)   52–3
1st Gloucestershire Regiment
      197, 200–1
2nd Coldstream Guards   126
3rd Foreign Regiment (French
      Army)   50–2
4th (Royal Irish) Dragoon Guards 26
5th Dragoon Guards   81
8th Foot Regiment   81
8th King's Royal Irish Hussars   195, 197,
      198–9, 200, 204
9th Queen's Royal Lancers   79
10th (Irish) Division   129–30, 131–4, 135
15th *Bandera* (Spanish Foreign
      Legion)   156–9
16th (Irish) Division   143–4
18th King's Irish Hussars (formerly Light
      Dragoons)   26
24th Foot Regiment   79
27th (Inniskilling) Foot Regiment 26
28th (North Gloucestershire) Foot
      Regiment   31, 35–6, 38, 39, 71, 82
33rd Battalion of the Irish United
      Nations   205, 206–9
35th Battalion of Irish United
      Nations   211–17
36th (Ulster) Division   136, 138–43
38th (Irish) Brigade   170–3, 174–80
42nd Rainbow Division (US)   146, 227
44th (East Essex) Regiment   76–7, 78
60th Rifle Brigade   80, 81
61st (South Gloucestershire) Foot
      Regiment   72–4, 75–6, 80, 81, 82
63rd Regiment (US Army)   86
67th (South Hampshire) Regiment
      77

69th Infantry Regiment (US
      Army)   219–20, 226–30, 231–2
69th Regiment (US Army)   85, 87, 145
71st Highland Regiment   55, 56
78th Infantry Division   172, 174
88th New Yorkers   92
90th Perthshire Light Infantry   78
95th Rifle Brigade   30–1
116th Pennsylvania Infantry (US
      Army)   84, 87, 89
165th Infantry Regiment (US
      Army)   145–50
256th 'Tiger Brigade' Louisiana   226–7

A
Abwehr (German military
      intelligence)   183–5, 186–7
Act of Union (1801)   25–6, 27, 84
Afghan National Army (ANA)   232, 233,
      234, 236
Afghanistan   221, 231–7
Algiers *see* North Africa
Allen, Captain John   49–50, 51
America *see* South America; United States
      of America
Andrews, John   169–70
Anglo-Dutch alliance   12, 13–14, 16
Anglo-Irish Treaty   154–5
Anzac troops   130, 131, 132
Artigas, José   57–8, 59–60
Astorga, Siege of   48–50
Atlee, Clement   169
Auchinleck, Lieutenant Daniel   114, 115,
      116, 117, 122
Austria and Austrians   21, 23, 62, 84, 180,
      194

B
Bace, George Alexander 72–5
Badajoz, Siege of (1812) 32–6, 50
Ballytrain Barrack attack 154
Baluba tribe 205, 206–9, 210–11
Baptiste, Gerard 220
Barker, John 146
Barnes, Corporal Jimmy 178
Bautzen, Battle of (1813) 51
Bayer, Stig von 206, 210–11
Beattie, Captain Doug 223, 232–3, 234,
    235, 236
Belfast 60th Squadron (Imperial
    Yeomanry) 120
Belgium and Belgians 13–15, 16, 18–19,
    196–7, 198, 206, 211–12, 214
Benteen, Captain Frederick 105
Beresford, William 79
Berwick, Duke of 11
Blake, Colonel J. Y. F. 112
Bloomberg, Michael 230
Boer War 110–11, 112–19, 120–2
Bolívar, Símon 60–1
Boyne, Battle of the (1690) 1–6, 16, 138
Bradley, Private Danny 205, 210
Brazil 62–4
Bredin, Colonel Humphrey 'Bala' 178
Britain 16–17, 21–2, 41–2, 43, 44, 71–3,
    161, 162
    see also Boer War; **British Army
        regiments by name**; Churchill,
        Sir Winston; Fenian Brotherhood;
        First World War; Imperial
        Yeomanry Force; James II, King;
        Peninsular War; Second World
        War; Wellington, Duke of;
        William of Orange
Browne, Trooper 209–10, 211
Bryan, Colonel Dan 185
Bryant, Private L. J. 121
Buller, General Redvers 114, 116, 117
Bunworth, Colonel 209
Burnside, General Ambrose 88, 93
Bush, George W. 219, 221
Bussaco, Battle of (1810) 50
Byrne, Miles 47–8, 50, 51, 52, 53

C
Caernarvon, Lady 134–5
*Call to Arms to Irishmen in South
    Africa* 111
Campbell, Lieutenant David 129–35
Campbell, Peter 55–60
Canada and Canadians 96–9, 100–1, 148,
    174, 178–9
Carson, Sir Edward 137, 138
Catholics

Battle of the Boyne 1–6, 138
    exclusion from British Army 26–7
    sectarian conflict in British forces 30–2
    Siege of Limerick (1691) 7–8
    soldiers meet Pope Pius XII 179
    the 'Wild Geese' 8–9, 11, 12–13
    see also Spanish Civil War (1936)
cavalries 4, 5, 11, 14, 17, 38, 77, 96, 101,
    102, 103–7, 120–1
Cavendish, Lord Frederick 109
Chambers, Corporal Tom 80, 81, 82
Chancellorsville, Battle of (1863) 93
Chillianwallah, Battle of (1849) 73–4, 75
China and Chinese 76–7, 196, 197–9, 200,
    201–2
Churchill, Sir Winston 167–9, 170, 174
Civil War, American 83–4, 85–94, 96, 102
Civil War, Irish 154–5, 160
Coghill, Nevill 78–9
Cold War conflicts 193–204
Collins, Colonel Tim 221–2, 223
Communism 153, 155, 160–1, 185, 201–3
    see also Korean War; Spanish Civil War
Confederate Army, Irish in 92
Congo civil war 205–17
Congressional Medal of Honour (US) 94,
    150
Connaught Rangers 25, 26, 27–30, 32–5,
    37, 38, 50, 56, 113, 115, 124, 128, 130,
    143, 145, 164
Conway, Kit 162
Cooper, Major R. J. 124
Corbet, Captain Thomas 45, 46
Corbet, William 45–6
Costello, Sergeant 51
Cranborne, Viscount 168–9
Crazy Horse, Chief 104, 105–6
Cremin, Cornelius 208–9
Crimean War 78
Cromwell, Oliver 1–2, 20–1
Cushing, Thomas 'Red' 160–1, 162–4,
    165–6, 191–2, 194
Custer, Lieutenant Colonel George
    Armstrong 102, 103, 104–6, 107

D
Dardanelles Campaign 130
Davidson, Major C. J. Lloyd 116
de Valera, Eamon 145
Devereux, John 60, 61–2
Devoy, John 79–81, 82
Distinguished Flying Cross 129
Donnelly, Charles 161–2
Donovan, Lieutenant Colonel William
    J. 148, 149–50, 151
Dooley, John Edward 92
Downing, Private Thomas 107

Driscoll, Lieutenant Colonel Daniel
  Patrick 117–19, 122
Dublin 61st Squadron (Imperial
  Yeomanry) 120
Duffy, Father Francis Patrick 145–8,
  149–50, 151, 230
Dundalk Democrat 154
Dutch 3, 4–5, 7, 12, 13–14, 16

E
Earl, Trooper 120–1
Easter Rising 122, 144, 145–6, 154, 186
Elizabeth I, Queen 20
Emmet, Robert 47, 87, 96
Emmet, Thomas Addis 42–3, 44–5, 47
Engeldrum, Staff Sergeant Christian
  P. 227
England *see* Britain
Essex Regiment 76–7, 78

F
Farrell, Private Richard 107
fascism and fascists 155, 159, 160, 161
  see also Second World War
Fenian Brotherhood 79–82, 96–100, 111,
  112, 148
'Fighting 69th' 85, 87, 145–50, 219–20,
  226–30, 231–2
Finley, Sergeant Jeremiah Finley 103, 107
Finucane, Brendan 168
First World War 122, 125–8, 129–36,
  138–51
Fitzgerald, Peter 174
Fitzmaurice, Sergeant 79
Fitzpatrick, Private Joseph 207–8, 210
flags, Irish 79, 84, 89, 90, 97, 110, 112, 156
'Flight of the Wild Geese' 8–9
Flynn, Captain Sean 229
Foreign Legion of Patricios 66
France and French
  3rd Foreign Regiment and 1st
    Battalion 50–3
  and the Americas 21–2
  Battle of Ramillies 16–17
  Battle of the Boyne 2–3, 4, 5
  Battle of Waterloo 38
  French Revolution 22, 41
  invasion of Belgium 13–15, 16
  and the Irish Legion 43–5, 46, 47,
    48–50, 60
  Peninsular War 29–30, 32–5, 47–50
  Siege of Limerick (1691) 7–8
  and the United Irishmen 41–2, 44
  the 'Wild Geese' 8–9, 11, 12–13
  see also Louis XIV; Napoleon Bonaparte;
    O'Connor, Gerald; Sarsfield,
    Patrick

Franco, General Francisco 153, 156–7,
  159, 164, 184
Fredericksburg, Battle of (1862) 89–93,
  101
French Foreign Legion 79, 163, 225

G
Gallagher, Ambassador Brian 209
Gallagher, Captain Patrick 45–6
Gallipoli 130, 131–4, 135
Garibaldis, Piedmont and Giuseppe 102
Gaynor, Sergeant Hugh 205
George V, King 129
George VI, King 181
Germans and Germany 3, 51, 62–3, 64,
  122, 156, 159, 162, 164
  see also First World War; Second World
    War
Gibbon, Major General John 106
Gillingham, Solomon 110–11, 112
Giordano, Private Carlo 229
Gleeson, Lieutenant Kevin 205, 206, 207
Glyn, R. W. 118
Goertz, Hermann 184, 185
Goff, Colonel Ion 177
Gorman, Private John 213, 214, 215–17
Gough, General Sir Hubert 167
Grattan, Henry 25
Grattan, William 25, 28–9, 30, 32–3, 34,
  36, 37–8, 50
Great Famine 76, 80, 83
Great Transvaal Irish Conspiracy 110–11
Great War *see* First World War
guerilla warfare 113, 118, 121, 154

H
Hagans, Sergeant Dominic
  'Brummie' 222, 223, 232, 233–7
Hales, A. G. 119–20
Hamilton, Sir Ian 130
Harris, Benjeman 30–1
Hart, Major General Fitzroy 113, 115
Hitler, Adolf 162, 185
  see also Second World War
Hogan, Corporal Martin J. 150–1
Holland, Lieutenant John 145
Home Rule Bill 137–8, 144
Hope, Lance Corporal John
  Kennedy 139–41
Hoven, Jupp 189–90
Hughes, Sergeant Robert 107
Hughes, Thomas 145
Hussein, Saddam 221
Huth, Major Henry 198–9

I
Imjin River, Battle of (1951) 197–200

Imperial Light Infantry (colonial South
    Africa)   115
Imperial Yeomanry Force   119–21
Independence, American War of   22
India   73–6, 78, 82
Indians, Native American   104–7
Inniskillin, General Johann-Sigismund
    Maguire   22–3
IRA (Irish Republican Army)   154–5, 160,
    161, 169
and Nazi Germany   181–6
Iraq   221–4, 225, 226, 227–9
Irish bandera (Spanish Foreign
    Legion)   156–9
Irish (5th) Brigade   113, 115, 116
Irish Brigade (Second World War)
    see 38th (Irish) Brigade
Irish Brigade, American   84, 85–93
Irish Brigade, French   13, 16, 18, 19
Irish Brigade, Transvaal   112–13, 114–15,
    119, 122
Irish Free State   154–5, 164, 165
Irish Freeman   110–11
Irish Guards   117, 124–8, 173, 174, 189,
    223–4, 225, 226
Irish Independent   153, 216
Irish Inniskilling Dragoons   19
Irish Legion, Napoleon's   43–6, 47, 48–50,
    60
Irish National Brotherhood   111–12
Irish National Invincibles   109–10
Irish Protestant Unionists   137
Irish Republican Army (Irish-
    American)   97
Irish Republican Brotherhood
    109, 111
Irish Volunteers   143–4, 145
Irish War of Independence (1919   154
Irizarry, Staff Sergeant Henry   227
Italy and Italians   102, 155, 162, 174–80,
    183

J
Jadotville, Siege of (1961)   212–17
James II, King   2–4, 5–7, 8, 11, 12, 138
Jurgens, Thomas   220

K
Katangans   206, 210, 211, 212–14,
    216
Kenneally, General John   173–4
Kenny, John   186–8
Kenny, Private Thomas   207, 208, 210
Keogh, Captain Myles   101–7
Kitchener, Lord   113–14
Korean War   193–203, 204
Kruger, Paul   112, 118, 119

L
La Hougue, Battle of (1692)   12
Latin America see South America
Lawless, William   51–2
Leinster Regiment   130, 143, 145, 164–5
Lenon, Lieutenant   77–8
Limerick, Siege of (1691)   7–8, 87
Limerick, Treaty of (1691)   8, 13
Lincoln-Washington battalions   160–1
Little Bighorn, Battle of (1876)   105–7
London Gazette   77
London Irish Rifles   136, 169, 170–2,
    174–5, 176, 177–8, 179
Los Angeles Examiner 181
Louis XIV, King of France   2–3, 8, 11–12,
    13–14, 16, 20, 21
Lowry, Quarter-master-Sergeant J.
    G.   127
Luchsinger, Staff Sergeant
    Brandon   231–2
Luxembourg, duc de   13, 14, 15

M
MacBride, John   111–13, 114–15, 119, 122
MacSheehy, Adjutant Commander
    Bernard   45, 46
Mahon, Lieutenant General Sir Brian
    T.   131, 133
Mail on Sunday 221
Majury, Captain James   201, 203, 204
Malone, Lance Corporal Ian Keith   224–6
Malplaquet, Battle of (1709)   17–18
Manning, Private John   213
Margesson, David   168–9
Marlborough, Duke of   16–17
Martyr, Captain J. F.   129, 134
Mashonaland Irish Association   215
Mathews, Sergeant Jon   235
McCarter, William   83–4, 87–92, 93, 94
McCarthy, John   183
McCleland, William H.   92
McGrath, Colonel John   189–92
McGrigor, Surgeon General James   28, 36
McWheeney, Sergeant William   78
M'Dougall, Lieutenant   77–8
Meagher, Thomas Francis   84, 85, 86–8,
    89, 91, 92, 93–4
medals of honour   49, 77–9, 94, 124, 127,
    129, 135, 143, 145, 150, 151, 173–4,
    178, 199, 209, 226, 232, 237
Melvill, Teignmouth   79
Merritt, General Wesley   103
Meuse-Argonne campaign (1918)   146–51
Mexico and Mexicans   64–9
Monaghan, Sergeant John   212
Monte Cassino, Battle of (1944)   177–8
Moors   22, 157, 158

Morning Rire 126–7
Mosley, Lieutenant Nicholas 175
Mulholland, Colonel J. A. 141–2
Murphy, Major Daniel 100
Mussolini, Benito 155, 174
mutinies 18–19, 62–4, 75–6, 80–2

N
Nagle, Captain William J. 92
Napoleon Bonaparte 22, 23, 38, 43–4, 46–8, 51, 52–3, 55, 57
Nation 71–2
National Volunteer Force 144
Native American Indians 104–7
Nazis see Second World War
New York militia 84–5
New York Times 85, 86, 128
North Africa 170, 171–3
Northumberland Fusiliers 198, 200–1
Nowlan, Lieutenant Henry J. 103, 105
Nugent, Major General Sir Oliver S. W. 138, 139, 141–2

O
O'Connor, Arthur 42–3, 46
O'Connor, Gerald 1–5, 7–8, 9, 12, 13, 14–15, 17, 19–20
O'Connor, Thomas Power 123
O'Donovan, Brigadier Morgan 170
O'Duffy, Eoin 153–9, 161
O'Higgins, Bernardo 60
O'Kane, Private Henry 194, 196, 197, 198, 199, 200, 202–4
O'Leary, Daniel 128
O'Leary, Sergeant Michael 123–4, 125, 126–9, 135
O'Neil, Charles 31–2, 35–6, 38–9
O'Neill, Captain John 95–7, 98, 99–101
O'Reilly, Alexander 21–2
O'Reilly, John 186–8
O'Rourke, Count Iosiph Kornilovich 23
O'Shaughnessy, Father Thomas 190, 191
O'Sullivan, Edmund 'Ted' 170–2, 173, 174, 175, 176, 177, 179, 180
O'Toole, Sergeant Edmund 79
Orange Order 6, 138, 179
Oxford riots 19

P
Paris 13, 109, 119
Parker, Robert 15–18, 19
Pedro I, Emperor of Brazil 62–3, 64
Penal Code, Catholic 8
Peninsular War 26, 27–30, 32–6, 47–9, 50
Phoenix Park murders 109
Picton, General Thomas 28–9, 33, 34, 35
Pius XII, Pope 179

Polish and Poland 176–7
Portugal see Peninsular War
POWs (Prisoners of War), Irish 189 92, 201–3
Prendergast, James 162
Prendergast, Sergeant Jack 213, 214
Protestants 7, 26, 75, 179
    Battle of the Boyne 1–6
    sectarian conflict in British forces 30–2
    Siege and Treaty Limerick (1691) 7–8, 13
    Ulster Volunteer Force 137–8
    see also 36th (Ulster) Division
Prussians 21, 38, 47, 51, 52

Q
Queen's Own (Canadian Army) 98, 99
Quinlan, Commandant Patrick 211, 212–13, 214, 215, 216–17

R
Ramillies, Battle of (1706) 16–17
Redmond, John (16th Irish Division) 143–4, 145
Redmond, John Patrick 75–6
Reno, Major Marcus 105, 106
Ricardo, Lieutenant Colonel 142, 143
Rickord, Major General 193–4, 195, 196, 197, 198, 199–200, 204
Riley, John 64–5, 66–7, 68–9
Roberts, Field Marshal Lord 113–14, 124
Robertson, John Parish 58–9
Robertson, William 59–60
Rodriquez, Lieutenant Michael 220
Rogers, Lieutenant Robert Montresor 76–8
Ronn, Private Kenneth von 227
Route Irish 228–9
Royal Barracks, Dublin 80–1
Royal Dublin Fusiliers 113, 116, 124, 130, 143, 165
Royal Inniskilling Fusiliers 113, 114, 115–17, 121, 122, 124, 130, 141, 142, 143, 164, 165–6, 169, 170, 178, 194
    see also 38th (Irish) Brigade
Royal Irish Fusiliers 56, 116, 130, 138, 165, 169, 170, 178, 189, 204
    see also 38th (Irish) Brigade
Royal Irish Regiment 221–3, 232–7
Royal Irish Rifles 113, 129, 130–3, 135, 138, 139–42
Royal Munster Fusiliers 130, 143, 165
Royal Regiment of Ireland 16, 17–19
Royal Scots Dragoon Guards 224–5
Royal Ulster Rifles 165, 170, 178, 193–201, 202, 204
Royle, William 189

Russell, Brigadier Nelson   170, 171, 172, 173, 174, 175–6
Russell, Sean   181–5
Russia and Russians   52, 159, 185
Ryan, Captain Frank   161, 162, 163, 164, 184–6, 191

S
Samuels, Captain Arthur   142
San Patricio battalion   65–9
Sarfield, Patrick   6–7, 8, 11, 12–13, 14–15, 16, 19
Scotland Yard 109
Scott, Brigadier Pat   175, 176, 179
Scottish and Scotland   1–2, 6, 19
Second Sikh War   73–4
Second World War   128–9, 151, 163–4, 165, 167–80
    the IRA and Nazi Germany   182–5
    Irish Abwehr agents   186–8
    Irish POWs and German forces   189–92
Shapiro, Michael   202
Sicily   174
Sinn Féin   119, 154
Slack, Lieutenant Colonel Geoffrey   220, 226, 228–9
Somme, Battle of the (1916)   138–43, 145
South Africa   110–11, 112–19, 120–2
South America   55–69
Spain   16, 20–2, 32, 37, 48–9, 55, 57
Spanish Civil War (1936)   153, 155–9, 160–3, 164, 184, 191
Spanish Foreign Legion   156–9
St Patrick's Day   37, 85, 117–18, 120, 195, 231
St Paul Pioneer Press   107
Stanley, William   20
Steenkirk, Battle of (1692)   13
Sweeny, Captain John   45, 46
Sweeny, General Thomas William   97, 99

T
Taliban   232, 233–5, 236
'Task Force Wolfhound'   227–9
Taylor, Sergeant Bryn   224, 225
The Times   61, 81, 82, 97–8, 124, 142–3, 167, 200–1
Timlin, Sergeant Major   157
Toole, Captain   74, 75
Transvaal *see* Boer War
Transvaal Irish Volunteers   111
Tugela Heights, Battle of (1900)   115–17
Turkey and Turkish   130, 131–4, 135
Tynan, Patrick J. P.   109–10, 111

U
Ulster Volunteer Force (UVF)   137–8, 143

uniforms   4, 18, 30, 44, 71, 86, 89, 97, 117, 120, 124–5, 145–6, 156, 170, 173, 195, 231
United Irishmen, Society of   41, 42, 44, 47, 79
United Nations *see* Cold War conflicts; Congo civil war
United States of America   72, 82, 95, 109, 111–12
    cavalry   96, 101, 102, 103–7
    Civil War   83–4, 85–94, 96, 102
    Fenian Brotherhood   79–80, 81, 96, 97, 100–1, 111, 148
    First World War   145–51
    frontier conflicts   104–7
    and the IRA   181–2, 185
    Korean War   195–6, 198, 201, 202
    New York militia   84–5
    pre-independence   21–2
    Second World War   164, 172, 174, 179
    Spanish Civil War   160–1, 162–3
    'War on Terror'   221, 226–8
    war with Mexico   64–9
    World Trade Center attacks   219–20
    see also US Army Regiments by name
Urbina, Private Wilfredo   227

V
Venezuela   60–2
Vessenmayer, Dr Edmund   183–4
Victoria Crosses   77–9, 124, 127, 143, 145, 173–4, 178, 226
Victoria, Queen   76, 117, 124

W
Wallace, Colonel Alexander   28–30
'War on Terror'   221–4, 225–9, 230–7
Waterloo, Battle of (1815)   38
Wellington, Duke of   25–6, 28, 29, 30, 32–3, 34, 36–7, 38, 50, 74
'Wild Geese'   8–9, 11, 12–13
    see also Irish Brigade, French; O'Connor, Gerald; Sarsfield, Patrick
William of Orange   2–4, 5, 6, 7, 11, 13, 14, 15, 16, 138
Winn, Captain   198–9
Wolfe Tone, Theobald   41–2
World Trade Center attacks   219–20, 230
    see also 'War on Terror'

Y
Young Irelander Rebellion   80, 84

Z
Zulu War   78–9